Rob Wiser is a native c
a resident of Las Vegas
University's film prograı
include the crime thriller
the Toronto Film Festival before enjoying nationwide release in the US. He also writes for magazines including *FHM*, *Cigar Aficionado*, *Casino Player*, *Hard Rock Magazine* and *VEGAS*.

In addition, Rob is the co-author of *M.A.C.K. Tactics* – described as 'the ultimate dating manual for single guys'. *The Cheat Sheet* is his second book collaboration with Christopher Curtis, with whom he is also developing film and television projects. You can contact Rob Wiser at rob@macktactics.com.

Christopher Curtis was born and raised in Queens, New York. At the age of seventeen he joined the US Marines and was later stationed at embassies in Venezuela, Yugoslavia and Paraguay. On his return to the United States, he earned a degree in Criminal Justice and joined the Las Vegas police force, where he entered the field of Hostage Negotiations and subsequently served in countless armed and barricaded situations. Currently, he is a member of the elite Crisis Intervention Team.

While making the streets safer (and being featured on occasional episodes of *Cops*), he works part-time as a model and is the unofficial 'Date Doctor' for the Las Vegas Metropolitan Police Force. You can contact Christopher at chris@macktactics.com.

The
Cheat Sheet

Sex, lies and undercover
adventures in adultery

Rob Wiser and
Christopher Curtis

RANDOM HOUSE AUSTRALIA

Random House Australia Pty Ltd
20 Alfred Street, Milsons Point, NSW 2061
http://www.randomhouse.com.au

Sydney   New York   Toronto
London   Auckland   Johannesburg

First published by Random House Australia 2006

National Library of Australia
Cataloguing-in-Publication Entry

Wiser, Rob.
  The cheat sheet.

  ISBN 978 1 74166 144 6.

  ISBN 1 74166 144 7.

  1. Men – Sexual behavior. 2. Man–woman relationships.
  3.Adultery – Prevention. 4. Mate selection. I. Curtis,
  Christopher. II. Title.

646.77

Cover photograph courtesy of Getty Images
Cover design by Darian Causby/www.highway51.com.au
Typeset by Midland Typesetters, Australia
Printed and bound by Griffin Press, Netley, South Australia

10 9 8 7 6 5 4 3 2 1

Contents

A man took his wife to the rodeo and the first exhibit they stopped at was the breeding bulls. They walked up to the first pen and there was a sign attached that read: 'This bull mated 50 times last year.'

The wife nudged her husband in the ribs and said playfully, 'He mated 50 times last year.'

They walked to the second pen, which had a sign that read: 'This bull mated 120 times last year.' The wife jabbed her husband and said, 'That's more than twice a week! You could learn a lot from him.'

They walked to the third pen. It had a sign attached that read: 'This bull mated 365 times last year.' The wife, so excited that her elbow nearly broke her husband's ribs, said: 'That's once a day! You could *really* learn something from this one!'

The husband looked at her and said, 'Go over and ask him if it was with the same cow every time.'

Introduction

Do you suspect your spouse of cheating? Are you losing sleep at night, tortured by the thought of him having affairs behind your back? Do you want evidence of his infidelities, but can't afford to hire a private investigator? For only $49.95 (all major credit cards accepted) we'll arm you with state-of-the-art technology that will reveal the truth – no matter how hard he tries to hide it.

online advertisement

'Semen test kits.' Run an internet search on those three words and you'll find a number of websites giving a similar sales pitch. Home-use semen detection kits let any suspicious woman play CSI detective. Just dab the chemical solution anywhere you think your man may have left some 'evidence' – the back seat of the Volvo, your sister's bed sheets, his secretary's desk – and if the spot turns purple within fifteen seconds, you'll know he has made a deposit at the wrong bank.

One spurned wife offers an icky testimonial:

It was a Sunday afternoon and Roger told me he was meeting his buddies for a round of golf, but I suspected he was paying his ex-girlfriend a visit. When he came home I snatched his underpants while he was in the shower and performed the test. Semen leakage was detected. When he came out of the shower, I confronted him and showed him the proof. How was he supposed to explain the spill – that he'd been wacking off on the golf course with his pals? My woman's intuition, combined with this handy home testing kit, gave me all the proof I needed.

While it may sound like an appalling episode of *Jerry Springer*, these cat-and-mouse games are occurring every day in the homes of people you know. According to Dr Bonnie Eaker Weil, author of *Adultery, the Forgivable Sin*, eight out of ten marriages fall prey to some form of adultery – an inevitable result perhaps when you consider the findings of a recent *Playboy* magazine survey, that 86 per cent of married men said they regularly flirt with the opposite sex. (And these were just the guys that admitted to it.)

The subject of adultery has intrigued experts and researchers for decades. Back in 1953, sex researcher Alfred Kinsey concluded that 50 per cent of husbands had had a least one affair by the time they were 40 years old. And this was long before the arrival of the internet, which has given cheaters a whole new universe of opportunities.

Can you be absolutely certain that your relationship is adultery-proof? If your answer is yes, then it's a good thing you picked up this book – because

no woman is immune to cheating. Not you, not the hottest starlets in Hollywood, not your friend who scored the 'perfect husband' and had the fairytale wedding. Cheating can destroy any relationship, and it often occurs in ways and for reasons that you would never see coming until it's too late.

The Cheat Sheet: Sex, Lies and Undercover Adventures in Adultery approaches the subject of infidelity from a unique angle. As the authors of *M.A.C.K. Tactics*, a book that aimed to teach guys how to meet and form relationships with the opposite sex, we bring an insider perspective to the topic of why men stray. When *M.A.C.K. Tactics* came out in 2005, my co-writer Christopher Curtis and I started to attract a lot of media attention, as a result of which we received tons of emails through our website from guys asking for advice. And whenever we hung out at nightclubs or bars, people who recognised us as 'the Mack guys' would hit us up for tips and share their own stories. This is when a rather alarming discovery dawned on us: many of these men were already in committed relationships but were interested in using the Tactics to cheat on their wives or girlfriends.

This bothered us, since the intent of *M.A.C.K. Tactics* was to help men develop self-confidence and build bonds with women, not to deceive them and cheat on them. While some of the cheaters we knew liked to brag about their conquests, others were clearly ashamed. They claimed they still loved their partners and had tried to remain faithful, but their relationships had deteriorated to the point where they felt they had to seek happiness elsewhere.

As Christopher and I heard these stories, and spoke

to more and more guys about their troubled relationships and their affairs, we realised we were gaining a
perspective on infidelity that had never been expressed
in a book. While women have a lot of assumptions
about cheating – why guys do it, how they get away
with it, and how to detect it – they really only know
half the story. And here's the reason: **the only times that
guys are truly honest about their affairs are when
they're discussing them with other men.**

It's true. We were hearing the stone-cold reality as
no woman has ever heard it. Even when a man
confesses to you, his partner, that he cheated (and
receiving a confession, as we'll explain later, is highly
unlikely), there's no way he's going to come completely
clean. He's not going to explain the true reasons behind
his actions, or articulate the things he felt were missing
in your relationship. And he's certainly not going to tell
you any of the down-and-dirty details. Instead, he'll
spin the truth or downplay his behaviour. He might try
to deflect the blame away from himself and onto you.
In any case, you're only going to get a fraction of the
truth from a cheating man. The rest will remain a
mystery. This torments a lot of women who've been
cheated on, and they wind up dumping the guy but
wondering for months (or even years) afterwards what
they did to deserve it. It also poisons their future relationships, since they're paranoid about being cheated
on again.

This book is meant to enlighten women and deliver
the truth about cheating men, in all of their various
forms. In the course of writing *The Cheat Sheet* we had
hundreds of candid discussions with unfaithful guys –
in locker rooms, on barstools, at strip clubs, bachelor

parties and other 'male bonding' environments – in order to gather the facts and report the reality. To understand other aspects of cheating, we went undercover and plunged into the strip clubs, the swingers' parties, the internet chat rooms . . . all the places that test the boundaries of fidelity.

A lot of women say that for men, it all boils down to sex. They believe that we guys can't help ourselves, that we don't have the same respect for fidelity that women do, or that our primitive brains are overpowered by the urges emanating from below our waists. This may be true in a lot of cases. But by exploring the subject from all angles, we found out that the truth is usually more complicated. We learned the *real* reasons why guys cheat, and very often these reasons have little to do with sex. We found that many men feel they've been driven to cheat because of various problems in their relationships – problems that could have been rectified, if only their partner had been more in tune with the situation. The information we uncovered is going to surprise you, no matter what kinds of relationship hell you've suffered through, how many couples you've watched sobbing on Dr Phil's couch, or how many books or articles you've read about infidelity.

We're sure to catch some grief from our fellow men for airing their dirty secrets, but by sharing them with you, our hope is that it will help men and women understand each other better and build stronger relationships in which cheating is not an option. Believe us when we tell you, very few guys enter into relationships expecting to cheat some day, or wanting to. None of us looks forward to the day when we'll ignore our wives and spend our nights prowling the internet in search of hook-ups. But relationships change. Lines of communication break down. And once a guy cheats, it's a slippery downhill slope that can only end in heartbreak.

But it doesn't need to reach this point, and there is hope. We wrote *M.A.C.K. Tactics* because too many men have grown disillusioned with women and their own dating prospects. We realised that the average man was in desperate need of more information about women: what the opposite sex truly wants, what makes them tick, and how to build relationships with them. *The Cheat Sheet* is meant to lend similar help to women. We'll take you inside the hearts and minds of men to help you arrive at solutions you can use in your own relationships.

Women need this information now more than ever. We're not going to sugar-coat the state of affairs; our *Cheat Sheet* research led us to a number of disturbing discoveries. So be prepared to learn some shocking facts, hear some outrageous tales, and find out some unsettling truths about men. At points, this story descends into dark territory. Certain chapters may force you to ask questions about yourself, and your relationship, that you're not comfortable asking, because the fact remains that adultery is even more prevalent than women realise – so much so that we formed a controversial but undeniable conclusion . . .

There are three types of men:
- Those who cheat.
- Those who have cheated in the past.
- Those who will cheat if placed in the right (or wrong) circumstances.

So how, exactly, is *The Cheat Sheet* going to help

you? This book is about two things. First, it's about understanding why men today *really* cheat, and the path that led them to this point. After all, it's a whole different ballgame today from what it was back when our parents hooked up.

Second, this book is about helping you before it's too late. Whether you want to make your current relationship adultery-proof or enter into a new relationship on solid ground, it's critical that you understand the realities before infidelities start coming between you and your man. We'll teach you the pre-emptive actions you can take to prevent cheating from happening to you. Instead of wasting your time and energy worrying who he's flirting with in cyberspace, or setting traps to try to catch him, we'll explain how you can work on making your relationship 'cheat-proof'. Relationships are a two-way street, a fact that a lot of female-authored books on cheating overlook. Particularly over the course of a marriage, you'll need to put forth a daily effort to keep the pulse of your relationship beating strong. When things settle into a dull, predictable routine, it's the beginning of the end. This book will show you how to keep the fires burning hot.

While we don't make excuses for our fellow males, there is a lot to be learned – and much value to be gained – from understanding their motivations for seeking love, sex and attention from other women. We heard wild tales of adultery from guys of every age and background; we also quizzed women about their affairs, to understand the other side of the equation. And just as important, we met couples who are doing it *right* and pumped them for inspiration and information. In the end, after hearing endless stories of lies and betrayal, we actually found ourselves arriving at some optimistic conclusions. We learned that you *can* build a foundation of trust, avoid the pitfalls of cheating, and keep the flames of passion roaring. But it takes work. It also takes awareness and a keen understanding of what really makes men tick.

So take the lessons in this book to heart, and you can establish a relationship in which cheating is not an option your man is ever going to seriously consider. Let's face it, this is certainly more gratifying, and less messy, than detecting a purple stain on his boxer shorts.

The goal of having a loving, fulfilling, faithful relationship can definitely be attained. You've now got to channel the same amount of effort you put into finding the right man, into staying together. But you can't do this alone, of course, so we're also going to show you ways to encourage and inspire your man to become a better partner and lover. The kind of guy who's so focused on you that other women disappear from his radar.

We hope this book will inform and inspire you, and if it scares you at points, that's a good thing. The stories contained in these pages are going to help you in the long run. Take it from us, a couple of guys who've dwelled among the cheaters and spent time behind enemy lines – in this day and age, no woman can afford to enter into a relationship with her eyes closed.

Rob Wiser
Las Vegas, May 2006

Chapter 1
The Entrance Exam

Marriage is like twirling a baton, turning hand springs or eating with chopsticks. It looks easy until you try it.

Helen Rowland

Okay, ladies. Before we begin this journey, we're going to have you take our 'Entrance Exam'. This is a series of provocative questions we want you to ask the man in your life. They're designed to illuminate both of your views on fidelity and cheating. (These are also great questions to discuss among your girlfriends.)

While you're supposed to have some fun with this exam, encourage your man to be thoughtful and honest. Don't let him off the hook – make him answer. Then, flip the questions and have him pose them to you. Just change the names and the genders around. (Question 3, in particular, is almost always answered differently by men and women.)

Christopher Curtis, my co-writer on this book, is a police officer trained in interrogation techniques. He put a spin on these twenty questions to make them as effective as possible. While there are no 'right' answers, each is designed to provoke an honest answer.

Some questions are going to make your man pause and think. Some of them might make him squirm. Chances are, this test is going to reveal some surprising differences in the way the two of you view infidelity – and if he's honest, some of his answers might shock you. But don't freak out if you don't agree with his responses. The idea here isn't to spark arguments. His answers will point out issues in your relationship that this book will help you work on, and generate discussions that are going to get the two of you on the same wavelength.

When answering these questions, the only ground rule is that you're not allowed to say 'It depends.' Tell your man to give a straight answer – many of these questions require a simple yes or no. When it's his turn to pose these questions to you, follow the same rule.

So without further ado, here is the Cheat Sheet Entrance Exam.

1. John and Marie have been in a committed relationship for five years. While at a party with their friends, someone proposes a game of truth or dare. John gets a dare to make out for ten seconds with Annabelle, who is their mutual friend. John goes through with the dare. Does this make him a pig, or is he just being a good sport and playing by the rules?

2. Jesse and Emily are newlyweds. Emily discovers evidence that Jesse, while on a business trip right before they got married, had a one-night stand. She confronts him and he admits it. Emily says the marriage is over and she wants Jesse out of

the house immediately. Do you agree with Emily's decision?

3. What would make you more upset: catching me in bed with another man, or overhearing me on the phone saying 'I love you' to another man?

4. Your best friend tells you he's been cheating on his wife with a girl from his office. He sees this girl every Saturday night. As an alibi, he told his wife that Saturday night is now poker night at the house of one of your friends. He's relying on you to back up his story if his wife ever asks. Would you agree to cover for him?

5. Your best friend just got married to the woman of his dreams. You've never seen him this happy. One day, while at the mall, you see his wife accompanied by another man. They're walking together hand in hand, laughing and chatting. Do you tell your best friend what you saw?

6. Name a female celebrity you would love to have sex with. If you had the opportunity to sleep with her, and I gave you permission, would you do it?

7. Stephanie and Joe have been dating for two years. One day Stephanie comes across the password to Joe's personal email account. She proceeds to check through all his emails and discovers that Joe's ex-girlfriend, whom he says he hasn't talked to in months, has been writing him flirtatious notes on a regular basis. She confronts Joe about this and breaks up with him. Was she wrong to invade his privacy?

8. Imagine you live in a world where all couples have 'open relationships'. You're allowed to have sex with other women, I'm allowed to have sex with

other men, and this is considered perfectly normal. Which of the following comes closest to your reaction?

    a)   'This could work. Sounds interesting.'

    b)   'Beam me back to Earth!'

9. Do you feel monogamy is an unnatural state for men to live in?

10. You meet a couple who have been married for 50 years. They lost their virginity to each other when they were eighteen and have been together and monogamous ever since. Do you think this is inspiring, or do you think it's strange?

11. Would you rather find out that I cheated on you, or have me find out that you cheated on me?

12. Lately, whenever Frank has sex with his wife he finds himself thinking about his hot new secretary. He feels ashamed about this and confesses it to his wife. Is he a fool for opening his mouth, or does he deserve credit for being honest?

13. You and I are having sex, and as I climax with an amazingly powerful orgasm, I scream out another man's name. What is your immediate reaction?

14. Tony, a married man, meets an attractive woman at a company party. She is flirting with him but he stays faithful and doesn't take advantage of the opportunity. When he goes home that night, his wife is already asleep. He masturbates while thinking about the woman he met at the party. Is this wrong?

15. Bob is in a dead-end marriage and hasn't had sex with his wife in months. They're only staying together for the sake of their kids. He happens to run into his former high school sweetheart one

night, who is also married, and they wind up having sex. She feels guilty and confesses it to her husband a few days later, but Bob says nothing about it to his wife. Who made the better decision?

16. Eddie and Tanya have a great relationship. One day while cleaning up their apartment, Tanya finds a box full of photos of naked women. She recognises some of the women as Eddie's ex-girlfriends. She decides to put the photos back in the box and say nothing. Is she doing the right thing by leaving it alone, or should she handle the situation differently?

17. Ted and Cindy have been married for six years and have always enjoyed a hyperactive sex life with each other. But Cindy now has a medical condition that prevents her from having sex for one year. She gives Ted the okay to have sex outside their relationship as long as he is discreet and safe. Is Cindy being a super-woman or a super-fool?

18. Let's say I admit to you that sometimes I'm attracted to other women. I want to see what it's like to have sex with a woman and I'll allow you to pick who it's going to be. The catch is, you need to leave us alone and can't come into the bedroom. Would you agree to this?

19. I asked one of my male co-workers to estimate what percentage of his guy friends cheat on their mates. He said 50 per cent. Would you agree that 50 per cent is the average for men?

20. You're at your buddy's bachelor party. You've rented a hotel suite in Las Vegas. You guys wind up at a nightclub and the groom-to-be hooks up with a girl. He wants to take her back to the suite to

have sex. He tells you, 'It's just one last fling – it doesn't mean anything.' Would you try to discourage him? If so, what would you do if he gets angry and tells you to mind your own business?

Chapter 2
Defining the C Word

Women might be able to fake orgasms, but men can fake whole relationships.

Sharon Stone

The way men and women define cheating is a distinct difference between the sexes. Ask men to explain what constitutes cheating, and nine times out of ten they'll tell you it's sex with another woman. In their view, cheating is a physical act and defined in sexual terms. Women, on the other hand, define cheating in more emotional terms. They feel that a man doesn't need to act on his desires to be branded a cheater; that desire and lust can be forms of infidelity.

Ask a guy how he'd feel if he caught his woman cheating, and his temper flares because he equates the C word with her having sex with another man. But for women, it usually isn't the thought of sex alone that makes them upset. It's far more distressing for them to think about their man *loving* another woman. In a survey we carried out while researching this book, 80 per cent of women said they would rather catch their man having sex than overhear him on the phone saying 'I love you' to another woman. The following story puts this dichotomy into practice.

JAY, 37: 'I work in advertising. Recently I was working on a big account and spending late nights at the office. One night, my co-worker Christina and I took a dinner break together and went to a restaurant down the street from our office. We split a bottle of wine and had some laughs and a great meal. Although Christina is attractive, I had no romantic intentions whatsoever. We were simply blowing off steam towards the end of a very long and stressful workday. Besides, I'm getting married to my fiancée, Jennifer, in a couple of months, and Christina has a boyfriend.

'Well, one of Jennifer's friends happened to see us dining together and ratted me out. She called Jennifer to tell her. While we're finishing dessert, she comes storming into the restaurant, cursing me out and causing a scene. It wasn't like she caught me screwing Christina's brains out on my office desk – we were just sitting there eating!

'Now Jennifer expects me to come crawling back to her and apologise, but I feel her behaviour was immature and ridiculous. Maybe this was the signal I needed to break up with her. I can't deal with jealous and possessive women.'

We're betting that Jay wasn't being completely truthful when he related his story. Any guy knows his fiancée isn't going to be pleased if she finds out he's been having cosy dinners with an attractive female co-worker. When confronted about it, of course he's going to use the old excuse 'I didn't think I was doing anything wrong.' And because his fiancée never specifically told him that this type of behaviour was unacceptable to her, a guy like Jay can stick with that excuse. In fact, he'll probably turn it around and accuse her of being insecure, of making a big deal out of nothing.

The moral of the story is this: **when it comes to the boundaries of fidelity in your relationship – what is acceptable to you and what is not – it's important to define them, and the earlier, the better.** If you don't verbalise these boundaries to your man, expect him to test them. If you see him with another girl on a nightclub dance floor, catch him on the phone with his ex-girlfriend or find out he went for drinks with a pretty co-worker, he can always use the excuse 'I didn't know you felt that way' or say 'I didn't think it was a big deal.'

Trust us, guys will play dumb even when it's obvious they're doing something they know you wouldn't approve of. Sometimes they'll go to absurd lengths. 'One time I caught a boyfriend of mine, Bob, in bed with his ex-wife,' recalls Melanie, 33. 'He told me it wasn't technically cheating, because they had kids together and needed to stay close for the children's sake.'

Other times, men honestly believe they haven't crossed the line, yet their spouse feels deeply betrayed. Let's talk about these boundaries for a moment. How would you feel about your man maintaining a friendship with his ex-girlfriend? Would it be okay for them to occasionally hang out, even if he swears to you that it's just platonic? What about him visiting a strip club with some business colleagues? How about if he joined in the fun and had a lap dance or two?

Would it upset you to know that he surfs porn websites? How about if he's meeting girls online in chat rooms – flirting over the internet, but never meeting any of them in person? If it's a guy you haven't been dating for very long, have you discussed whether the relationship is exclusive? Or, could he play dumb when you catch him going out with other women?

If you're like the majority of women, all of the above scenarios would disturb you to some degree. But does your man know your stance on them?

A woman we know, Diane, ran into this exact problem. 'I didn't want to have the "Are we boyfriend and girlfriend?" chat because I didn't want to seem like I was pressuring him,' she told us. 'But we'd been hooking up almost every night for three weeks, and I thought it was understood that we were a couple now and we were going to be with each other exclusively. Then I found out that he'd been sleeping with another girl we both knew. When I confronted him about it, he lied and tried to cover it up, so obviously he knew he'd done something wrong. Then, when he knew he couldn't squirm out of it, he told me he didn't think it was a big deal because I wasn't "technically" his girlfriend. I felt like a fool.'

With a happy, monogamous couple, both parties are in tune with the parameters of their relationship. If she doesn't want him hanging out with other women in certain environments, he is aware of her opinion on the matter and respects it. While in the above story, Jay's fiancée handled the situation poorly – causing a scene in public is never the right way to handle things – he had to know that his intimate dinner was inappropriate, and that it would upset Jennifer if she were to walk into the restaurant and see them sharing a bottle of wine. But as most guys will do, Jay played dumb and tried to make her feel as if she was wildly overreacting, that *she* was the one who had issues.

Jennifer was entitled to feel the way she did. While guys like Jay might claim dinner with a female co-worker is 'no big deal', what do you think would happen if *he* walked into a restaurant and found Jennifer sharing a candlelit dinner with her hunky personal trainer? We're the first to admit that guys have double standards when it comes to these para-meters – if you don't define the boundaries upfront.

Pop quiz

Would you rather catch your man having sex with your best friend, or have him confess to you that he's in love with a woman he works with – even though she's unaware of his feelings?

In the stories we heard from couples affected by cheating, we recognised a number of common themes. One was that the 'cheating boundaries' in their relationships were often blurry and undefined. Obviously, it's cheating when you catch him between the sheets with someone else, just as there are no acceptable excuses when you overhear him on the phone planning a romantic weekend getaway with some girl he met online. These are both clear-cut, black-and-white situations. But it's the grey areas that create the most confusion – the 'minor' infidelities he feels he can justify, or get away with, because you've never expressly forbidden them.

We know a cool couple, George and Gina, who have a rule for the situation that caused problems between Jay and Jennifer. George knows it isn't okay for him to have dinner at a restaurant, or even drinks, with a woman other than his wife. This isn't because Gina thinks George is going to tumble into bed afterwards with the woman. It's simply because she isn't comfortable with the idea. George respects that, and knows that he wouldn't feel comfortable if his wife was out with one of her male co-workers having martinis. It simply would not be appropriate.

'Have a conversation with him about boundaries before he tries to test them,' Gina advises. 'Don't lecture him or lay down your rules; he's much more likely to listen and be honest if you frame it as a casual "what if?" conversation. Ask him where he draws the line at cheating, and then explain how you view things. Don't make any allegations or accusations, just ask him his thoughts on the subject and go from there. The two of you will probably learn some new things about each other, and that's how a relationship grows.'

Linda, who found out her husband David was having online chats with other women, wished she had discussed her feelings on the subject with him upfront. When she confronted him about it, he told her she was blowing things out of proportion, insisted that he'd done nothing wrong, and accused her of being insecure. 'David would always twist things around and try to make it seem like *I* was the one with the problem,' she says, 'or the one trying to start arguments, even when I caught him doing totally inappropriate things. I have to admit, this tactic would work sometimes. I'd start questioning my own feelings and wonder if I *was* making too big a deal out of it.'

By setting parameters, you won't leave him any wiggle room if he tries to get away with more than he should. If you find out he went bar hopping with an ex-girlfriend, he can't use the excuse 'I didn't think you'd care.' If you catch him flirting with women in online chat rooms, he can't try to justify it as harmless fun when you've already mentioned that you find such behaviour unacceptable.

Some would define cheating as doing something with a man or woman that you wouldn't do if your partner was present. Essentially, this makes sense. But a new form of infidelity has added another shade of grey and made infidelity more difficult to define.

EMOTIONAL CHEATING

Dr Judy Karianski, sex and romance columnist for the *New York Daily News*, says emotional cheating is defined by the three As: when you give your **attention**, **attachment** and erotic **attraction** to some-one other than your mate. The phrase 'emotional cheating' became a hot topic in the media during the meltdown of the Brad Pitt–Jennifer Aniston marriage in 2005. It isn't known whether he was having sex with the other woman, Angelina Jolie, while he was still married. But members of Aniston's inner circle said that he became emotionally invested in Jolie shortly after they met on the set of their movie *Mr. and Mrs. Smith*. Though Pitt may have been physi-cally present in his marriage, he had 'checked out' emotionally.

Speaking with Katie Couric on *The Today Show*,

Vanity Fair contributing editor Leslie Bennetts described an interview she did with Aniston: 'Jennifer said to me, "You know, from the moment Brad started filming *Mr. and Mrs. Smith*, he was gone." He was just not there for her.' Courteney Cox, Aniston's former cast-mate on the sitcom *Friends*, said of Pitt: 'I don't think he started an affair physically, but I think he was attracted to [Jolie] . . . there was a connection, and he was honest about that with Jen. It was attraction he fought for a period of time.'

The Pitt–Aniston–Jolie scandal inspired a lot of discussion about emotional cheating. The TV show *Showbiz Tonight* even polled its viewers, posing the question 'Angelina, Brad and Jen: Do you believe in "emotional cheating"?' Eighty per cent of the 2772 internet users who took part voted yes. Meanwhile, in another online poll, 30 per cent of men thought emotional cheating was worse than sexual cheating. With women, the numbers were reversed: 70 per cent thought emotional cheating was worse.

For the married women we spoke with, the idea of emotional cheating was scarier than their husband having sex with another woman. 'When guys have a sexual affair and get caught, they say "It didn't mean anything,"' says Kendra, 36. 'And that's actually true in most cases. Guys will cheat sometimes just because they're horny, and they'll feel no emotional connection to her afterwards. But if I found out that my husband was bonding with another woman on an emotional level, sharing feelings that he wasn't sharing with me, that would be devastating. Our marriage is based on the fact that we're supposed to be best friends.'

Emotional cheating is real, but don't get paranoid

about it. And don't jump to conclusions. Don't feel that your man is emotionally cheating just because he has female friends. But if he has a female friend who acts as his confidante – someone he shares his ups and downs with, instead of you – you do have cause to be concerned. This type of intimate emotional bond can easily erupt into a sexual affair.

On a final note, keep in mind the three categories of men that we stated in the Introduction to this book: those who cheat, those who've cheated in the past, and those who will cheat when placed in certain circumstances. For men, it's that last category that they need to remember if they're truly committed to staying faithful. When men willingly place themselves in sexually charged situations – such as dining out with sexy co-workers, or flirting with other women during a boys' night out – it's often the prelude to cheating. The slope can become slippery in a hurry, as the following story illustrates.

AMANDA, 31: 'I was deeply in love with my husband, Robert, and I was determined to make our relationship last. All of my girlfriends were so controlling with their husbands, barely letting them spend any time with their friends and barking at them if they even looked in the general direction of another woman. They treated their husbands like dogs that had to be housebroken and beaten into obedience.

'I never wanted to be like that. I trusted Robert and let him have his own space. If he wanted to stay out late at the bar with his friends, I never gave him a hard time about it. If he needed to bring some business clients to a "gentleman's club" [a strip club] once in a while in order to close a deal, I didn't like it, but I trusted he would behave himself. I never thought in a million years he would cheat on me. His buddies would tell me how cool and understanding I was, and how they wished their wives were more like me. That made me feel like I was doing the right thing.

'Well, it blew up in my face when I found charges on his credit card for a motel room. He rented the room during a weekend when he was supposed to be out of town visiting his sick father. I hired a private investigator to find out if he had a mistress. It turned out to be worse than that. He checked into that motel regularly to have sex with prostitutes.

'I'm not the cool wife any longer. I'm the one who's going to sue him for half of everything he's got, and then some.'

Christopher Curtis says . . .

As a police officer, I often respond to domestic violence calls where all hell is breaking loose because someone is being accused of cheating. As a result, I have a rule: I don't visit the homes of my married buddies if they're not there. Even if it's a friend of mine I knew long before he got married, I won't visit his house if I know his wife is home alone.

I remember one time, my friend John was out of town on business. His wife called my cell phone one evening and asked me if I could come by and help her set up her new DVD player. It was an innocent request, but I made up an excuse and told her I was busy. All I could think of was her casually mentioning to John that I came by at 11 pm to help her out, and him getting the wrong idea.

But it was one particular call that made me set this rule for myself. A woman was home alone when a pipe burst in the bathroom off from her bedroom. It was late at night and she couldn't call a plumber. Frantic, she saw one of her neighbours outside and asked him if he could come in and do something about the pipe. 'Sure,' he said, and went inside; he was a nice guy and just wanted to help out.

A few minutes later, her husband returned from work. He walked in, saw the Good Samaritan coming out of his bedroom, and beat the crap out of him. The neighbour wound up with a broken orbital bone and lost partial vision in his right eye, and the husband wound up getting arrested for assault and then sued.

So, the message I'd give to the guys out there is this: it's cool to be friends with your buddy's wife, but respect the boundaries.

Chapter 3
Let Your Man Be a Man

Il is as absurd to say that a man can't love one woman all the time as it is to say that a violinist needs several violins to play the same piece of music.

Honoré de Balzac

One weeknight in Las Vegas, we were hanging out at a bar with our usual gang of friends. This evening, there was a special addition to our posse: Tom, an old pal of ours who'd been 'on lockdown' for the past eight months since taking up with a very possessive girlfriend named Christie. She didn't like Tom hanging around us. She didn't approve of him going to bars, unless she was at his side holding on to his arm and restricting him to only a few drinks. But tonight, he'd managed to secure a pass from Christie on account of the fact that his favourite football team was playing a big game. He was eager to watch it, but she didn't want to miss that night's episode of *Desperate Housewives*. Ground rules had been laid down by Christie: three beers, tops, and he was to return immediately after the game (and pick up a pint of Häagen-Dazs for her on the way home).

When Tom walked into the bar, the difference in his appearance was striking. His goatee was shaved; his once-shaggy hair was cut and coiffed. In place of his customary heavy metal T-shirt and baggy shorts, he wore a button-down polo shirt and slacks. Obviously, Christie had given Tom a full makeover – but although he may have looked more mature and polished, his old hard-partying instincts quickly emerged.

The beers started flowing and he was deliriously happy when his team roared off to an early lead. Then his mobile phone started ringing . . . and ringing . . . and ringing. Every 30 minutes or so, Tom would have to duck away from us to update Christie on his evening. 'No honey, I'm not drunk. I'm having water,' he told her as we fed him another shot of tequila. 'I'll be home as soon as the game is over. What flavour ice cream did you want again?'

Cheat Sheet fact

In Spanish, the word for 'wife', *esposa*, also means 'handcuffs'.

Christopher and I felt the guy's pain. Tom was a nice, good-natured guy who avoided confrontations. He was ill-equipped to put up any resistance to a girl like Christie. Every time he hung up and returned to our group, the other guys would crack jokes and rib him about how 'whipped' he was. About how Christie kept his balls in her purse. About how she'd removed his testicles and replaced them with a tracking device so she could watch his every move. Tom smiled along, but clearly he felt embarrassed. Each time his phone rang, it became more awkward and uncomfortable for him. And he had no choice but to answer – otherwise, he knew he'd catch hell when he got home.

By the end of the game, Tom was hammered . . . and he wasn't ready to go home. As the DJ started spinning music and the post-game party kicked off, we lost track of him. Then we spotted him on the dance floor – sloppily making out with some young blonde.

We were stunned when Tom stumbled back to us a few minutes later and proudly displayed a cocktail napkin with a phone number written on it. 'I got her digits,' he crowed. The other guys gave him hand-shakes and 'You're the man' back-slaps. In a flash, Tom had gone from hopeless wimp to the stud of the group.

Then, to their shock, Tom crumpled up the napkin and discarded it. The guys flipped out. 'Dude, that chick was hot!' 'What are you thinking? She's totally into you!' As for Christopher and I, we completely understood the reasons behind Tom's actions. At this point, we were deep into our research for this book, and we knew why a safe, faithful boyfriend like him had suddenly crossed the line. And it wasn't the booze (though it did help grease the wheels).

The next day, Tom called me and stammered out an apology – he didn't know what he was thinking, he'd been an idiot, he'd never cheated on Christie before – but the way I saw it, his actions the previous night had been inevitable. And it could have been a whole lot worse. By leaving that girl on the dance floor and throwing away her number, he'd shown more restraint than a lot of guys would.

I knew that ever since they'd started dating, Christie had worn down and trampled on Tom's sense of masculinity. Threatening it in front of his buddies had been the final straw. His booze-fuelled make-out session with the blonde had been an effort to prove to us, and to himself, that he was still 'one of the boys'.

The male ego, you see, is a delicate thing. As a woman, you've got to understand and respect it if you're going to keep a relationship faithful. Men live in a confusing and frustrating age, one that is constantly chipping away at their sense of masculinity. They're forced to question their natural instincts, suppress desires, and follow the lead of women instead of playing the role of protector and provider. How did things get to this point? It's a question that a lot of men are asking themselves these days. One thing is for certain: guys aren't what they used to be.

WHERE HAVE ALL THE COWBOYS GONE?

Over the years, 'the ideal man' has become progressively softer, more sensitive and more feminine. Just look at the top male movie stars of past generations. In the 1960s we had two-fisted icons like Steve McQueen, Frank Sinatra, John Wayne and Clint Eastwood. In the '70s, despite the popularity of more rounded leading men like Dustin Hoffman and Robert Redford, hairy-chested he-man Burt Reynolds was the top star in Hollywood. In the '80s, pumped-up action heroes like Sylvester Stallone, Arnold Schwarzenegger and Bruce Willis constantly saved the world from imminent destruction and their films reaped billions at the box office.

How things have changed. For fans of 'guy movies', a pivotal moment came in 2000 when Mel Gibson – once the star of bad-ass classics such as *Mad Max* and

Lethal Weapon – starred in *What Women Want*. In this fluffy romantic comedy, Gibson played a chauvinistic advertising executive who loses a promotion to a female co-worker because he doesn't understand that it's a 'woman's world'. An accident then gives him the power to hear women's thoughts. Only by understanding their needs and tapping into his own feminine side is he able to regain his success.

Even before the release of *What Women Want*, but especially since then, there's been a never-ending parade of softer, more 'vulnerable' stars. Keanu Reeves, Leonardo DiCaprio, Justin Timberlake, Tobey Maguire, Joaquin Phoenix, Orlando Bloom . . . the list goes on. And even the so-called heir to Schwarzenegger's action-hero throne – wrestler-turned-actor The Rock – is waxed, buffed and polished to the point where he could moonlight as a Chippendale. We still have the occasional scruffy, testosterone-fuelled star (Russell Crowe comes to mind), but they're a rarity; and all of the major male stars, from Tom Cruise to Tom Hanks, cry and emote on-screen in ways that the stars of past generations would never have dared. In her hit song of the same name, Paula Cole asked 'Where have all the cowboys gone?' We've been wondering this ourselves lately.

Masculinity used to be a virtue; now, the media encourages men to downplay their inherent masculine traits and show a more delicate side. This shift has spawned a new breed of men, dubbed **metrosexuals**: straight guys who take as much care in their appearance as women do, sometimes even more so. For men, hairy chests and bulging muscles are out; body waxing, tanning beds, manicures/pedicures, lean or rail-thin physiques and even cosmetic surgery are in. Companies have sprouted up to sell make-up for men, with products such as 'face and body bronzer', eyebrow glaze and lip gloss. (Christy, a single and frustrated 24-year-old, told me: 'I'd just like to meet a guy who takes less time to get ready for a date than I do.')

The message is clear: it's no longer socially acceptable for men to look, or behave, the way men of past generations did. Women aren't looking for men in the mould of their fathers; our society is coaching them to seek cuter, feminised versions who are 'in touch with their feelings'.

Television sitcoms provide clear evidence of this trend, as 'the guy's guy' is now something to be mocked. The formula for many hit TV shows in recent years has involved a bumbling, rough-around-the-edges husband who would be hopeless without his sexy, sassy, competent wife. In *The King of Queens*, comedian Kevin James portrays a lug who is constantly set straight by his wife, played by Leah Remini. (Only on television would a woman that attractive marry such a schlub.) On *Everybody Loves Raymond*, Ray Barone (played by Ray Romano) was a henpecked wimp. Constantly belittled by his wife, Debra, poor Ray was regularly denied sex and scolded for wanting to hang out with his pals. The only thing keeping him from sleeping on the couch was that he invariably came to realise the error of his ways and apologised – not exactly an inspiring role model for the modern man, or his kids.

This shift began to take shape in the late 1970s with the rise of the feminist movement. Their agenda resulted in a number of important triumphs for women. Equal pay for equal work; equal opportunity; the end of gender-based discrimination; zero tolerance for sexual harassment. But some serious problems surfaced when radical feminists began to paint male sexuality as a crime. Some even equated penetration (and any sexual intercourse at all) with rape. To the members of this 'Sisterhood', all men were oppressors to be overthrown. 'Gender equality' basically meant that men should start behaving more like women. Chivalry suddenly became offensive. Holding a door open for a woman was no longer polite; it was an insult, a sign that he considered her weaker and inferior. And forget about paying a female co-worker a friendly compliment on her dress; this constituted sexual harassment.

What began as a positive movement wound up being hijacked by radicals with an axe to grind against the small percentage of men who actually are sexist creeps. As a result, men became bewildered and intimidated. How were they supposed to act? Were they allowed to take the initiative with women, or were they supposed to wait for mysterious 'signals' that it was okay to ask for a date, or try for a kiss? **Most damaging of all, men were no longer sure what role they were supposed to play in their relationships.** The role they'd played for thousands of years – that of the protector, the provider and the partner who took charge in the bedroom – had been thrown out the window. Their natural inclination to admire and acknowledge beautiful women now made them a sexist pig. **In short, men became ashamed of being men.**

While the hardcore feminists of that era have fallen by the wayside, their impact on relationships remains profound. Today, there's a direct correlation between this emasculation of the modern man and the depressing cheating statistics. Men are more confused than ever, and when men get confused they tend to stray towards comfortable territory. This territory is often the arms of another woman, one who props up his ego and makes him feel like he's allowed to be in control.

As a sensible modern woman, you don't need to buy into the hype and the propaganda. If you're looking for a man with masculine qualities (and the vast majority of women, in their hearts, are) then find that guy and make him feel good about his inherent male qualities. Let him play the role he was born to play. He likes it when you help polish his rough edges, but don't try to convert a guy's guy into a metrosexual. And don't attempt to isolate him from his close male friends. He needs these friends in his life; when he's around them, he gets to act like a man and assert this side of himself.

THE POLARITY PRINCIPLE

Self-help guru Tony Robbins says that **polarity** is the key to sexual attraction and is the basis for intimacy. *Webster's Dictionary* describes polarity as 'the tendency to turn, grow, think, etc. in contrary directions, as if because of magnetic repulsion'. *Magnetic repulsion?* We know, it doesn't exactly sound like the recipe for everlasting love, but the way Robbins explains it, it makes perfect sense.

Everyone exudes either masculine energy or feminine energy. It's not dependent on gender. A woman can have a masculine energy to her, and a heterosexual guy can have a feminine energy. But in order for a couple to feel a strong **sexual connection** to each other, each has to fulfil one of these roles in the relationship. In other words, they need to be polarised. If both people are masculine or both are feminine, there's not going to be any spark. It's the difference between trying to press two rocks together (which will come apart the moment you let go) and pressing two magnets together.

As a woman, you can be assertive, independent and opinionated. You can be the boss at your workplace. And yet you can still be the feminine partner in your relationship – meaning you require a man who fulfills the masculine role.

Likewise, there are big, strong guys who are confident and successful in their careers. But when they're alone with their girlfriend or wife, they don't play the masculine role. They allow the woman to take the leadership position and make the important decisions. During arguments, they'd rather seek compromise than take a stand. Now, if a feminine woman is with a guy like this, it's a turn-off. Over time, she's going to lose respect for this type of man and grow bored with him.

Feminine women prefer to follow the lead of a *masculine* male. They take comfort in knowing that their man can handle situations and make the important decisions. This is not to say that guys should always call the shots and not respect their spouse's opinion. In order for a relationship to work, both people need their voices to be heard and respected. But the feminine woman wants to feel that when it comes down to it, her man is always ready to step up, make decisions and protect her.

It can work equally well when a masculine woman is in a relationship with a feminine man. This type of polarity can be just as powerful. By 'feminine', we're not saying he has gay tendencies or that he likes to dress a certain way. It has nothing to do with any of that. It's about the energy he exudes when he's with his woman. There are strapping, totally heterosexual men whose personalities are more feminine than masculine, just as there are petite, softly spoken women who have a masculine energy.

Jerome is a 270-pound nightclub bouncer who could pass for an NFL lineman. Seeing him, the last word you would think of is 'feminine'. But when he's around his wife, Jackie, he defers to her and lets her run the show. He's a pussycat around her, and this arrangement works well for them. Jackie, a tiny dynamo who barely weighs 100 pounds, is the masculine partner and Jerome is the feminine partner. They've been married for eight years and adore each other.

So how do you know whether a man is more masculine than feminine? Tony Robbins explains that masculinity is about taking big things and making them small. Men want two things in their life: peace and freedom. In order to feel at peace, and therefore free, they tackle problems head on, resolve them, and put them to bed. They don't want to fret and debate over issues that they consider minor.

Femininity, on the other hand, is about taking small things and making them big. For individuals with a more feminine personality, this can mean turning a minor problem into a source of great drama (such as getting deeply upset over squabbles with friends or family members). But turning 'small into big' can also be a wonderful feminine quality. It means you're more sensual and emotionally tuned in to the world around you. You have strong emotional reactions to scents, colours, songs – you see beauty in things that masculine

people overlook. Feminine women want to feel appreciated, loved and protected. And only a masculine partner
can fill this need.

Put a feminine person and a masculine person
together, and there's potential for an attraction to
develop. Put two feminine people together, and while
they might have lots in common and enjoy each other's
company, there aren't going to be sparks. And if you
put two masculine people together, they might become
buddies – but in a romantic relationship, they're only
going to wind up butting heads. They both want to
lead, they both want to make the decisions, and it
winds up resulting in constant arguments. Homosexual
or lesbian relationships work the same way. There
has to be a masculine partner and a feminine partner
in order to create a strong mutual, sexual attraction.
There needs to be polarity.

Have you ever been on a date with a guy who was
good-looking, polite and fun to be around – a totally
'nice guy' – but you felt absolutely no sexual attraction
to him? Again, it's about polarity. If you're feminine,
chances are this guy failed to project the masculine
energy that you instinctually need.

Most women are feminine and desire masculine
men. If this is the case with you, then find a masculine partner and encourage that side of him. Make
him feel like a protector. Don't nag him, order him
around or belittle him; making him feel like his
masculinity is being threatened is a quick way to turn
him against you. **And *always* make him feel like a
man in the bedroom.** We can't stress that point
enough. There are occasions that call for tender lovemaking, and there are other times when you should

coax out his inner animal. What's more of a turn-on, a partner who isn't afraid to initiate hot, passionate sex or a timid guy who's always waiting for you to make the first move? If you're a feminine woman, it's never going to work out long-term with guy number two.

Know what kind of role you need your man to play. And don't get too hung up on the idea of finding someone you're completely 'compatible' with, since it's the differences between two people – the polarity – that keep sexual attraction alive. It's great to share interests and hobbies, but it's that fundamental push-and-pull between masculine and feminine energy that creates real passion.

'I'll always adore my ex-husband Carl,' says Vivica, 26. 'My friends all thought I was crazy to divorce him. He was tall, handsome, made good money, and he was a total sweetheart. He worshipped the ground I walked on and would have done anything for me. I just wasn't passionate about him. It sounds weird, I know . . . I can't explain it.'

But when Vivica described her relationship with Carl to us, her lack of passion for him made perfect sense. Their marriage lacked polarity. Carl could have been the sweetest, most loving guy in the world, but he also constantly put Vivica in the driver's seat. He preferred to let her make all the decisions. Whenever she was going through upsetting situations – whether she'd been passed up for a promotion at her job, or was feuding with a family member – he never had much to say about it. He never took an active role and suggested a course of action for her to take. Over time, she couldn't help feeling that Carl was weak. She craved masculine energy but she was living with a feminine spouse.

Another part of respecting your man's masculinity is allowing him to feel a sense of independence. He should respect you and never keep you in the dark, but don't make him feel that he constantly needs to answer to you. Don't keep him on a short leash; if you feel the need to do so, it's a red flag that there are problems in your relationship – or with your own self-esteem – that you need to work out. This is what causes 'nice guys' like Tom (the friend we described at the start of this chapter) to go over the edge and cheat. In a lot of cases, it isn't just a five-minute make-out session with some random girl at a bar, it's a full-blown affair that leads to a relationship meltdown. No guy wants to feel like a woman has him under a microscope. If you nag him and belittle him in front of his buddies, you're going to hurry things down the road to ruin.

When roles become blurred and a man feels his masculinity is under attack, he'll look for an escape. One of the challenges faced by 'power couples' – that is, relationships in which both the man and the woman are highly successful and respected by their peers – is that the woman often starts to view her husband as merely a partner instead of a man. Surely this factor came into play in the relationship between Bill and Hillary Clinton, when he was in the White House and allegedly engaging in affairs left and right. It's hard to imagine hard-charging, masculine Hillary allowing Bill (also a masculine personality) to be the man at home, or in the bedroom. We'd venture to say this also played a role in the break-up of Brad Pitt and Jennifer Aniston. When you're a famous actress starring in Hollywood movies – where every day you have men fawning over you and you're in a position of total control – it must be difficult to come home and allow your husband to feel like a masculine protector, a man that you *need*.

Back when Ben Affleck was dating Jennifer Lopez, how was he supposed to feel like a man when she was constantly surrounded by handlers and bodyguards who took care of everything for her? **A masculine guy needs to feel needed by his woman.**

At the time of writing, the Britney Spears–Kevin Federline marriage is reportedly on the rocks. (If they're still married by the time you read this, we owe our bookies money.) Their relationship is an example of how polarity can pull two people together who don't appear to be compatible – and how it can destroy a relationship when the feminine/masculine roles become blurred. It's easy to see why Britney fell for the guy. She was surrounded by people who catered to her every whim, and along came this swaggering 'bad boy' who projected a strong masculine energy. (He was virile as well, which is another sign of masculinity; he'd already had two kids with another woman.) Around 'K-Fed', she didn't feel like an untouchable superstar – she felt like a girly-girl who wanted to be loved by him and protected.

She was into this arrangement, but the situation wound up crushing his sense of masculinity. He became a laughing stock in the media: an unemployed leech living off his wife's wealth and fame. The disparity between them was so obvious that he started jetting off to Las Vegas to party without her, so that he could reassert himself as a man.

We'd speculate that it's also why, back in June 1995, Hugh Grant snuck away from his drop-dead sexy girlfriend, supermodel Elizabeth Hurley, for a tryst with a street hooker (Divine Brown). As for the break-up of Jessica Simpson and Nick Lachey, for us the writing was on the wall when we saw the involvement of her father, Joe, who manages her career with a heavy hand. Talk about emasculating: not only was his wife a zillion times more successful than him, but his father-in-law was constantly hanging around and calling the shots.

It's always difficult for a highly successful female to maintain a relationship with a less successful guy, a point that Halle Berry made after splitting from her cheating husband, R&B singer Eric Benet. It makes men feel demoralised and emasculated when their basic functions – to protect and provide for their mate – are no longer required.

Today, guys will tell you that women have achieved more than equality; they've now got the upper hand. As females, you've got more opportunities than ever, at the workplace and in how you approach your relationships with men. But if you want to maintain a healthy relationship in which *both* people feel respected and comfortable in their roles, you've got to simply let him be a man sometimes – and love him for it.

Chapter 4

Love and Marriage, Generation X–Style

In Hollywood, an equitable divorce settlement means each party getting 50 per cent of publicity.

Lauren Bacall

While the stories and lessons in this book apply to women of all ages, this is the first book about adultery written from the Generation X perspective (which we define as anyone who came into adulthood with MTV and the internet). It's a whole new ballgame for this generation, as the options for adultery and consequences of divorce are dramatically different from what they were in the past.

Our parents and grandparents approached relationships very differently. Back in their day, you were *expected* to marry in your early twenties, have kids right away, and stay together until the (sometimes bitter) end. If you were still single at the age of 28, people suspected there was something seriously wrong with you. As for divorce, it was seen as an absolute last resort. Women trapped in lousy marriages would suffer in silence and put up a happy facade, able to remain content in the knowledge that they were maintaining the household and raising the children.

In Canada, there weren't even divorce laws until the 1960s. Prior to that, the only way to get divorced was to file an application with the Canadian Senate, where a special committee would investigate the request for a divorce. If they found that the request had merit, it took an Act of Parliament to officially dissolve the marriage. Now, compare that to the United States' modern divorce laws, which permitted Britney Spears to get hitched to her first husband in Vegas, grab a billion dollars' worth of free publicity, and dump the befuddled groom 55 hours later.

Or, consider the trash-TV abomination of 2000, *Who Wants to Marry a Multi-Millionaire?*, in which female contestants in the United States competed to marry some rich dude they'd never even met. The 'winner', Darva Conger, tied the knot with creepy millionaire Rick Rockwell on live television – then sought to have the marriage annulled a few days later. (At least she wound up scoring a nice payday to pose nude in *Playboy*.) Naturally, the whole crazy fiasco generated great TV ratings.

In prior generations it was rare for a woman to leave her husband for reasons other than abuse. There were two major reasons why. Women didn't have the career options that they have today and were often completely dependent on their men; and from a social standpoint, no one wanted the stigma of being a divorcee. It was a shameful and embarrassing thing.

Today, if somebody decides to seek greener pastures with someone else, they can file the papers and move on. We all have divorced friends who are happy to have us join their 'team'. And for women, modern divorce laws – which are weighted heavily in their favour – can create a major *incentive* to terminate a troubled marriage. Rather than being cast off to fend for herself (which was usually the case for divorced women in previous generations), now she can take half the man's assets in court. If the husband is wealthy, a woman can get sweet revenge *and* set herself up financially for life.

Pop quiz

Christina wonders if her husband, Peter, would cheat, given the opportunity. She asks her sexy friend Michelle (whom Peter does not know) to approach him when he's out at a bar with his buddies. She instructs Michelle to flirt with Peter and see if he'll agree to go home with her, just to find out whether he'll take the bait. Is this 'test' fair, or is Christina playing dirty?

MATRIMONIAL MADNESS

Why has the institution of marriage fallen apart? Why does the sacred vow to stand by each other 'till death do us part' now mean, 'Let's give it a shot, and see if it actually works out'?

It's interesting to note that the concept of marriage wasn't invented for reasons of love. The first 'marriages' took place when a primitive man went into a primitive woman's cave, scooped her up and carried her off to be his mate. Back then, it was mainly about finding someone to share the workload. After a long day spent hunting for food, a guy needed someone to tend to the cave and cook up the brontosaurus burgers.

Cheat Sheet fact

On 27 May 1996, the *Los Angeles Times* ran a front-page story on efforts to reform no-fault divorce laws. According to the *Times*, in approximately twenty US states, 'it is easier to break the marriage contract than it is to fire an employee or back out of buying a car.'

In ancient Greece, marriages were arranged by the parents and 'approved by the gods'. It was customary for girls in their early teens to marry men well into their thirties. A man had to purchase his wife from her father. On the night before the wedding, her hair was cut off and she was bathed in holy water from a sacred fountain. The toys she played with as a child were then taken away and offered as sacrifice to a goddess. The Greeks owned their wives in every sense – they could even lend or sell them to another man. (Ancient Romans also viewed their wives as 'property'; the groom carried his bride over the threshold of their new home to symbolise his ownership of her.)

The Spartans believed that athletic ability determined whether two people were compatible for marriage. Before tying the knot, couples had to wrestle in public to demonstrate how well matched they were. Spartan women married in their twenties, and the groom's father chose his son's bride. Once he'd made his pick, the couple were married twelve months later. The ceremony was held in the groom's tent and was followed by seven days of festivities. (In a weird feminist twist, wealthy women were allowed to have a husband for each house they maintained.)

In medieval times, it was believed that Christian

church marriages were made in heaven and could never be broken. Therefore, you only got one shot at making it work. The father of the bride had to fork over a dowry of land or money to the groom. If the marriage fell apart, the wife – and the dowry – were returned to the father, and neither partner was permitted to remarry.

Unusual traditions still remain. Amish men need to ask a churchman to seek the approval of the woman's parents. Weddings take place on a Tuesday or Wednesday in November, following the harvest, and at the ceremony the bride wears white for the first and last time in her life. There isn't any honeymoon, and the newlyweds don't get to shack up together until the springtime.

Arab marriages are arranged between the families of the bride and groom. They work out the amount of money that will be paid to the bride's family for her *trousseau*, a special wardrobe the bride needs to purchase before marriage. An ancient ceremony (in which no men are allowed) is held to celebrate the bride's wedding; her hair is covered with a red dye and her body is elaborately painted by her friends. At the conclusion of the ceremony, the women dance together.

In France, three separate marriage ceremonies may be involved. The first of these is a civil ceremony, performed in the town hall with the mayor officiating. The second is the religious ceremony, conducted by a priest. If the couple live in the countryside, a third ceremony is held in which the people of the village host a ten-course banquet for the bride and groom. The villagers bang pots and pans to remind the couple of the difficulties of marriage, just as, in the Italian tradition, newlyweds are showered with confetti made of sugar-coated almonds, to symbolise the bitterness and sweetness of being married.

Child marriages are still common in parts of rural India, with brides as young as seven years old. On the big day, the groom rides into town on a horse, followed by a horde of friends and relatives, while the local wise man chants prayers. After the bride and groom walk around a ceremonial fire seven times, the bride goes to live in her husband's house for three days. Then she returns to her own home to await puberty, at which point she will be reunited with her husband.

In Japan, married couples didn't even live together until the 1400s. Husbands and wives lived in separate homes and could meet only at night. (Quite fittingly, the ancient Japanese word for marriage meant 'slip into the house by night'.) Today, the most common Japanese wedding tradition is the Shinto ceremony. A Shinto priest purifies the bride and groom, who then drink from cups of sake; the bride wears a white kimono, which symbolises the death of her ties to her own family, and a special hat (known as a horn cover) to cover her 'horns of jealousy'.

The Mbutis, a nomadic people who live in central Africa, take a pretty wild approach. The man must prove his worth to his beloved's parents by catching an antelope and offering it to them. He also gives them roots, nuts, birds and orchids from the tops of the tallest trees in the forest. When the couple are ready to be married, they build a house and live together, but the marriage isn't official until three days after the wife gives birth to their first child.

While marriage ceremonies and traditions vary, at the end of the day it's supposed to be about love between two people. But centuries ago, when the concept of marriage first began to take shape in the western world, it had nothing to do with making the ultimate commitment to your soul mate. For upper-class men and women, it was more about consolidating wealth or creating alliances between two families. Among the lower classes, families arranged marriages for their kids based on practical matters, such as whether the bride and the in-laws would be able to assist with the groom's family farm. Hopefully, love between the husband and wife would develop *after* the papers were signed. If it didn't, they stayed married regardless.

Back then, there was no paperwork and no official records. If a couple decided they were married, then they were. In the thirteenth century, marriage became more formalised. Men and women began to tie the knot in ceremonies that involved a priest and witnesses. By the 1500s, governments were creating laws around marriage, requiring couples to be licensed and registered. (Some of these laws were bizarre. In the Bavarian city of Nuremberg, for example, having pre-marital sex could get you a fine or jail time.) Basically, marriage had become a legal contract.

As economies in both Europe and the New World changed from agricultural to industrial, the lower classes no longer needed to consolidate their families for the purposes of farm labour. The eighteenth century saw society beginning to view marriage more in terms of companionship, love and intimacy. But with this new concept of marriage came the concept of divorce. Love and passion could wear off over time, and when it did, men needed a way out.

Many people feel that the 1950s represented the golden era of marriage, certainly in the likes of America and Australia. And married life was a lot simpler then, with family coming first and the roles of husband and wife clearly defined. In the so-called 'nuclear families' of this generation, the woman was the homemaker and the man was the breadwinner. Families were tight-knit units and the overall good of the household was more important than the individual needs of the husband and wife. Young men and women married out of love, but also because it was the socially correct thing to do. Marrying and raising a family enhanced your standing in the eyes of yours peers and the community. Once you were into your twenties, there was nothing hip about being single; it was time to grow up and begin building a family of your own.

Then, in the 1960s and '70s, everything got turned upside down. The feminist movement taught women to be more independent and to explore their 'sense of self'. Instead of the preservation of the family unit being the most important thing, it was now more about individual needs. Women were venturing out into the workplace and didn't *need* men to provide for them. Divorce laws were changed to reflect this new attitude, making it easier for couples to split up if they felt unful-filled in their relationships. Living with your mate without getting married, or simply choosing to remain single, became socially acceptable.

Today, if you're a dissatisfied husband or a desper-ate housewife, there's much less impetus to stay in a troubled marriage and work through the challenges. The well-being of the children is often the only consid-eration. Divorce is no longer a scandalous scarlet letter for women; it can be a sign of courage and independence. It spoke volumes when the marriage between Prince Charles and Camilla Parker-Bowles – both of whom were divorced – received Queen Elizabeth's blessing. Fifty years earlier she had warned her sister, the late Princess Margaret, that she would lose her royal status if she married the divorced man she was in love with.

These days, divorcees can shrug off the failed 'starter marriages' they entered into in their twenties and chalk them up as a learning experience. It's certainly not something modern men need to be ashamed of either, since many women find divorced men in their thirties or forties more appealing than men of that age who've never married. A divorced man has shown that he's at least capable of committing, and, it can be presumed, has gained some maturity that he'll bring to his next marriage.

It's now common for couples to abandon their once sacred vows and take up with other lovers simply because they feel they've 'grown apart'. Celebrities provide the most absurd examples of this, announcing through their PR flacks that they're divorcing after a few months (or in Britney Spears' case, *hours*) of marriage, but 'remain the best of friends'.

It should be pointed out that in this crazy marital merry-go-round, women are as deserving of blame as men. Far too many women place all the emphasis on *finding* the right man and not nearly enough emphasis on keeping him. We've all heard the saying about how maintaining a relationship takes work. But how many women are actually putting in the necessary work – and how many are folding their cards and filing for divorce as soon as the initial thrill of marriage fades?

As for cheating, it's no longer a last resort for desperate husbands and wives who've felt neglected for years. People nowadays are cheating right out of the gate. And the percentages of women who cheat and men who cheat are now nearly equal.

CELEBRITY PIMPS AND THE MEDIA FACTOR

A lot of Gen X women allow celebrity couples to influence the way they view their own relationships. Hollywood marriages are the stuff of girlhood fantasies; the media breathlessly reports every detail of the whirlwind courtships, eye-popping engagement rings, multi-million-dollar weddings and exotic honeymoons. But in the end these stars are human, like any of us, and there are lessons to be learned from their relationships and the way the public perceives them.

When Brad Pitt and Jennifer Aniston called it quits, women of all ages and backgrounds were genuinely affected, as if the golden couple had personally let them down. In the marital disaster zone that is Hollywood, their union was widely considered to be the one that would last. Despite the fact that they were ludicrously rich, famous and attractive, it was a marriage that everyday women took comfort in. If Brad Pitt, one of the world's most desirable men, could stand by one woman and resist all temptations, then certainly there was hope for any marriage to remain monogamous.

As we all know, their marriage crumbled in a very public, and ugly, spectacle. It was immediately assumed that another woman – Academy Award-winning sex goddess Angelina Jolie – was the reason why. From a public relations standpoint, Pitt played it smart by keeping his relationship with Jolie as low key as possible. It was only in January 2006, a year after he and Aniston split, that Pitt and Jolie went public, and that was to announce that they were expecting a baby together.

Interestingly, Pitt didn't draw the scorn of the media for leaving his wife for another, younger woman. The pairing of Pitt and Jolie was a match made in tabloid heaven; it was as if this impossibly photogenic couple transcended bad press.

In the immediate aftermath of the break-up, Aniston received more negative press than her straying husband. Many publications, quoting anonymous sources close to the couple, advanced the theory that Pitt had wanted children, but Aniston didn't, and that it was the chief cause of the break-up. He emerged from the split pretty much unscathed, free to continue pulling down $20 million* per movie and sending crowds of females into hysterics every time he ventured out in public. Aniston, on the other hand, was portrayed by the tabloids as the grieving, devastated 'woman scorned'. Her post-break-up interview with *Vanity Fair*, in which she wept over the split, became the best selling issue in the magazine's history.

In the end, Aniston's PR experts were able to spin her as a tragic hero. *GQ* magazine named her its first ever 'Woman of the Year'. From here on, even though she's already a fabulously rich A-list actress, her image will always be that of the gutsy phoenix rising from the ashes. Her handlers are, no doubt, determined for her to achieve the same level of success as Nicole Kidman –

---

* The reader should note that all dollar amounts given in this book are US dollars.

another woman scorned, who soared to incredible career heights after her divorce from Tom Cruise. (And another female celebrity who endured media allegations that she was too focused on her career to bear children with her partner.)

It was a different deal with actor Jude Law. His engagement to gorgeous 23-year-old actress Sienna Miller imploded when it was revealed that he'd been sleeping with his children's nanny. Law had met Miller on the set of the 2004 movie *Alfie*, around the time of his divorce from his first wife, Sadie Frost (with whom he had three children). In an unusual twist, instead of denying everything, the 32-year-old lothario issued a public apology to Miller. This scandal sparked a frenzy of tabloid headlines and discussions in the mainstream media about whether men are even *capable* of being faithful.

It's interesting to note that years ago, news of a superstar heart-throb like Brad Pitt getting hitched, or Jude Law being married with three kids at a young age, might have been swept under the rug. There was a time when the handlers of male celebrities urged their clients not to marry, so as to not dash the dreams of their love-struck fans. If they did tie the knot, it was kept quiet.

Ever heard of Cynthia Powell? Probably not, and there's a reason why you might not have done. She was John Lennon's first wife, and the mother of his son Julian, when the Beatles rocketed to superstardom. The Fab Four's manager, Brian Epstein, kept Lennon's family a secret because he didn't want to detract from his image as a heart-throb rock star.

Today, the situation has been reversed. A marriage, or a divorce filled with scandalous allegations, can be a quick-fix answer for any celebrity who wants to control the front pages of the tabloids. Marriages are orchestrated and timed to reap maximum PR. Reports about stars dating each other are often planted in the press by their handlers, in order to generate buzz for whatever movie they're appearing in. The effect is that the institution of marriage is cheapened; getting hitched to some Hollywood hunk-of-the-moment is glamorous and cool, but it's not something anyone in the real world is supposed to take too seriously.

Once married, female celebrities continue to flaunt their sexuality all over the place – striking porn-star poses in magazine spreads and sending the message that they're loose, horny and available. Nick Lachey, who at the time of writing has split from Jessica Simpson, epitomised this trend of the 'celebrity pimp' – guys who reap fortunes from the sex-bomb image their famous wives hawk to the public. In an appropriate move, when Britney Spears wed the trash-tastic Kevin Federline, the wedding party wore crushed velvet jumpsuits with the word 'PIMP' printed on the backs. (Federline's father had 'PIMP DADDY' emblazoned on his.)

The problem is that turbulent celebrity relationships have become models for impressionable young couples. The more dysfunctional the stars' behaviour, the more glamorous it all seems. The disastrous drug-addled sideshow that is the Bobby Brown–Whitney Houston marriage is seen by many young women as an example of true love: a wife standing by her man, no matter how many times he bounces in and out of jail and rehab.

For a period, rocker Tommy Lee and *Baywatch* pin-up Pamela Anderson were the hottest couple on the planet; their relationship was a three-ring circus of drunken brawls, domestic abuse, jail terms and fist-fights with paparazzi. The icing on the cake was their homemade porn video, which turned out to be the biggest seller in triple-X history. In the eyes of many young couples, this mess of a marriage couldn't have seemed any cooler.

The B-list version of the Lee–Anderson marriage is the one between rocker Dave Navarro and singer/actress Carmen Electra, who allowed MTV to turn their November 2003 march to the aisle into a lame reality TV show. While bad-boy Navarro and boy-band flunky Nick Lachey might not appear to have much in common, they made their millions the same way: by having their wives appear practically naked all over print and television.

Ironically, while no mother would approve of their daughter worshipping such dysfunctional celebrities, middle-aged women make up the chief audience of TV soap operas. On these shows, the most popular plotlines always involve steamy and scandalous affairs. Meanwhile, female viewers have turned *Desperate Housewives* into a ratings bonanza; this red-hot network drama draws tens of millions of viewers per week. Hollywood executives say that the show's adulterous storylines are the main reason behind its success. (A major plotline was the extramarital affair between a bored housewife and her teenage landscaper. This surely inspired plenty of sexually frustrated housewives to start viewing the hired help in a new light.)

The fat cats who run the television business know that sex sells, and that cheating sells even more. In 2001, the Fox network unleashed the ultimate cheat-fest with its reality show *Temptation Island*, a sexed-up twist on *Survivor* that saw young couples separated on opposite sides of an island and surrounded by horny, good-looking singles whose mission was to tempt and seduce them. Unsurprisingly, the show proved to be a huge hit.

As a society, we're far more fascinated by cheating than by the famous couples who've managed to make it work. The blow job that Bill Clinton received from Monica Lewinsky generated more media coverage and more public interest than any war George Bush can wage. While a distressingly low percentage of Americans can even find Iraq on a map, they can tell you the details of Kobe Bryant's extramarital sexcapades with the nineteen-year-old girl he was accused of raping in a hotel room.

In May 2005, Paris Hilton, the celebutante who epitomises the phrase 'famous for being famous', announced her engagement to Greek shipping heir Paris Latsis and, more importantly, got to boast about her $5 million ring. (If you actually believed she was going to make it down the aisle with that guy, I know a Nigerian banker who's got an investment opportunity for you.) An even bigger joke was Michael Jackson's 'marriage' to Lisa Marie Presley; I'm still scarred from the sight of those two tongue-kissing each other on stage at the 1994 MTV Awards, one of the more ill-conceived publicity stunts in the history of the entertainment business.

The end result of all of this nonsense is that the institution of marriage continues to lose credibility. Celebrity pimps, their sex-object wives, and a scandal-hungry media are only hurrying it down the road to ruin. As the average person loses respect for these supposedly sacred vows – viewing marriage as something you can do on a whim, figure out later, and end with a divorce as soon as you get second thoughts – cheating becomes even more widespread. There's less incentive to face the challenges and work things out.

So this is the state of relationships today. We know the situation sounds grim, and the divorce rates make it all the more depressing. The odds of anyone out there enjoying a happy, mutually fulfilling, monogamous lifetime relationship may not seem any better than the odds of leaving a Vegas casino up a million dollars. But the research we conducted for *The Cheat Sheet* showed us that there are solutions.

Quickie celebrity splits

You'd figure actress Robin Givens would have learned to pick her husbands more carefully after her hellish marriage to Mike Tyson. But on 22 August 1997, Givens and tennis instructor Syetozar Marinkovic married and separated on the same day.

Legendary Hollywood producer Robert Evans and sometime actress Catherine Oxenberg, his fifth wife, lasted all of twelve days together. (They married only four days after meeting each other.) Evans, 75, is now on his seventh marriage.

When Carmen Electra and Dennis Rodman got married in Las Vegas in November 1998, he sought an annulment nine days later but they wound up staying married for five months. Few believed the union would last — even fewer when Rodman admitted he was so drunk during the wedding that he didn't remember most of it.

After six weeks of dating, Drew Barrymore got hitched to bartender Jeremy Thomas in 1994. It didn't even last a month. In 2001 she lasted all of five months with husband number two, the incredibly unsexy comedian Tom Green.

In 1997, Jennifer Lopez swapped vows with waiter Ojani Noa. They lasted thirteen months, which was five more than her next marriage, to choreographer Cris Judd. (That one collapsed in 2002; she's now married to singer Marc Anthony.)

R. Kelly married the late singing star Aaliyah in August 1994. After three months, the marriage was annulled when a court found out she'd lied about her age in order to get married. She was only fifteen at the time.

Chapter 5
Infidelity Around the World

An archaeologist is the best husband a woman can have: the older she gets, the more interested he is in her.

Agatha Christie

Every country has its own views on adultery. In the United States, Bill Clinton's indiscretions with an intern nearly brought the American government to its knees. (If Monica Lewinksy had never gotten *on* her knees, the whole mess could have been avoided in the first place.) While in some Muslim societies wives who screw around still face the prospect of death by stoning – a sentence imposed on them by Islamic courts. On the other hand, in France, President François Mitterrand's mistress stood beside his wife at his funeral.

Harsh anti-adultery laws still exist for members of the US military, who are beholden to their own separate legal system and prosecuted for crimes by military courts. Cheating on your spouse can get you a dishonourable discharge (which means forfeiture of all

58

retirement pay) and a year in jail. This doesn't just apply to married service members who mess around with each other, but also to unmarried service members who have sex with married civilians. In a controversial case that gained national attention, Kelly Flinn, a 26-year-old unmarried Air Force pilot, was discharged in 1997 because she disobeyed orders to end her relationship with a married soccer coach.

But a soldier will rarely be prosecuted for adultery alone. The charge is usually folded into a list of other crimes, such as lying to a superior or sexual misconduct. And proving adultery under US military guidelines is extremely difficult; according to Article 134 of the Uniform Code of Military Justice, the prosecution must prove that the accused not only indulged in extramarital hanky-panky, but also that their conduct 'was to the prejudice of good order and discipline in the armed forces or was of a nature to bring discredit upon the armed forces'. Basically, it needs to be proven that the affair impaired the military's ability to operate effectively, or damaged the public's faith in the armed forces. This law is ambiguous for a reason: the well-being of the armed forces isn't threatened by a GI stationed overseas who visits a prostitute, but a couple of married service members engaged in a serious extramarital affair could explode into an ugly situation.

For ordinary citizens, the United States still has a number of anti-adultery laws on its books. America based its legal system on English common law, which outlawed adultery as well as sodomy (oral and anal sex) and fornication (sex between unmarried people). When the individual states wrote their own criminal codes in the mid and late nineteenth centuries, these laws were included, and today, 26 of the 50 states still have anti-adultery laws on the books. Although the definitions of adultery vary, the penalties are pretty much a joke. According to Maryland state law, for instance, adulterers face a maximum fine of $10; while down in Virginia, an attorney named John Raymond Bushey Jr pleaded guilty to a charge of adultery and was fined $125 plus $36 in court costs. Obviously, these laws aren't taken seriously. And, as for the military, it's an extremely difficult offence to prove (unless you've got photos of your hubby in the act of sexual intercourse).

Cheat Sheet fact

In a US court of law, a spouse can't be forced to testify against their wife or husband. Just as someone on trial can 'take the fifth' (invoking the fifth amendment to prevent them from having to incriminate themselves with their testimony), a spouse can take the fifth to avoid having to incriminate their partner. In court, when it comes to husband and wife, married people are considered one.

Some states define adultery as any sex outside marriage. Others say it's when a married person lives with someone other than their spouse. In North Carolina and West Virginia, adultery means 'to lewdly and lasciviously associate' with anyone other than your spouse. We're not exactly sure what that law means, but if it applied in Las Vegas, Nevada, 90 per cent of strip-club customers would be guilty.

Under the original Napoleonic Code, generally considered to be the first successful civil legal code, a man could ask to be divorced from his wife if she committed adultery, but the adultery of the husband was not a sufficient motive unless he had kept his concubine in the family home. In many countries (including Austria, Greece, Korea, Switzerland and Taiwan), although adultery remains illegal, the laws are usually not enforced. In countries where these laws are actually taken seriously – such as Nigeria and Pakistan – women are often punished far more severely than men. Several years ago in Nigeria, a Muslim woman became impregnated by a man other than her husband. She was convicted of adultery and sentenced to death by stoning. (This sparked opposition from international human rights groups, and ultimately the sentence was overturned.)

In Dubai, any sex outside of marriage is considered illegal. In 2003, a 39-year-old French businesswoman accused three men of raping her after they offered to drive her home from a nightclub. When she reported it to the Dubai police, *she* was arrested. Because one of the men claimed the sex was consensual, she was considered guilty of both adultery and making a false rape accusation.

JUDGMENT DAY

Malta and the Philippines are the only countries where divorce is still banned by law, leaving women unable to end their marriages and remarry no matter how abusive or unfaithful the husband. In both countries, the Catholic Church has tremendous influence and is opposed to lifting these restrictions.

Until 2004, divorce was prohibited in Chile. After years of debate, a new law was finally passed that allows couples to divorce one year after separating, if both partners agree to split up. (If one partner doesn't want the divorce, one can still be granted after three years.)

Elsewhere in the western world, the courts' attitude towards divorce and adultery has become downright nonchalant by comparison. In America, most states passed no-fault divorce laws in the 1970s. This meant couples were no longer required to state a specific reason why they wanted to split. Prior to these laws, adultery was sometimes the only reason why a court would grant a divorce. (However, in some cases, proving that your husband cheated can still get you a heftier divorce settlement.)

There are various theories that explain why adultery was ever considered a punishable crime in the first place. One is economic; the laws were intended to encourage monogamous relationships so that families would be established and there would be enough labour for farming. Others point to the Ten Commandments (the seventh of which states 'Thou shalt not commit adultery'), and say that Jews established this precept in order to unify their society and distinguish themselves from other, polygamous tribes. Either way, just as marriage wasn't originally about love, the laws that criminalised adultery weren't based on moral reasons. It was about more practical matters and creating a more cohesive, productive society.

In the Catholic religion, divorces still aren't considered legitimate, because the Church views marriage as sacred and permanent. (In Ireland, a staunchly

Catholic country, divorce wasn't legalised until 1997.) The Church considers divorced people to be living in sin, unless a church tribunal annuls the previous marriage. By granting an annulment, the Church is basically saying that the marriage was never real to begin with. In an odd loophole, adultery is grounds for annulment, based on the notion that if a person knew that their spouse had a predilection towards infidelity, the marriage would not have occurred in the first place. The Catholic Church used to grant annulments only rarely, but this has changed with the times. In 2004 it approved more than 60,000, of which 90 per cent occurred in the United States.

Global divorce rates paint an equally sobering picture, especially when you consider that over half of all divorces involve infidelity. A survey conducted in 2002 by the Heritage Foundation determined the percentages of married couples that buy a one-way ticket to Splitsville:

- Sweden 54.9 per cent
- United States 54.8 per cent
- Finland 51.2 per cent
- Luxembourg 47.4 per cent
- Austria 43.4 per cent
- Russia 43.3 per cent
- United Kingdom 42.6 per cent
- Norway 40.4 per cent
- Canada 37 per cent.

Even in famously repressed China, divorce rates are rising faster than Yao Ming during a teenage growth spurt. In 2004, more than 1.6 million Chinese couples split up, a 21 per cent increase over the previous year. A popular new career path in that country is private investigator – there are an estimated 20,000 private eyes working in China, usually hired by wives to follow their husbands and find out whether they're creeping around with an *er nai*, or 'second wife'.

Some experts say the country's adultery epidemic is the result of economic and political changes that have given Chinese men more money and personal freedom. Unlike in previous generations, they're pretty much free to live their lives however they want, as long as they don't challenge the Communist government. Another factor is that since 2003, couples have no longer needed approval from their employers to get married or divorced. (You think it's awkward asking your boss for a raise? How about asking for permission to get a divorce!)

Naturally, many of the divorces, prosecutions and annulments around the world are caused by guys who couldn't keep it in their pants. So is it realistic to even expect that the average married man won't stray at least once? A lot of cheated-on women will tell you that it's inevitable. They say that no matter how much you give, no matter how much you love your man, there are powerful primal forces that compel him to chase other tail.

Are men born to cheat, or can the right woman tame even the wildest horse? In this next chapter, we'll get down to the heart of the matter.

Chapter 6
Are Men Naughty by Nature?

I've had bad luck with both my wives. The first one left me and the second one didn't.

Patrick Murray

One summer afternoon in Las Vegas I was sitting poolside at a trendy resort, sipping beers with a bunch of my friends who'd come out for a bachelor party weekend. (Being a Vegas local, I'm constantly being called upon to help plan these types of festivities.) The groom-to-be was my buddy Michael, 29, whose *GQ* good looks and bold manner of approaching women had enabled him to rack up countless one-night stands over the years.

The previous night had been a blur of booze, strippers and outrageously bad behaviour, even by Vegas bachelor-party standards. Michael, inebriated and horny after receiving an endless string of lap dances at a strip club, wound up having sex in his hotel room with a prostitute (paid for by his best man). Another member of the bachelor party, Terry, was still missing in action. A married father of two young children, he was last seen around 4 am piling into the back of a taxi with a stripper. The official city slogan – 'What happens in Vegas stays in Vegas' – would certainly need to be the rule for this weekend.

Personally, I don't condone such behaviour, but while working on this book I knew a lot could be learned from observing it. Michael's younger brother, Paul, was engaged to be married to a girl he'd been dating for three years, and he was also among our group. Clearly, she was highly uncomfortable with the idea of him spending a weekend in Vegas with the boys. She'd called his mobile phone to check up on him at least ten times since he'd arrived. Paul was currently on the phone with her, nervously pacing around the pool while attempting to explain why he hadn't answered her calls last night. His excuse was that he'd been playing blackjack and didn't want to interrupt his winning streak; in reality, he'd lost 500 bucks, got blitzed on free casino booze, and wound up making out with some 22-year-old tourist on a nightclub dance floor.

We'd all had a discussion earlier, during which Michael and Paul aired their views on their pending marriages. Paul said that he'd slept with a number of other girls while dating his fiancée, Elaine, but was firm in his belief that once he got married he would be completely monogamous. 'It'll be totally different once we're married,' he explained. His attitude was that he might as well get his kicks in now, before taking a trip down the aisle.

Hearing this, Michael, his playboy brother, burst out laughing. 'There's absolutely no way you're going to stop messing around,' he said. 'Maybe you'll be able to hold off for a year or two, but eventually you're going to start cheating.' Michael proceeded to explain how cheating was what *allowed him to stay* with his wife-to-be, and what would allow him to stay married to her. 'She's a great girl, a total sweetheart,' he declared, 'the woman I want to have children with. But for me, the idea of sleeping with only one girl for the rest of my life is ridiculous. I'd go crazy. I'll always have some fun on the side, but she's the woman I love and the one I come home to.'

'What if she ever finds out about your side flings?' I asked.

'She already told me – she'd cut my balls off,' Michael smirked. 'But I'm not worried. I've been covering my tracks for years.'

Vegas is all about the odds. If I had to put money on it, I'd bet Michael's marriage would crash and burn before the five-year mark. He may have thought he'd figured out his own method for keeping a marriage intact, but I was convinced it was destined to blow up in his face. And it wasn't because Michael would eventually get caught. He was too smooth for that. He never let his flings get serious, never formed attachments with the 'other women', and always let them know the deal upfront: he was already spoken for, and only looking for a good time on the side. If they were down with that program, then cool – let's hook up.

'That's where these married guys screw up,' he once told me. 'They get stupid and fall in love with some other chick, or they mislead her and she starts thinking there's a future between them. That's when you get a *Fatal Attraction* scenario and your wife finds out. Me, I keep it no strings attached.'

Why, then, was I so sure that Michael and his wife would eventually split? Because of the fact that she was, as he described her, 'sweet and innocent'. It was a polite way of calling her 'naive and non-challenging'. Guys like Michael grow restless with this type of woman. Playboys love a challenge; for them, sleeping around is much more about the thrill of the hunt than it is about sexual gratification. Michael's doting fiancée had managed to get him to marry her, but there was no way she was going to keep him. Eventually he'd meet a woman who challenged him, who played hard to get and drove him wild with desire, and when that happened he would abandon his wife for the thrill of the *ultimate* hunt.

As for Paul, the guy who swore he'd never cheat once married, I'd bet his marriage would last considerably longer. His wife's constant monitoring, and his desire to placate her, would keep him in check. I could imagine them settling in for the long haul, staying together for a decade or maybe two, but it would be a frustrating, depressing routine. Just overhearing the way she interrogated him over the phone, his fiancée was obviously a jealous, insecure person who would never be able to fully trust him. (When a woman is calling her man ten times a day to check up on him, what does she really feel about his character and his commitment to her?) I could imagine that years into their marriage, he'd still have to explain himself every time he spent time with friends or missed one of her phone calls. Hardly a recipe for long-term romance.

So what's the answer for guys like these? Can a cad love his wife, raise children with her, and actually maintain the relationship through his occasional infidelities? If a woman is going to marry a guy like Michael, a handsome alpha male with a high-octane sex drive, is it even realistic for her to expect that he won't ever cheat? Not even *once*?

Cheat Sheet fact

The word 'cuckold', which is used to describe a married person whose spouse cheats on them, originally meant a wife who was pregnant by someone other than her husband. The term was inspired by the cuckoo bird, which prefers to lay its eggs in the nests of other types of birds – who are then shocked when a baby cuckoo hatches in their nest. A cuckoo clock plays off this same premise.

PRIMAL SCREAMS

Some say that cheating is hardwired into a man's DNA, that he's driven by primal urges that override his conscience and common sense. They feel that while monogamy sounds nice in theory, it's an unnatural state for a man to live in since he's biologically programmed to spread his seed in order to ensure genetic survival. They argue that men are hunters by nature, that for a lot of guys the thrill of the hunt – and the satisfaction of the conquest – is an instinct that's impossible to suppress. This theory holds that females, on the other hand, are programmed by nature to settle down and procreate with one mate.

Is there truth to this argument, or is it just a cheap excuse for men who can't keep their pants zipped? Is the concept of monogamy viable, or is it really just a wishful fantasy? We say it's both. **Monogamy certainly can work, but women need to realise that it's not a natural condition for men.** Understanding this is one of the first steps towards ensuring a healthy relationship. You need to be aware of the realities – that for men, staying faithful can be a daily struggle. Another reality is that you'll have to invest a fair amount of effort in order to keep him interested in you – not just as a partner, not just as the person who pays the bills and gets the kids to school, but as a sexy, vibrant, passionate individual. **You need to remind him that you're the same woman he fell madly in love with.**

You've also got to accept the fact that your man is going to be attracted to other women. One of the fastest ways to make him resent you is to get angry whenever he glances at a beautiful woman, or to hurl constant accusations.

Entering into a committed relationship with a man is not going to erase thousands of years of genetic coding. Throughout the history of humankind – regardless of laws, race or religion – men have always cheated like crazy. Historically speaking, the whole concept of monogamy is relatively new. In early Jewish culture, starting around 500 BC, the sole purpose of marriage was procreation. If no children were born, the marriage was dissolved – and if a man died without having sons, his younger brother was obligated to marry the widow and keep trying. Then there were the anything-goes Romans, who didn't believe any limits should be imposed on sex. Your sister, that hunky gladiator with the blue eyes, a cute farm animal . . . it was all fair game.

Perhaps the first attempt in a society to restrict sex

outside the marriage was in the sixth century, when the Arab prophet Mohammed encouraged his followers to only have sex with their wives. Mohammed did provide a convenient loophole, though: it was okay for a man to have up to four wives. Chinese and Japanese men had a similar arrangement, marrying multiple wives known as concubines.

Now fast-forward to modern times, to the age of true monogamy. One woman, one man, till death do us part. Is this arrangement working out for couples, or is it a recipe for failure? As discussed in the previous chapter, the country-by-country divorce rates make for pretty depressing reading, alarmingly so in the case of China, where in one year alone the divorce rate has risen by over 20 per cent.

The bottom line, it seems, is that Chinese women are learning an uncomfortable truth that western women have known for centuries: as men's careers flourish and they begin making the big bucks, men realise they have romantic options that they didn't have before. This is when a man might feel tempted to 'trade up' for a younger or more sexually desirable spouse. A relationship built on the right foundations will, however, avoid this pitfall.

COMBATING COMPLACENCY

Writing this book from the male perspective, we'll be the first ones to admit that men tend to get lazy. The courtship stage contains the thrill of the hunt – from the first kiss, to the first time he gets her into bed, to making her his girlfriend and getting her to accept his proposal of marriage. From this point forward, it's easy (and all too common) for men to become complacent. Taking her out to dinner after a hard week of work or planning a special Valentine's Day can begin to feel like a chore rather than an opportunity to enjoy special time together.

Men, by nature, are going to start taking a woman for granted once they know she's 'his'. They're no longer worried about getting laid; they know the sex is there to be had. Being lonely isn't a concern any more; they know they've got someone who's committed to them. They know they've 'beaten' all the other guys and taken her off the market. At this point, from the guy's perspective, there's not a whole lot of incentive to keep making the extra effort. The game is already won.

This is why it's important for women to take a more proactive approach to their relationships. If you want to prevent adultery, you need to keep your man engaged, stimulated and interested. **Don't let him forget that a woman like you *does* have other options if he starts neglecting you.** As long as he views you as a desirable, dynamic person with other interests and a social life outside of your relationship, it's going to keep him on his toes. It gives him an incentive to keep you interested in him, rather than assuming that no matter how unhappy you are, you're not going anywhere.

Ten years into a marriage, you can make your man feel like he's still courting you – and this is a turn-on for guys. Men never forget the thrill of the hunt. They love a challenge. If you can make him feel that even after all this time, he still needs to do the 'little things' to keep you into him, a good man´ – a man worth holding on to – is going to step up and do what's necessary.

On the other hand, if you're totally reliant on him and he's convinced that you would never stray and that no other man would make a play for you, then, yes, he's going to take you for granted and the situation is going to grow dreadfully stale. When things reach this stage, most women are inclined to hang in there, especially if there are children to consider. Men, however, will begin to look elsewhere. If you fail to challenge him, he'll return to the hunt with someone new.

In later chapters, we're going to explain some specific ways in which you can play off his competitive instincts and make him feel that you're a prize to be cherished – instead of allowing him to view you as a trophy on his shelf that's just collecting dust. But for now, it's time to meet the first of the true enemies of the monogamous relationship.

Chapter 7
Cyber Cheating

*Every man wants a woman to appeal to his better
side, his nobler instincts and his higher nature – and
another woman to help him forget them.*

Helen Rowland

Studies have shown that the global internet porn
industry generates around $57 billion per year. Some
$12 billion of this is generated in the United States,
which is more than the combined revenues of all
professional football, baseball and basketball fran-
chises – or the combined revenues of the three major
television networks, ABC, CBS and NBC. The
National Coalition for the Protection of Children and
Families states that approximately 40 million people
in the United States are 'sexually involved with the
internet'.

The number one topic searched on the internet?
Sex, by a landslide: 25 per cent of total search-engine
requests are sex-related, as are 8 per cent of all emails.
According to a poll conducted by Harris Interactive,
nearly a quarter of men view pornography in the

workplace. There are over 4 million pornographic sites on the internet and hundreds more are added each day.

Cheat Sheet fact

In 1997, the hottest cheating story of the year in the US involved former American football star Frank Gifford, husband of squeaky-clean talk-show host Kathie Lee Gifford. Frisky Frank was photographed cuddling a flight attendant in a motel room. He later admitted to having an affair with her. The story contained a twist: a tabloid newspaper had reportedly set Frank up, paying the woman $75,000 to seduce him in a room rigged with microphones and a tape recorder.

But the dangers the internet poses to your relationship go far beyond your man checking out dirty websites. The anonymity of the internet, and the instant access it provides to millions of available women, has spawned a new type of cheating epidemic: online affairs. Don't assume this chapter doesn't apply to you because he doesn't spend time on the home computer. A lot of guys conduct their online affairs at the office.

The internet has thrown open the floodgates for cheaters, giving them a vast new playing field where they can seek out women to fulfill their sexual and emotional needs. A man with cheating on his mind no longer has to sneak out at night, or try to flirt at the workplace or at bars. He simply logs on to his computer and prowls for like-minded females. Or, as this story illustrates, it begins with innocent online 'friendships' that morph into something more.

JERRY, 44: 'A few months ago, while checking out chat rooms on the internet, I met a woman online. What started out as innocent conversations about something we've got in common – we're both dog lovers and breed Pomeranians – turned into flirting. Over the next couple of weeks, it kept escalating until we were typing dirty messages to each other and describing what we'd like to do to each other sexually. I was spending hours every night in my home office with the door closed. I told my wife I was working on my book (I'm a writer). Now, every night I rush through dinner with my wife and kids so that I can get back on the computer.

'Our new thing is masturbating for each other on our web cams. It's not like my wife even notices that I'm sexually spent when I crawl into bed next to her after my "cyber-sex" sessions – she has always viewed sex as a chore. I feel like I'm almost doing her a favour, since I no longer need to pressure her for it.

'I know this all must sound pretty sordid, but my internet lover lives on the other side of the country and she's married with kids, like I am. Neither of us has ever even raised the possibility of meeting in person, and I doubt we ever will. I've never even heard her voice! Is this really so bad?'

Guys who start forming relationships with women over the internet often find it addictive, as they realise they've got an entire world of potential affairs at their fingertips. Jerry figures 'What's the harm?', since he's never actually met the woman on the other end of his modem – but chances are, it's only a matter of time before he gets the urge to do so. We've heard of men jumping on planes and abandoning their families for flings with women they've met online, having never even met them in person. Few of these adulterous internet relationships ever work out, yet every year they leave thousands of trashed marriages in their wake. In a poll conducted by CNN, divorce lawyers stated that in two-thirds of divorces the internet now plays a significant part.

The Ashley Madison Agency offers to facilitate 'romantic rendezvous' for attached adults. Their slogan? 'When monogamy becomes monotony.' This organisation boasts nearly 400,000 members. Apparently, the majority of the married men who use this service to hook up don't feel too badly about it; according to *Divorce* magazine, only 46 per cent of men believe that online affairs constitute adultery.

FLESH VS FANTASY

The majority of men who form romantic relationships online never actually meet these other women in the flesh. A lot of guys prefer it this way. Cloaked in the anonymity of cyberspace, they can claim to be as youthful, successful and handsome as they want to be. If their chat partner asks to see a picture, they can always send a phony one – or one that was taken ten years and many pounds ago.

'Sometimes I don't even want to see their picture,' says Joe, 46. 'When I meet women in chat rooms I'd rather think of them as being young and sexy. In reality, I know a lot of them are probably lonely, middle-aged housewives, but I'd rather enjoy the image in my head.'

But for a lot of men, emails and instant messages aren't enough. They're trolling the internet in search of real-life sex partners and lovers. If you've never surfed any of the sites where these people congregate, you'll be shocked by how graphic the ads can get. On adult personals websites it's a common practice for men to post nude pictures of themselves, or simply close-up shots of their erections. (Disturbingly, it's the fat guys that are hung like mosquitoes who seem to prefer this approach.) Call it the portrait of the internet-age family: while the wife and kids are watching *American Idol* in the living room, Dad is down in the basement snapping shots of his crotch to post online.

Guys tend to get so immersed in the world of cyber-sex that they fail to take the precautions they would take to conceal a traditional adulterous affair. One 38-year-old woman named Jackie had a sister who signed up for an online dating site. She discovered that Jackie's husband had a profile on the same site: he advertised himself as a 'hard stud looking for hot, nasty sex, S&M, bondage and water sports'. (That means urination, for all you squares.) 'Age and looks unimportant,' he added. 'Your house or mine.'

In his picture, he was naked except for a leather mask, and was gripping his erect penis. When Jackie's sister showed it to her, it was obvious that the photograph had been taken in their family room. According to the date and time stamped on the lower right-hand corner of the photo, it was taken on the night of Jackie's birthday, just a few hours after she blew out the candles on her cake.

Another woman we spoke with, Daisy, made an even more horrifying discovery about her husband's online activities. Suspicious about all the late nights he was spending on his computer, she checked his email inbox and learned that he'd been visiting a chat room devoted to organising gang bangs. Random men would sign up for these events, which were held in hotel rooms or at someone's home. In order to be invited to participate in one, you had to supply a woman for everyone else to enjoy at the next party. (Bear in mind, none of these women is doing it against her will; they all volunteer for the job because they love the thought of group sex with strangers.)

Daisy discovered that he'd submitted photos of her to the gang-bang club, taken during their honeymoon. Apparently, he hadn't got around to asking *her* if she'd be interested in the idea. She kicked him out of the house the next day.

THE DAMAGE DONE

When we asked married guys about their internet dalliances, a common response was: 'It's only flirting, it's harmless. It's different if you're meeting them in person.'

But the world of internet affairs is a dangerous Pandora's box. Our discussions with married guys showed that cyber-relationships, even ones in which the two parties never meet in person, can be *more* damaging to a marriage than an actual sexual affair. This is because the emotional bonds that form in cyberspace can be deeper and more powerful than a night of sex with some random woman. The anonymity of the internet encourages men to express themselves and reveal feelings they don't share with their wives – particularly thoughts about their sex lives and the things they wished their spouses would do in bed. This can create very intimate connections between virtual strangers.

On the internet, men can express their innermost sexual fantasies without consequences. There are no real challenges to maintaining an online relationship, none of the stress or awkwardness that comes with actual dating. You can just tell the other person what they want to hear. We know guys who are afraid to talk to their own wives about sex, yet online they'll proposition a woman with the most perverted, outrageous lines you could imagine. If she doesn't want to talk dirty, these wannabe 'cyber-studs' just move on to the next until they find one who does.

Of course, online romances hold a special appeal for married women as well. The convenience factor alone draws millions of women into this underworld of cheaters; flirting in cyberspace doesn't require them to put on make-up, choose an outfit or even leave the house. If she's self-conscious about her looks, no one ever needs to actually see her. Or, she can build an intimate friendship with a man first, then show him her photo once she's comfortable doing so.

For most women who use the internet as a means to cheat, their introduction to this world happens rather innocently. Typically, it begins with a woman visiting websites related to her interests or hobbies. She winds up entering chat rooms and joining group discussions, typing messages back and forth with others who share her interests. Some of these people are men who want to continue the discussion privately, so she agrees to exchange email addresses or instant messenger IDs. This is how the relationship is formed. 'They find somebody else who seems to think like they do, and then they gradually move from that to an instant message, and then they wake up one day and they cannot believe it happened to them,' says Peggy Vaughan, author of *The Monogamy Myth*.

Internet relationships accelerate much faster than regular ones, as, like men, women also feel encouraged to express themselves and divulge personal details that they would never share with a man they'd just met in the 'real world'. Innocent chats turn flirtatious in a hurry, and may grow blatantly sexual. Just as a bland middle-aged husband can reinvent himself as youthful, sexy, witty and rich, a bored housewife can portray herself as sexy, spontaneous and kinky.

In cyberspace, you can be whoever you want to be. Over the course of a few long internet chats, two people will often feel they're connecting on a deeper level than they would after weeks of hanging out in person. Sometimes these relationships culminate in full-blown affairs; other times, the flirting and sex talk is restricted to cyberspace. In some cases, when the two people finally meet, it's a disappointment, because one or both of them can't possibly live up to the online persona they'd projected. Men, especially, are notorious for using misleading photos online – sometimes the guy they're claiming to be is a completely different person.

CAUGHT IN THE ACT

We checked out a number of websites devoted to the topic of cheating, and read a lot of stories by women who claimed their marriages had been wrecked by internet affairs. As terrible as some of these tales were, we couldn't help but chuckle at the pitiful excuses offered by husbands when their wives confronted them about their online girlfriends.

'I only talk to her about the problems in our marriage,' one 55-year-old lamely explained to his wife. (The woman he was corresponding with was 21 years old.) 'I'm writing a romance novel and I needed to do research,' another guy stammered.

'I never *start* conversations on IM [instant messenger],' one guy fibbed, after his wife installed software on the computer that recorded his flirty chat sessions. 'I just respond when people write to me. I wouldn't want to seem rude.' 'I thought it would spice up our sex life,' said another man to his wife. He'd been trading X-rated emails with women in the Philippines, three of whom were under the impression he was going to marry them.

Our favourite was the housewife from Kansas who said she'd found photos on the computer that her husband had taken of his erect penis. Obviously, he'd been using them in his quest for sex partners online. When she printed out the photos and showed them to him, he claimed they were for a special Valentine's Day card he was putting together for her. Valentine's Day was seven months away.

SPY GAMES

To combat this tidal wave of internet infidelity, wary wives and girlfriends are turning to surveillance technology once reserved for CIA operatives. Scores of companies have cropped up to sell 'cheating detection devices'. If you suspect your darling husband has been having naughty internet chats while you've been away at yoga class, you can shell out $300 for the Micro Hardware Keystroke Recorder. This handy device will record every keystroke typed on a computer keyboard, so that when you come home you can review his online conversations. The device is virtually undetectable; he'll have no idea his typing is being monitored.

If you're a suspicious spouse on a tight budget, perhaps you'll want to go with the $99 Spector Pro, which records all online activity for later viewing. There's also the eBlaster, a powerful weapon in the war against philanderers. Once this software is installed on a computer, it will broadcast everything typed on the machine to a remote computer. Install this bad boy on your home computer, and while he's composing love notes to someone else, you can sit in the other room and watch it transpire on your laptop.

If you suspect he's been having late-night phone chats while you're at work, you might consider ModemSpy. It's described as: 'your solution to monitoring ALL incoming and outgoing phone calls in your home, office, apartment, anywhere. ModemSpy will secretly save all calls unknowingly to anyone on the phone and save the conversations in compressed format for small file size.' And for the wife on the go, Realtime-Spy offers 'Remote installation and access! Realtime-Spy allows you to remotely install the software on any computer as well as view the log files from anywhere in the world via your own personal Realtime-Spy webspace!'

You don't need to visit spy-gadget stores or to search the back pages of *Soldier of Fortune* magazine to find these devices. Do a simple internet search on the words 'cheating detection' and they'll pop right up.

Just imagine that right now, as you read this, there are hundreds – maybe thousands – of attractive, intelligent adult women scrambling to install surveillance devices on their home computers and poring through their spouse's emails, searching for the one that will deal the deathblow to their marriage. Women who might usually struggle with the TV remote are installing phone taps and conducting semen tests on boxer shorts.

It's sad, it's absurd, and it's a tremendous waste of time, energy and money. When a relationship reaches this stage, it's doomed, whether the man is actually cheating or not. No trust remains at this point, only the woman's desire to catch and humiliate him, to shove the proof in his face and show him he's not as slick as he thinks. In the end, what does a woman gain from this? Absolutely nothing. She's already lost the effort to keep their relationship faithful; now, it's just a sleazy game of cat and mouse as she attempts to catch and punish him, as was the case with Marcy and Bob's relationship.

MARCY, 35: 'My husband, Bobby, and I had a strong marriage until he set up a home office with an internet connection. Every night he started spending hours on the computer and I started to think he might be chatting with girls online. Whenever I would walk into the room, he would minimise the screen and pretend to be playing a video game. Well, one night, I snuck up behind him and caught him looking at a singles website for "casual sexual encounters". He tried to flip it around and blame it on me! He said the only reason he was on the site was because he was checking to see if I had a profile on there.

'I didn't, but I later found out that *he* sure had one. I hit the roof when I saw it. First off, he used a picture of himself that was of me and him on vacation together in Hawaii two years ago – except I was cropped out of the picture. Then he said in his profile that he was a married guy who was trying to find out if his wife was cheating with guys from the site. Obviously this was his lame way of making women feel sorry for him and to justify what he was doing on the site.

'I purchased some "keylogger" software that enabled me to record any messages he typed. I discovered he had not one, but *four* different internet girlfriends that he'd met and spent time with. He was paying for these women to fly in from different states and putting them up in nearby motels. He'd been telling each of them that he was in the process of getting a divorce and would soon be free to marry again (completely untrue). I was able to read all the ridiculous love letters he was sending them, and I also saw the credit card transactions he was making online to set up their travel arrangements.

'I printed up all the emails, threw them in his face, and filed for divorce. He's gone now, but he did leave me with something to remember him by: an STD which he picked up from one of his cyber-sluts and passed along to me.

'All you women out there, be very careful about your husband's computer usage. In my next relationship, I don't even want a computer in the house. The internet destroyed my marriage and ruined my life.'

We sympathise with Marcy. But she, like many women affected by the online cheating phenomenon, is vilifying the internet when she should be looking at the root problem.

The internet, on its own, never ruined a single marriage. It simply served as the vehicle that got their man where he wanted to go. Being able to prowl cyber-space gives cheaters a new world of opportunities and possibilities, and enables them to get away with flings they might have otherwise been afraid to attempt – but the bottom line is, they're out there looking for something they feel they're not getting at home.

This is why it's crucial to understand how you can prevent adultery from coming between you and your man. Men don't cheat on a whim; they cheat because of the cumulative effect of a number of factors, which range from lack of sex to the need for a sympathetic listener. If you take certain measures that we explain in this book, your relationship shouldn't ever reach this point.

We'll try to end this chapter on a happier note. Here's a story about a woman who used internet flirting to take her sex life with her husband to another level.

MARY JANE, 28: 'A friend of mine at work, Harvey, had been exchanging erotic emails with a woman he met on the internet. His wife, Kim, got hold of his password, checked his email account, and discovered what was going on.

'Kim could tell from their correspondence that they'd never actually met; Harvey was just getting off on all the dirty talk. So she took an interesting approach to her discovery. She set up a new internet account under a fake name and began to anonymously send him erotic emails. Harvey took the bait. Thinking the emails were coming from a stranger, he replied in detail about his sexual fantasies and desires. Basically, he said he was dying for a woman to talk dirty to him in bed. He explained that he loved his wife, but she was always quiet and passive in bed.

'Kim, now knowing what her husband secretly wanted, talked dirty to him that night in bed. *Very* dirty. It blew Harvey's mind, and they had the best sex of their marriage. Ultimately, she confronted him about the emails he'd been sending to the other woman. Harvey was embarrassed and apologised. He quit using the internet for that purpose, and doesn't need to any more. Now, Kim knows exactly what to say in the bedroom to send him into orbit.'

Chapter 8

Husband Hunters: Why Some Women Prefer Sex With Married Men

There is so little difference between husbands that you might as well keep the first.

Adela Rogers St Johns

It's a Saturday night in Los Angeles at a trendy bar/restaurant. Thirty minutes until last call. The room pulsates with sexual energy; a sense of urgency sets in around this time of the evening, when the crowd is well lubricated with booze and those without romantic companionship are scanning the remaining options.

We'd showed up tonight wearing suits and a special accessory: wedding bands on our ring fingers, purchased from a pawn shop. These rings were supposed to mean we were 'off the market'. But would women see it that way? we wondered. If we were to go about our normal Saturday night routine, 'macking' on women in the hope of sparking a romance, would our 'married' status serve as a deterrent . . . or an advantage?

When we told a female friend of ours about this experiment, she scoffed. She said we didn't stand a chance; any guy who's clearly married and out at a bar hitting on women is a sleaze. She was certain that women would want nothing to do with jerks like us.

But we knew this wasn't necessarily true. We knew plenty of married guys who regularly cheat with women who are fully aware they've got wives at home. In fact, we know guys who claim their married status makes them *more* desirable. We stated in our book *M.A.C.K. Tactics* that women, by nature, want what they can't get; when a man strolls into a nightclub accompanied by attractive female friends, he automatically becomes more desirable to other women. They're intrigued by him, because he's obviously got something to offer – there has to be a reason why beautiful women hang around him. But does this hold true with married guys? Does the fact that a man has a wife at home make him more desirable on the open market? This evening, we aimed to find out.

Our undercover operation was simple: party and flirt as we normally do, but do it as married men. The backstory: we were businessmen from New York in town for a conference, each with a wife and a couple of kids back home.

For the past few hours we'd been chatting up women of various ages and backgrounds, from wannabe actresses, to corporate climbers, to punk-rock chicks tossing back shots. We made no attempt to hide our rings or our supposed married status. Quite the opposite, in fact, and we made a point of following up any mention of our wives with a quip about how we had to enjoy our 'night of freedom' while it lasted.

For a number of women we flirted with, the fact that we were married didn't present an obstacle. One woman did make the memorable comment: 'You're cute, but I want to be the main course – not a side dish.'

One plain-looking 25-year-old, the type who probably doesn't get much attention at the singles bars, told us she'd had relationships with married men in the past. She said married guys come with a number of benefits. 'There's no guessing about their intentions,' she said. 'They have no reason to play games, and when it comes to finding a girl, they're not super picky and critical. They're grateful for what they can get because they're lacking attention at home.'

It reminded us of a story we'd heard . . .

BRANDY, 26: 'I just ended a relationship I'd been having with a married man named Danny, for the past year and a half. I'm young, attractive, educated, confident and intelligent – not the kind of girl you might think of as a typical "mistress". I could have my pick of single guys, but I've found that I prefer to be with married men.

'Danny lived in another state with his wife and three kids. His company would send him to my city once a month on business and he used to hang out sometimes at the bar where I worked. We struck up a friendship and it grew from there. He had no expectations of me and I had none of him; it was simply about having fun and awesome sex. We would hole up in his hotel and go wild on each other. At first I felt a little guilty knowing that he had a wife and children, but when he explained how the love was gone from his marriage, I didn't feel bad any more.

'I was adamant about one thing, though: I didn't want him to develop serious feelings for me. If he ever started talking about leaving his wife for me, I would have broken it off immediately. I'm not a "home-wrecker". This was supposed to be fun, that's all.

'Eventually, Danny was the one who had to break it off, because his company stopped sending him out here. We parted as friends. I'm currently dating another married guy, and frankly I don't see the upside of dating single guys at this point. The single guys I meet either get jealous and possessive, or else they play games and are trying to screw other girls the minute you turn your back. They're phony and insincere. Married guys are generous, fun and grateful to be spending time with you. And why should I feel bad about it? They wouldn't be with me if their wives took care of them the way they're supposed to.'

Cheat Sheet true crime

Clara Harris wed her husband on Valentine's Day. After eleven years of marriage, the 45-year-old woman was arrested for repeatedly running over her orthodontist husband with her Mercedes-Benz. The murder occurred in a parking lot outside the hotel where he'd been holed up with his mistress (which, ironically, was the same hotel where their wedding took place). The murder was caught on videotape by a private investigator who Harris had hired to investigate her husband's affair.

The jury convicted Harris, but decided that she had acted with 'sudden passion' due to the furious confrontation she'd just had with her husband and the mistress. According to sentencing guidelines, this special circumstance could have reduced her sentence to probation. Instead they recommended the upper limit of the sentencing guidelines, and Harris was given twenty years in prison and a $10,000 fine.

MODERN MISTRESSES

The possibility of a mistress or 'other woman' entering the picture is a fear that nearly every woman grapples with at some point during her marriage. For some women, particularly those who are insecure about their age or looks, this fear crosses over the line into paranoia. You know the type. These women will trust their girlfriends with their deepest, darkest secrets, yet won't trust them alone with their man for five minutes. They suspect that virtually *any* female – whether it's their maid, best friend or sister – would jump their man's bones, given the chance. As a result, they keep their husband on a tight leash, which only makes him want to break loose that much more.

'I had to end my friendship with Valerie, who'd been my best friend for over ten years, because of her crazy jealousy,' says Naomi, 24. 'She has a boyfriend named Seth, and every time we'd all be out partying together she would get drunk and start thinking that Seth and I were flirting with each other. The last time it happened, we were all at a bar and she screamed at me and caused a scene. I've known Seth for years and there's no way I would ever do anything with him. He's like a brother to me. It really sucks that Valerie is so insecure that she would trash our friendship over something that's all in her head.'

The common perception is that mistresses are needy, unstable women who inevitably grow more needy and start pressuring their married lover to get a divorce. The movie *Fatal Attraction* scared up a fortune at the box office by showing the psychotic lengths one mistress went to, to force a married man to ditch his wife.

Another assumption is that married men who cheat are lying to their mistresses and pretending to be single. It may be hard for you to imagine a married man having a girlfriend on the side who knows he's got a wife, doesn't mind, and just wants to have fun and screw his brains out when he's available. No guy could possibly pull that off, right?

Wrong. These relationships do exist, and they've become far more commonplace than most wives could imagine. There is a growing pool of single women who actively seek out married men for affairs and *expect* them to stay with their wives. For these women, it's the guys who *don't* have rings on their fingers that they don't want to waste their time with.

THE MAGIC OF MARRIED MEN

'Married guys are just a lot easier to deal with,' says Sarah. 'I always know where I stand with them. They don't play the games that single guys my age do.'

Sarah is one of thousands of single, attractive **husband hunters** – women who desire relationships with married men and prefer this route to conventional dating. 'It's never boring,' smiles Tori, a 31-year-old personal trainer who is involved with another woman's husband. 'There's an element of intrigue built in to everything we do, even if it's just going to the movies together. I feel like we're a couple of kids sneaking around after curfew – which makes the sex twice as hot.'

Husband hunters feel they get the 'better part' of these men. While the wife is stuck with the part of him that's bored and burned out, the girlfriend gets to experience his adventurous, spontaneous, youthful side. In effect, they're seeing what these men were like with their wives back when the two of them were dating, before the routine of a bad marriage dulled their enthusiasm and passion.

When a husband hunter offers the promise of a drama-free, no-strings-attached sexual relationship, it's an ideal scenario for a married guy on the prowl. 'It's like a win–win situation,' says Tony, 43, who admits he's cheated on his wife with over 30 women. 'They know I'm married, they tell me it's not an issue, and all they want is a good time – which I'm happy to show them. As long as they're cool with it, I'm cool with it.'

'All of my friends who date "regular guys" are constantly getting upset,' adds Sarah, 'because the guy lets them down or breaks their plans, or may or may not be cheating on them. With the married guys I date, I know what to expect from them and what not to expect. We have fun together, and if the sparks die out, then we both move on. I don't want to waste my time trying to mould some guy into the perfect boyfriend, like my friends try to do with their men. And I don't want to worry about whether he's being faithful; I know he has a wife, so of course he's not sleeping only with me. When I date a married guy, it is what it is.'

While some husband hunters grow possessive and desire a one-on-one relationship, women like Sarah take the opposite approach. 'If he even mentioned leaving his wife for me, I'd tell him we're through,' she says. 'I'm not looking to marry him, nor am I looking to destroy anyone's marriage. Besides, divorce makes him a single guy again – and those are the types of men I've been trying to avoid in the first place.'

Does she ever feel guilty about being with a married man? 'The guilt is on him, not on me,' she replies. 'I'm not the one who's married.'

MOTIVATIONS OF HUSBAND HUNTERS

There are other reasons why these men are appealing to husband hunters. A married man who normally keeps his wallet clenched may be generous, even extravagant, with his girlfriend. Because she doesn't spend time at his house, she isn't aware of his true financial situation. He can spend money on her when they're together and feel like a big shot – boosting his own ego – without her realising that at home, he's struggling to make ends meet.

Guys have boasted to us about the gifts they've lavished on their other women, yet they couldn't recall the last time they'd surprised their wives with any token of affection. In fact, one of the most common reasons these extramarital affairs come to a crashing halt is that the wife finds out about these secret purchases. Often, it's jewellery. (A jeweller actually told us once, 'If it wasn't for married guys with girlfriends, we'd only sell engagement rings.')

Sometimes these affairs ignite because a man finds he's able to communicate with his mistress more honestly than he does with his wife. 'Sure, it was mainly about the sex, but there was more to it,' says Rick, a married 28-year-old who enjoyed a six-month relationship with a single female ten years his senior. 'I felt like I could talk to her about anything because she never judged me. She knew I was married, and I knew she was seeing other guys, so there wasn't any need to put up false fronts. We just enjoyed our time together. I started to think she knew me better than my wife did.' For a lot of married men, feeling that they're truly being listened to – plus great sex on demand – is a formula for happiness, at least in the short term.

Interestingly, many husband hunters can accept the fact that their boyfriends are going home to their wives and sharing a bed with them every night. *Other* women, however, are off limits. They can share their man with his wife, but if he looks for any additional sex, *that's* cheating.

KEEPING HIM OUT OF THEIR CLUTCHES

We asked the husband hunters themselves what women can do to prevent their husbands from straying. These comments represent the three most frequent responses we received, and we believe they're the most important.

1. '**Take it up a notch in the bedroom.** Every time I had sex with my married boyfriend, my goal was to make him have a bigger orgasm than the last time. Try making it your goal and see what happens. Go all out to pleasure your husband – really blow his mind one night – and he'll look at you in a whole new light.'

2. '**Listen.** Ask him about his day and let him vent if he needs to, instead of starting in on your problems and issues that need to be addressed the minute he gets home. The reason men stop talking to their wives, and reach for a beer and the remote control, is because they don't want to deal with the aggravation.'

3. '**Make him feel like a man.** We both know he doesn't have the biggest penis and he's losing his hair, but

I build him up to believe that if George Clooney walked in the door, I'm not going anywhere. Make a man feel this way and he'll be hooked on you.'

One of the most common complaints that married women have about their husbands is that they have trouble communicating; either they refuse to or they don't know how. But the truth is that men *do* know how to communicate. Furthermore, they have a need to express themselves and talk about their feelings. This means that **if your man isn't opening up to you, there's a good chance another woman is fulfilling that need** – whether it's a female friend he's developing feelings for, the stripper he's been buying lap dances from while you think he's working late, or a husband hunter who's willing to give him exactly what he needs.

Chapter 9
Confessions

Marriage is not a ritual or an end. It is a long, intricate, intimate dance together and nothing matters more than your own sense of balance and your choice of partner.

Amy Bloom

Through talking to guys from all walks of life, we realised a truth about cheating and how men confess (or avoid confessing) their affairs. No matter how sure a guy is that he'll be forgiven for his actions, he'll never be totally honest with his wife about the details of his affairs or the reasons why he strayed. Even when a couple is in marriage counselling and a therapist is encouraging open communication, a man is bound to leave out certain details because he fears reprisals.

With us, however – a couple of fellow guys who can supposedly relate to what they're going through – you'd be shocked at how freely men discuss the most intimate details of their affairs, and how honest they are about what spurred them to cheat. Now we're going to pass this 'intel' along to you.

We recall hanging out at a pool party last summer, checking out beautiful women as they frolicked about in the water. A guy in his mid-thirties, whom neither of us had seen before, walked over and joined us in admiring the view. 'Dude, I would *love* to hit that,' he grinned, pointing to a hot brunette in a bikini.

For guys, pointing out a girl we'd all love to have sex with is an instant ice-breaker. It's like a secret hand-shake, a sign that we're all in the same brotherhood. We started chatting with the guy, whose name turned out to be Glenn. He mentioned that he was married and that his wife had accompanied him to the party. She was inside the house somewhere and he seemed intent on avoiding her for as long as possible. So we grabbed some beers from our cooler and got talking.

When the discussion inevitably turned back to the subject of women, Glenn started telling us about a hot new girl at his office and how she'd been giving him 'vibes'. He said his wife had been breaking his balls lately and he was seriously thinking about putting the moves on this new girl.

Then his wife emerged from the house and approached us. She was an attractive woman in her twenties that any guy would be proud to be seen with. Glenn's demeanour instantly switched, however, from outgoing party guy to uptight pansy. The two of them immediately started bickering about something, Glenn started whining, and they walked off together.

'More good stuff for the book,' I said to Christopher, with a smile. He nodded. It was yet another example of the way that a man will pour out his sexual secrets to a couple of other guys, even if he's only known them for five minutes. We'd met countless guys like Glenn.

With us, he wasn't afraid to open up and talk freely; but the instant his wife showed up, he shut down and got frustrated and flustered.

TRUE CONFESSIONS

It's guys like Glenn that inspired this chapter. We asked seven cheaters to each write a letter to his wife confessing the truth about their wayward ways. We changed the names, of course, and promised to never reveal their identities. These letters were never shown to their women. It was simply an exercise for them, a way for them to express their true emotions on paper.

Read these letters, but don't rush to judgments. Listen to what these guys are saying and see if you can understand where their feelings are coming from. This is an opportunity to get inside the heads of cheating men . . . and to see if there's anything to be learned that can save *your* relationship before it's too late.

South of the border

Gina,
We have discussed this a million times and you just don't get it. Our sex life is boring as hell. I have tried to get you to spice it up a little. The dirty videos and magazines I sometimes leave around the house aren't just for my enjoyment; they're also a hint. I have a high sex drive and I desperately want you to make more of an effort.

I'm tired of feeling like a pervert every time I want sex, but you say you're tired. I wish you would try watching a video with me to see what turns me on, instead of just saying it's 'disgust-ing'. And when we do have sex, I wish you would try some positions other than missionary without me having to ask.

Okay, so here's the confession: my monthly business trips to San Diego always include a night in Tijuana. It's just twenty minutes away, right over the Mexico border. It's the highlight of my month. For a hundred bucks I get the wildest sex that I can imagine. I don't feel any guilt, either. I pay our bills and work my ass off. I've always been a supportive husband. All I want is to feel like you want me sexually. I'm at the end of my rope, Gina. It's time for you to get with it, or else we need to end this.

Tim

Boredom in the bedroom is a very common complaint among guys. Even when they're getting a healthy dose of sex at home, they regularly fantasise about other women – and about the possibility of having *different kinds* of sex from what they're accustomed to.

You wouldn't want to eat chicken for dinner every night, so why take the same approach in the bedroom? To a lot of men, sex is just as important as eating (and only slightly less important than breathing). Be receptive to new ideas and trying out new things. Be willing to venture outside of your comfort zone. There are boundaries, of course; you should never feel degraded or violated. If Tim's fantasy involves taking his wife down to Tijuana for a three-way romp with a hooker, then she's well within her rights to tell him to go to hell. But in most of these situations, it's not about a guy wanting to explore his weird fetishes or perversions. He just wants the sex to be a little hotter, more intense, to know that his woman is enjoying it as much as he does. Nothing turns on a guy like knowing he's rocking his woman's world in bed.

Look at it this way . . . If the average couple is together for five years and has sex four times a week, that's over 1000 lovemaking sessions. You might as well loosen up and have fun with it. Try new positions, and be the initiator instead of letting him direct how every session goes. **Good sex is when it's enjoyed by both people.** And on that same note, don't fake it – *ever*. This is deceptive and sets a bad precedent. You need to work on genuinely pleasuring each other; you should *desire* sex with your man, instead of feeling obligated to 'give him some' once in a while. If the sex is lacklustre, you're both missing out.

It's all about feeling free and comfortable enough to express what makes you feel good, and not being afraid to tell him what adjustments you want him to make. Say one of these words in his ear while you're going at it (or when appropriate, scream them!), and you'll accomplish two things: he'll get turned on and want to do the job right; and you'll direct him to give you the satisfaction you need. Here are the five prompts:

1. 'Harder!'
2. 'Faster!!'
3. 'Deeper!!!'
4. 'Slower!!!!'
5. 'YES!!!!!!'

These five simple

can imagine!

The size issue

Tammy,

Since I'm sure you ar...

I guess I should let it ...

weight you've gained I ... ...u you sexy a...

more. I resisted the urge to cheat for a long time,

but over the past few months I've been with

several women. I don't invite you out with me

because it embarrasses me. The final straw was at

my company Christmas party, when I heard a

couple of my co-workers make a comment

behind my back about your size. I know this

sounds horrible and mean, but I'm writing down

my honest thoughts because I do love you and I

wish we could fix this situation.

You keep saying you are trying to lose weight,

but your actions show me something completely

different. Chips, candy, ice cream and fast food are

not the way to shed pounds. When I am with other

women it's partly because of my physical attraction

to them, but deep down, part of it feels like a

revenge act towards you for letting yourself go.

When we first hooked up, I told you how impor-

tant it is for me to be physically attracted to the

person that I am with. People can talk all they want

about beauty being 'skin deep' and how 'it's what's

inside that counts', but let's be honest: a man like

me, who takes pride in his appearance, is going to

want to be with a woman who does the same.

...definitely for the best that Tammy never read this
...etter. But in his own (admittedly harsh) way, Gregory
was trying to express his true feelings, and it seems he's
honestly frustrated that this issue has come between
them.

The reality is that when either spouse gains a drastic
amount of weight, it can cause tension and resentment.
There's no denying that both partners need to be physically attracted to each other in order for there to be
sexual chemistry.

The United States is the fattest country in the world,
and guys are just as guilty as women when it comes to
letting waistlines expand. But while women tend to be
more accepting when their husbands pack on the kilos,
men can get downright contemptuous when their wives
gain weight. They'll use it as a reason to stop having
sex with their wives, creating a justification for themselves to eventually cheat. One guy we know, whose
wife had become heavy since he'd married her five
years before, told us he felt like he'd 'bought a lemon at
the car dealership'.

It sounds horribly insensitive, we know. But this is
the reality of how some guys think. Not only do men
want their woman to remain physically attractive to
them, they're also concerned with how other guys
perceive them. If they feel their wife has lost her looks,

These five simple words wield more power than you can imagine!

The size issue

Tammy,

Since I'm sure you are not going to read this, I guess I should let it all out. Because of all the weight you've gained I do not find you sexy any more. I resisted the urge to cheat for a long time, but over the past few months I've been with several women. I don't invite you out with me because it embarrasses me. The final straw was at my company Christmas party, when I heard a couple of my co-workers make a comment behind my back about your size. I know this sounds horrible and mean, but I'm writing down my honest thoughts because I do love you and I wish we could fix this situation.

You keep saying you are trying to lose weight, but your actions show me something completely different. Chips, candy, ice cream and fast food are not the way to shed pounds. When I am with other women it's partly because of my physical attraction to them, but deep down, part of it feels like a revenge act towards you for letting yourself go. When we first hooked up, I told you how important it is for me to be physically attracted to the person that I am with. People can talk all they want about beauty being 'skin deep' and how 'it's what's inside that counts', but let's be honest: a man like me, who takes pride in his appearance, is going to want to be with a woman who does the same.

I am tired of hearing from you that your problem is genetic. Both of my parents are overweight, and look at me. Even with my work schedule I keep in shape. Lose the weight or get used to me being on the prowl.

Gregory

It's definitely for the best that Tammy never read this letter. But in his own (admittedly harsh) way, Gregory was trying to express his true feelings, and it seems he's honestly frustrated that this issue has come between them.

The reality is that when either spouse gains a drastic amount of weight, it can cause tension and resentment. There's no denying that both partners need to be physically attracted to each other in order for there to be sexual chemistry.

The United States is the fattest country in the world, and guys are just as guilty as women when it comes to letting waistlines expand. But while women tend to be more accepting when their husbands pack on the kilos, men can get downright contemptuous when their wives gain weight. They'll use it as a reason to stop having sex with their wives, creating a justification for themselves to eventually cheat. One guy we know, whose wife had become heavy since he'd married her five years before, told us he felt like he'd 'bought a lemon at the car dealership'.

It sounds horribly insensitive, we know. But this is the reality of how some guys think. Not only do men want their woman to remain physically attractive to them, they're also concerned with how other guys perceive them. If they feel their wife has lost her looks, it's going to cause them embarrassment. Guys in this position are likely to be unrepentant when they embark on extramarital affairs. They use the weight gain as a justification; if she's not willing to put effort into staying sexy, then why should he put effort into staying faithful?

The guy who made the 'lemon' comment also pointed out a difference between buying a defective car and marrying a woman who lets her weight get out of control. If you bring a defective car back to the dealership, they'll usually make some effort to make things right. A lot of women, on the other hand, have been conditioned by our politically correct society to think that they're entitled to gain weight, especially after having children. They figure it's the *guy* who has the problem – that he's insensitive and superficial for even making it an issue.

It's a sensitive subject. But mutual sexual attraction is critical to a relationship. You can't expect your man to remain turned on by your body when it's a radically different version from the one you had when the two of you got married. Whether it's fair or not, a man will usually equate your weight gain with laziness and a lack of interest in *him*. He might figure you no longer even care about turning him on.

Men will, however, be more accepting of the situation if they feel that their partner is making an effort. We have a friend whose wife had a perfect figure four years ago. We recently saw them at a restaurant and couldn't help but notice how much weight she'd put on; the last time we'd seen her was two kids and at least 15 kilos ago. But she still had a sexy, healthy glow about her, and she was fashionably dressed, as always.

Later on, our buddy told us that he's equally attracted to her at this size. He explained that she eats right and visits the gym a few times a week. 'She tries, and that's enough for me,' he said. In fact, they're more in love with each other than ever.

Effort goes a long way with men. They realise that it's difficult for a woman to maintain her figure as she has children and grows older (if not impossible), and that there are other priorities in life besides slavishly working out. But making an effort, even if it just means eating healthier, shows that you care about maintaining the mutual attraction. And if his waistline is slipping as well, then you should make diet and exercise a goal for both of you. **Let's not forget,** *both of you* **staying healthy and in decent shape is certainly going to make for better sex.**

Keeping it in the family

Jenn,
I feel like you might already be suspicious about this and several times I have almost come out and admitted it. This is driving me crazy. I had sex with your sister, Kate. For some reason I don't feel like this is coming to you as a surprise. For five years I have been faithful to you. The sex with Kate only started happening recently. But all throughout our relationship there has always been inappropriate behaviour between me and your sister. You have witnessed it. You even seemed to encourage it sometimes. I'll never forget the first time you intro-duced me to her: she pinched my butt and said how cute I was, and you both laughed. You were

always telling me what a 'freak' she was with guys and how much she loved sex.

Do you remember the time she stayed with us for a week when she got in the fight with her husband? Every night she was walking around our house in your negligees that I bought for you. Then, remember when she got her boob job? She took her top off to show me her implants and she even took my hands and made me feel them. You guys giggled and thought it was funny. Did you really think this was all innocent fun, or did you think it was funny to see me squirm and feel awkward?

Well, my lust for your sister built up over the years. On the night of your birthday, after you passed out, she put you to bed and led me back into the guest room and we went at each other like animals. We did it a few more times before she went back to Chicago. I knew it was wrong and I promised myself it would never happen again. But now I can't stop thinking about how good it was. You were right. She is a freak. And it was the best sex I've ever had.

Alex

We've heard a lot of guys say they want to have sex with their partner's sister or best friend. Is it a weird fantasy? The 'ultimate challenge'? We're not sure. But you've got to be aware of this, and make sure you're not placing your man in situations where he's tempted to cross the line. Never forget there is always another woman that will sleep with your husband if given the chance, and yes, as hard as it may be to imagine, this may include your own sister.

Alex's wife wouldn't have permitted (or encouraged) him to feel the breasts of other women. She would've been a fool to let friends of hers prance around in front of her husband wearing negligees. Therefore, she never should have allowed her sister to behave this way in front of him.

That said, some couples do enjoy allowing each other to do some flirting when they're out socially. We've got a friend named Ben whose girlfriend, Hailey, loves to wear tight outfits and show off her body. When we go out to bars together as a group, Ben gets a kick out of letting other guys chat and flirt with Hailey. These other men will buy her drinks or ask her to dance, thinking she's single; sometimes a guy will even slip her his phone number. Hailey humours them for a few minutes, but then walks back over to rejoin Ben, and they chuckle about it. For Ben, it's a turn-on to know that his girlfriend is in such high demand. And the fact that Ben is getting turned on turns *her* on. It's fun for them.

Other guys would flip out if another man bought his girlfriend a drink. We all have different parameters for what we consider harmless fun, and what constitutes inappropriate flirting. The point is, your man needs to be aware of what the boundaries are so that he can respect them. Men, by nature, thrive in environments where there are set rules, whether it's playing in a sports team or serving in the military. So without getting hostile, let him know when he's out of line, or when a friend of his is behaving in a way that you wouldn't want him to.

I remember being at a cocktail party with my girlfriend at the time, and a very buxom woman walked in wearing a tight red dress. Many of the guys stopped and stared and whispered comments to each other. One of my buddies standing next to me made a crude joke about her breasts, and I chuckled. I didn't think anything of it. But a moment later, my girlfriend gently took me aside and told me, in a non-hostile way, that she didn't appreciate those types of comments and that they made her uncomfortable. I respected the fact that she was open about it, and ever since then I've found myself telling my buddies to chill out when they start making those types of comments when women are present.

Massaging the guilt

Kim,
First off, most of the married guys I know cheat. Rod, Anthony and Miguel all see other girls on the side. Even Lenny, who you are convinced would never cheat on his wife, no matter what, has been sleeping with a new girl he hired.

I've never cheated on you. But every Friday when me and the boys go out drinking after work, we swing by a massage parlour at the end of the night. I have a little Asian girl that rubs me down and gets me off with a hand job. There is no chance of disease, falling in love, or her coming by the house. It gives me a sexual release that I need. Honestly, I do not have any interest in pursuing outside relationships with women the way my friends do.

I promised to be faithful to you and I am keeping that promise. I don't consider going to a

massage parlour 'adultery'. But I know you'd
blow it up into some huge deal if you found out,
so I'll just keep this little secret to myself.
   Winston

If you ask ten men and ten women to explain their
definition of cheating, you're liable to get twenty different answers. Even with couples who've been together
for long periods of time, there is often confusion about
where, exactly, the line is. As we've said before, this
line needs to be clearly defined in your relationship and
you need to make your man aware of it.

Winston, in his heart, knows that getting a 'happy
ending' at the massage parlour constitutes cheating; he
admits in his letter that his wife would flip out if she
knew. But he rationalises that because his wife never
specifically forbade this behaviour, he's not technically
cheating. It's a flimsy excuse, but it's one that men will
use.

Women don't generally sit their men down at the
kitchen table and tell them that massage parlours are
off limits. You don't need to present him with a list of
every act under the sun that you consider to be
cheating. But you *do* need to have an honest conversation with him about boundaries. As we said in our
'Defining the C Word' chapter, one catch-all is to tell
him: 'I don't want you doing anything with a woman
that you wouldn't do if I was present.'

If Winston's wife had told him this, would he go to
the massage parlour anyway? Maybe. But he wouldn't
do it with a clean conscience. He'd know that he was
committing adultery, as it is defined in their relationship. He would no longer be able to tell himself that he

was 'faithful, technically'. He'd be a cheater, and he'd know it.

We've asked some of our guy friends if they consider phone sex cheating. Most of them said the answer was 'No'. Then we asked some of our female friends, and they answered with an emphatic 'Yes' – phone sex is *definitely* cheating.

Winston's letter brings up another issue that women should be aware of: if a guy has cheating friends he is much more likely to cheat. In the first sentence, he mentions that most of the married guys he knows are sleeping with other women. He tells himself that compared to their affairs, his trips to the massage parlour are harmless. Maybe soon he'll be telling himself that his one-night stands with other women 'aren't so bad'; hey, it's not like he's actually *dating* other girls, like his married friends do.

If your husband has friends who cheat – even if he tells you he disapproves of their behaviour – he shouldn't be hanging out with them when you're not around. And if you're just getting involved with a new man, it's a red flag if he's got cheating pals. As the Japanese proverb says, 'When the character of a man is not clear to you, look at his friends.'

A fair trade?

Theresa,
I have been cheating on you since the day we started dating. I think you've known for some time that I haven't been faithful, but I'm never going to come out and admit it. I want it both ways, I guess – the security of a faithful girlfriend,

and the excitement of sleeping with different partners.

This is going to sound messed up, but you enable me to live like this. You found the condoms in the glove compartment of my car even though we haven't used protection in years. I told you they belonged to a friend, and you bought it. I come home at any hour of the night and tell you that I was out with friends, and you don't even ask where.

Don't get me wrong, I prefer that you maintain this laid-back attitude. My friends think I'm lucky to have such a cool girlfriend. And I am sure that if you started arguing and fussing with me about my behaviour, I would break up with you. But I know you would never confront me, because you're afraid to find out the truth, and you'd be even more afraid to lose me.

Now that I think about it, I play on this leverage. I know that without me, you would go back to waiting tables instead of living in my big house and having me support your child. I work hard so that you can enjoy this lifestyle, and frankly I resent the fact that you don't work at all any more, even though we don't need the money. I feel guilty sometimes about my behaviour but I tell myself that it's a fair trade.

Sean

Healthy, long-term relationships are about more than mutual attraction. It's also about mutual *respect*. This is why it's important for couples to 'excel equally'. This doesn't mean you need to climb the corporate ladder as quickly as he does, or bring home an equal pay cheque. But a good man will expect you to grow. He wants to be proud of you. Maybe this means you learn to invest, or take some classes, or take up a new hobby. The more you grow and evolve as a person, the more impressed he'll be with you – and the 'fresher' your relationship will feel. Intelligent men, especially, love to feel like they're learning and growing as a result of their relationship.

A girlfriend of mine once decided, on a whim, to start studying photography. She bought a camera, enrolled in some classes, and discovered she had a real talent for it. Instead of sitting around at night watching television, we would look at her work and talk about it. I found myself learning things from her, and I loved how passionate she was about it. It gave our relationship a new dimension, and being an artistic person myself, I gained a new level of admiration for her.

The thrill is gone

Cindy,
Let me start by saying I do love you. Don't ever forget that. Our sex life is good, and after having three kids I still find you attractive. I still want to be with you, but I have been sleeping with someone else. One night a few months back I was out with Ken and I met a girl. Her name is not important. Friendly conversation at the bar led to us making out. We exchanged numbers at the end of the night. It took me two weeks to work up the courage to call her, but once I did, we started having sex regularly.

I know that you will not understand, but she really is not a threat to our relationship. As the mother of our children, no one can compete with you. But what I have found is that through the years you have become an A+ mother but a mediocre partner. The problem is that you always place the kids before me. How many times have I wanted to have sex, but you didn't want to wake the kids? How many times have you let one of the kids sleep in our bed, when it was supposed to be a special evening just for us?

I guess it is pretty much inevitable for a relationship of eleven years to lose momentum. Just look at all of our friends who've gotten divorced. Sometimes I feel like our relationship is more of a business arrangement rather than the fun romance it used to be. When I'm with my new girlfriend, it is stress free: sex, laughs, and I'm gone. She knows about you and the kids, and we both feel a little guilty about what we are doing, but she and I both know that you will never find out, so I am going to continue. What you don't know won't hurt you.

Vince

This letter expresses some of the most common gripes we've heard from men. The spark and passion of the early years have given way to monotony and routine. The guy has stopped viewing his spouse as a lover, and now only sees her as the caretaker of their home and children.

Your children are of paramount importance. But you cannot allow the kids to control your sex life.

While your maternal instincts might allow you to put sex aside and always place your kids' needs first, your husband is going to grow frustrated by this situation – and he's not entirely wrong to feel that way. At night, once Mummy and Daddy close their bedroom door, it needs to be understood that you should only be disturbed in case of an emergency.

You can be Supermum, and you can also be the sexy, passionate woman he fell in love with. These roles are completely separate. When women are in 'mum' mode, men appreciate and respect that side of them; no guy watches his wife change a diaper and thinks, *Man, I can't wait to go wild with her tonight . . .* Men's minds don't work that way. He wants to admire you as a mother when you're in that element, but he also wants to know that you'll be passionate, sexual and focused on him when the two of you are alone together.

In order to find the balance between your kids, your career and the needs of your man, you have to be more than just one woman. In order to keep the passion in your relationship alive, you can't allow motherhood to engulf the side of your personality that first attracted him.

Back in the 1970s, there was a commercial for a woman's perfume. A woman enters her apartment after work and sings a flirtatious little number to her spouse. The song went: 'I can bring home the bacon, fry it up in the pan, and never ever let you forget to romance . . . 'cause I'm a woman.'

Walking tall

Gwen,
It is obvious that you don't respect me. I still

haven't gotten over my birthday party, when you made a joke in front of my friends about how little money I make and said one of these days I'll need to get a 'real job'.

Looking back, I realise that you've been making me feel bad ever since we got together. You know that from the time I was young, I was picked on because I was short. You knew my mother babied and henpecked me. You said you understood, but you've become even worse than her. You're always telling me what I can and can't do, who I can and can't hang out with, and making comments in front of friends that embarrass me. The 'jokes' you make about my height really hurt. You love to dish it out, but you can't take it; the one time I mentioned that you've gained some weight, you went totally ballistic. It's bullshit.

Well, I found someone who respects me as the 35-year-old man that I am. Michelle doesn't know that I am married, but so what? It doesn't matter. She allows me to be me. We have fun together and she makes me feel like a man.

For the last few months you have been asking me why we haven't been having sex. Well, the answer is simple: my loyalty is now to Michelle. I have not confronted you yet, because I want to make sure things are going to work out with Michelle. I am now confident they will, so very soon you and I will be having a discussion about going our separate ways. And if you think you're keeping the house, you're out of your mind.

Richard

This guy's anger is palpable. A man who feels emasculated by his woman, especially in front of his friends, is going to build up this type of pent-up aggression. Whatever his wife was looking to accomplish by needling Richard in his sensitive areas, it only drove him straight into the bed of another woman – one who restored his sense of manhood.

A loving woman will encourage her man's sense of masculinity, not destroy it. If you have a tendency to henpeck or belittle him with snipy comments, you're better off getting a puppy. They respond better to this type of treatment, and it's impossible for them to cheat on you – which is usually what a guy will wind up doing under these circumstances.

Chapter 10
Let's Talk About Sex

For me, the highest level of sexual excitement is in a monogamous relationship.

legendary ladies' man Warren Beatty

We've all heard the same old story . . . In the early years of the relationship, it was fabulously romantic: wine, roses, dinner dates and passionate sex. He would show up at her door for dates, always on time, showered, shaved and looking his best. He would take her out for nice dinners and whisk her away for romantic getaways. They would talk for hours while gazing into each other's eyes. Sometimes they finished each other's sentences. It was amazing how much they had in common.

The relationship became exclusive. They had sex twice a day or more – doing it on the beach, in the back of the car, anywhere they got the chance. When he proposed marriage, it was the ultimate confirmation of their love for each other.

Now fast-forward five years. When he comes home from work, they don't discuss their day; he plops down on the couch and starts watching TV. They have sex maybe once a week, with no foreplay; he just wants to roll on top of her and get off. She's frustrated and wants out, but they've now got two young children to consider.

We've seen this happen to too many couples. Lovers become partners, in the business sense, nothing more. Passion is replaced by complacency. A connection based on sexual desire has become a duty to maintain mortgage payments and raise the kids. It's the great irony of most relationships: while marriage is supposed to be the ultimate symbol of love and commitment, it often symbolises the beginning of the end.

The way we see it, there are three stages to the average relationship:

1. **Passion.** Both parties are usually eager to get into a relationship; they've been struggling with the dating scene for a while and are tired of all the games. They're looking to commit to the right person. Once these two people hook up they're channelling all of their energy and desire into each other. Emotions are running high. The thrill of being in a new relationship, and having frequent sex, creates a powerful rush.

2. **Realisation.** As time goes on, they both realise they have needs, desires and personal goals that neither of them has made the other one fully aware of. She hasn't shown him 100 per cent of who she is, and he's been putting on airs as well. It starts to become obvious that the two of you are a lot more different than you originally thought.

3. **Boredom.** Assuming they ride out the 'realisation' phase and settle in for the long haul, chances are the

relationship is going to settle into a state of complacency and boredom. The thrill is gone, the sex is probably fizzling out, but at least the relationship feels comfortable and safe.

Women who allow their relationships to reach stage 3 are often the ones who get cheated on. A lot of men in the 'boredom' stage begin scouting around for other options. And nowadays, you can't feel secure just because your man isn't the type to draw looks from other women, or isn't a flirt. We've explained how the internet can draw any married man out of his shell. In cyberspace, anyone can get back on the horse and feel like a sexed-up single person again. With millions of lonely women out there looking for a mate – even one who's already married – you can't afford to assume that your man isn't going to take a look around. Even guys who are completely clueless about computers can become cyber-Casanovas in no time.

In short, where there's a will, there's always a way for a bored man with cheating on his mind. Sometimes it's as simple as discovering a next-door neighbour, as the following story illustrates.

JASON, 27: 'My wife Tracy and I have been together since college and we've been married for four years. Until a few months ago, I'd never seriously thought about being with another woman. Even if I'd had the chance to cheat, my conscience wouldn't have allowed me to.

'This changed recently when my next-door neighbour's nineteen-year-old daughter, Chera, came home from college for spring break. Every day I'd see her walking their dog wearing skimpy shorts and bikini tops. I found myself fantasising about her during sex with my wife (which at least gave our sex some extra juice, something it had been missing for quite some time).

'But I was eager for the real thing. I started to flirt with Chera, and to my surprise she flirted right back. I started making excuses to go next door to borrow things from her dad. One day I was returning some tools and there she was, standing in the garage wearing those sexy little shorts, smiling at me. I couldn't resist. We started kissing and moments later we were having the kind of hot, wild sex that Tracy and I used to have.

'We had sex on two other occasions, at my house while Tracy was out shopping. Then Chera went back to college and I've been unable to stop thinking about her ever since. She's probably forgotten about me. But for me, it re-awakened a part of me that felt like it had burned out. It made me feel alive again. The sex with Chera gave me an unbelievable rush. I literally felt high afterwards. Now I want to feel that rush again.

'I do feel guilty and I know it was stupid to risk my marriage on a fling with a nineteen-year-old. But how is a young guy with a huge sex drive supposed to resist that kind of temptation? It's not like I was out there looking for it. It came to me.'

We see this story as a metaphor for what many men face these days. While few of them have half-naked nineteen-year-olds parading past their homes, all men are bombarded by sexual imagery on a daily basis. Some guys are able to cope with it, while others see cheating as a foregone conclusion because of it. Either way, we live in a culture drenched in sex, and the temptations for men to cheat are more in your face than ever.

We liken Jason's situation to a hungry man sitting at a dinner table. He hasn't eaten in days. A juicy steak is placed in front of him, but his hands are tied behind his back and he is unable to taste it. He can only sit there, stare at the meal, and salivate. If you were to observe this situation, it would look like some sort of cruel and unusual punishment.

Now consider the average married man. Even if he consciously avoids temptation, it's impossible for him to avoid a daily barrage of in-your-face female sexuality. Modern technology has taken sex out of the bedroom and into the living room. An endless universe of internet porn is only a mouse-click away. From flesh-filled music videos playing on MTV, to raunchy sex scandals dominating the headlines, to barely pubescent girls flashing bellybutton rings and thongs, men are kept in a constant state of arousal – their brains flooded with images that can only make their own wives and sex lives seem inadequate by comparison.

A strong marriage with a proper foundation can keep a man faithful despite temptation from every angle. But many marriages these days are especially vulnerable to cheating because they're entered into with a defeatist attitude, as discussed previously. Rather than being truly committed to making the marriage work, and making the sincere effort to remain faithful no matter what, the modern mentality is more along the lines of 'Let's give it a shot and hope it works out'.

As we all know, more than half the time it doesn't. For the majority of couples, the vows 'For richer or for poorer, in sickness and in health, till death do us part' might as well be spoken with fingers crossed.

A MATTER OF TRUST

Couples often talk about the trust and respect they have for each other, as if these virtues provide a form of armour against adultery. Rabbi Shmuley Boteach, an author and relationships expert who's been described as 'Dr Ruth with a yarmulke', makes the claim that trust and respect are the two greatest *enemies* of marriage.

In his book *Kosher Adultery* he writes: 'Indeed, spousal trust is the most damaging aspect of every marriage. Marriages that are based on trust become boring, routine, and predictable. Husbands who "respect" their wives usually treat them like their mothers or sisters. They may look up to them, but they don't want to make love to them.' The rabbi makes a valid point. While there needs to be an underlying level of trust and respect for a relationship to work, too much of it can actually be toxic. If your man completely trusts that you would never in a million years cheat on him – no matter what the circumstances, no matter who comes along – he'll no longer feel any pressure to keep you happy. In his eyes, you're permanently 'off the market' and you're going to stick with him no matter what.

At the same time, women are often guilty of placing way too much trust in their men. They assume that once they've turned him into a married man, other women cease to be interested in him. Asked whether she still considers her husband Jimmy desirable to other women, a 34-year-old named Samantha told us: 'Of course he's not desirable. He's married!' We could show her some husband hunters who would strongly disagree . . . Jimmy is tall, handsome, has a great sense of humour, and pulls down a nice salary. Although he's very much in love with Samantha, and we doubt that he'd cheat, she's naive to think that other women wouldn't sleep with him if they had the chance.

The outside threats to your relationship aren't just posed by single women. Quite often, it's other men's wives that you need to look out for. Rabbi Boteach writes in *Kosher Adultery*:

> *The great majority of married women who enter into adulterous affairs do so not with single, but with married men. Peggy Vaughan (*The Monogamy Myth*) estimates that 80 per cent of wives' affairs are entered into with married men, while Carol Botwin (*Tempted Women*) writes that 'the overwhelming majority of wives get involved with someone else's husband . . . women feel that a married man is safer, less likely to pose a threat to their own marriages.'*

SEX DRIVES

Sex is of major importance to men. We all know this. Women love to joke about how guys can only think of one thing, and how they're always thinking with their 'little head' instead of the big head. Women laugh about how men live in a constant state of horniness.

But why do so many women treat their man's horniness like a medical condition that is expected to go away over time? And why don't they see the warning signs when the frequency of sex with him diminishes over time, from twice a day . . . to twice a week . . . to maybe a few times a month?

As you both settle into the routine of your relationship, it's natural for you to have sex with each other less often. Whereas your man used to crave it morning, noon and night, he might only want it occasionally now. *You* might want it more than *he* does. But here's what you need to remember: he's still got the same sex drive he had the first time you two hooked up. **Unless there's a medical explanation for his lack of 'performance', it's not as if his sex drive has subsided; it's that the thrill of having sex with someone new has gone.**

When his libido seems to cool off, it's often because he's growing bored with the relationship sexually. If you're concerned about preventing adultery from occurring, understand that this is a red flag, and something that needs to be addressed. When a relationship reaches the complacent, bored stage, a man's sex drive can be like a sleeping tiger – and it might be another woman who unleashes it.

Many guys start channelling their libido in other directions. For some, watching porn provides an outlet. Others log onto the internet and start flirting. The majority of men try to behave themselves, however, and have every intention of staying faithful. But there's always the risk of those pent-up urges erupting if the opportunity to cheat arises.

You know your man's sexual appetite. When your sex life was at its peak, you knew exactly how often he wanted it and how he liked it. You *can* recapture that heat, but this will require you to try new things in order to make the sex feel exciting and new. We'll provide you with some ideas as guidance in Chapter 12 – but, of course, if 'exciting' and 'new' are the goals, the effort and the will have to come from you. For now, though, we're going to hear from a man who's well qualified to discuss cheating from a big-picture perspective.

Chapter 11
Lights, Cameras . . .
Adultery!

Love is a fire. But whether it is going to warm your heart or burn down your house, you can never tell.

Joan Crawford

If you haven't already heard of the reality TV show *Cheaters* you're missing out on one of television's greatest guilty pleasures. Described as *Cops* meets *Jerry Springer*, this exposé on adultery is the brainchild of Bobby Goldstein, 48, an attorney turned television producer. Each episode features a man or woman whose significant other is suspected of cheating. Goldstein unleashes a team of private detectives to place the suspect under surveillance and gather footage of their trysts, then sets the cheater up to be ambushed by their furious spouse along with a camera crew.

Some have called *Cheaters* the rock bottom of reality TV; others revel in watching these adulterers get busted in the act. But there's no denying the show's watchability. Just as we all slow down on the highway to check out a flaming car wreck, it's awfully hard to change channels when an enraged housewife is en route to bust her husband and his gay lover while they're between the sheets at a downtown motel.

Goldstein seems to believe he's performing an important social service. 'The purpose of this show, really and truly, is to draw out of men and women the palette of emotions,' he declared to the *Dallas Morning News*. This palette just happens to result in screaming matches, emotional breakdowns and, in some cases, violence. In one notorious episode, one of the aggrieved parties pulled a knife and stabbed the show's host, Joey Greco, on camera.

Amazingly, all parties involved nearly always agree to sign consent forms that enable *Cheaters* to air their episodes. Sometimes a modest 'consideration', as Goldstein calls it, is paid to gain their permission. But in most cases, these folks are taking their fifteen minutes of fame any way they can get it – even if it means being caught on national television with their pants down. Literally.

One thing is for certain: *Cheaters* is a show that will never run out of storylines. Goldstein, an eccentric fellow who speaks in a Texas drawl and is fond of hyperbole, says adultery is 'like the Visa card – it's everywhere you want to go'. Though the show has been dogged by controversy since the start and is a magnet for litigation, it has now been on the air for seven years, with episodes showing six nights a week, and is seen in around 90 countries. For Goldstein, adultery is big business.

We phoned him at the *Cheaters* offices in Dallas, Texas, to pose some questions about adultery, which he's witnessed in every imaginable shape and form. Now on his third marriage, he admits that his show is somewhat autobiographical. Although in interviews he tends to wax philosophical about *Cheaters* and its positive aspects, he's a showman first and foremost; he knows he's giving audiences what they want. Or, as he once explained his show's appeal, 'I think that people are just fascinated by what other people do with their crotches.'

Bobby, what inspired you to create this show?
I've told so many lies about this, I'm not even sure which one is true any more. I'll tell 'em all to you, and you pick one. Number one is I was sitting naked on a couch, stoned, at my girlfriend's house, and I thought I saw my wife peeking in the window. I got paranoid and thought I was being observed, and afterwards I thought, *What a good idea for a TV show*. Another story is I was in a restaurant and a guy walked in who looked like my grandfather, but the woman he was with wasn't my grandmother. I started thinking about getting some hush money from my ol' Grandpa. When I realised it wasn't him, I had a good laugh, but I thought I could turn that idea into a revenue-producing venture. Or, maybe I was once cheated on by a girl. I saw her kissing another gentleman through a window and it upset me . . .

Could the inspiration have come from a combination of all three?
Could've been. You'll never know. *(chuckles)*

How do you select your subjects for each episode?
Cheaters receives close to 300,000 requests annually for 'domestic relations investigations'. We receive

these requests by email, telephone and regular snail mail, most of which comes from prisoners. These requests are scanned to see what jurisdiction they're coming from, what kind of parties are involved, and how difficult it would be to take the case. We put them in different piles based on what kind of case we're looking for that day. Then they're dispatched to private investigators that are licensed in the jurisdiction where the case is coming from. These guys make initial contact with the complainant and it's up to them to chase down whether [the case has] merit or absence of merit. They decide after meeting with the complainant, and maybe spending time doing surveillance, whether it's a case that is meritorious. Once a case is ripe and ready to pick, we'll put our crew on it. Then we take the complainant with us [and confront the cheater] at a time and place where there's more than likely to be some hanky-panky going on – which is easy to ascertain, based on the patterns and practices of the suspect we're following.

Can episodes of Cheaters *be used as evidence in a divorce case, when someone is trying to prove adultery?*
Yes. In the United States, in the past, one had to prove certain reasons or justifications for divorce. Now there are 'no-fault' divorces. You can just get one. But [a *Cheaters* episode] can matter in states where the community property is going to be divided. One of the considerations that a court will look at, when deciding which spouse to award property to, is who's at fault in the break-up of the

marriage. This footage would be admissible in a divorce case. It's happened before.

What was the most memorable case you ever got on film?
I'll never forget the first episode. It was like Los Alamos. If you've ever read the accounts of those scientists who exploded the first atomic bomb, they didn't know what was going to happen – if the Earth would split in two, or if the environment would collapse. Hell, I didn't know what was going to happen either. All I knew was I had a bunch of guys [with cameras] dressed in black and we descended upon this woman, and I was honestly freaked out. I didn't wear a Depends [diaper] that day but I probably should have. I didn't know if the cops were going to arrest us, or if gunfire was going to erupt. It was also memorable because the woman that we converged on had never heard of *Cheaters*. The show had never been on the air, so no one had any awareness of it. People were stunned, shocked and completely blown away by what we had done. It was similar to what Native Americans felt when Europeans first arrived on their shores riding horses, which they'd never seen before. It was phenomenal.

What's the lamest excuse you've ever heard a cheater come up with?
One time we showed this guy the footage we had of him in his car, with a girl's ass going up and down [as she gave him oral sex]. He said: 'That ain't me. That's my twin brother!'

We're guessing that excuse didn't fly.
His wife said, 'Ray, you don't have a twin.' Later on
he said to her, 'You gotta forgive me – Hillary
forgave Bill!' I think she wound up keeping him.
They had two or three young kids.

*Is that common? Do you see spouses forgiving their
cheating mates even after they've been busted on
camera?*
It's a lot easier to forgive someone for adultery than
you think, because adultery is really not the problem
– it's a symptom. A lot of time adultery occurs
because there's other things going on. It's a lot easier
to forgive that than, say, abuse or cruelty. You can't
always forgive it, and you can't keep forgiving it –
once every ten or twelve years, maybe, because it
takes a lot of time to heal from it. When you have
kids, there's a bigger picture.

*When you set up the showdowns between the
cheated-on and the cheater, how concerned are you
that it's going to erupt into serious violence?*
Once the camera's on them, there's a much smaller
likelihood that they're gonna act out and do something. With a lot of these passion crimes, where a
murder results, if they knew there were cameras
there they would have kept their composure. It's
when they think they can get away with it that the
really bad stuff goes down. Once somebody's been
caught on film, they're in a petri dish. They know
they're being watched and they freeze like a deer in
headlights. Every sensational crime of passion that's
occurred in the last decade or two, I guarantee you if

those people had called *Cheaters* there would not have been a murder.

Too bad OJ Simpson didn't have your number handy. So, with cheating being a universal problem around the world, are you going to do spin-offs of the show for other countries?

The format of *Cheaters* is not very conducive to other cultures where the privacy rights and legal considerations are different – like in Europe, or in Muslim countries, where this wouldn't work. Then there are the 'romance cultures', where having an affair or a girlfriend on the side is a way of life. I will say that it's a very popular program even in cultures where they wouldn't allow such filming. I think part of the shtick is that [foreigners] like to watch stupid Americans, and they like the subject matter.

Reality TV shows constantly come and go, but Cheaters *seems like it could continue forever. In your case, adultery seems to be a growth industry.*

I've always said we're going to run out of tape and money a lot sooner than we run out of adulterers.

Chapter 12
Becoming a Bad Girl to Keep Him Faithful

Every woman should have four pets in her life. A mink in her closet, a jaguar in her garage, a tiger in her bed, and a jackass to pay for it all.

Paris Hilton (quoting Mae West)

In our book *M.A.C.K. Tactics* we devoted a chapter to the subject of 'bad boys' and why so many women find them irresistible. Rather than dating 'nice guys' who offer comfort, security and stability, they'd rather risk their hearts on men who live life on the edge. Whether it's the rocker who rides a Harley or the millionaire playboy who's broken a thousand hearts, women are drawn to these types of men like moths to a flame – and the more tumultuous the relationship, the hotter their passion for these men grows.

In *M.A.C.K. Tactics*, we explained ways that the average nice guy can incorporate certain bad-boy aspects into the way he interacts with women, in order to make himself more alluring. As we wrote, a successful Mack always has a bad-boy edge to his persona. While he is never disrespectful of women, he conveys the sense that he doesn't *need* a woman to complete him. He never acts with a sense of urgency or desperation. Women know he has other options – places to be, people to see, and no shortage of potential girlfriends. The less available he seems, the more sexually desirable he becomes.

For women – especially attractive ones, who have men hitting on them all the time – this type of man is far more alluring than one who makes it immediately obvious that he's interested. A friend of mine, Carolyn, recently told me about the guys she'd been meeting through an internet dating site. Some of these men appeared to be great catches: good-looking, successful and polite. But every one of them made a fatal error that caused her to reject their requests for a second or third date: they exuded desperation.

'You're the kind of girl I could see myself marrying,' one guy told her on their first date, before they'd even finished their appetisers. During another dinner date, a man explained to her how wealthy he was, and assured her that if she became his girlfriend, she'd never have to worry about money. Then there were other guys whom she'd enjoyed meeting, but the next day they called to press her for a second date as soon as possible. In all of these situations, Carolyn's instincts told her these guys weren't right for her.

Why? Because they presented absolutely no challenge. How desirable could these men have really been, if they were so obviously desperate to find a companion? Carolyn admitted to me that it's the guys who play their cards close to their chest, who retain an element of mystery and *don't* seem interested and available, that pique her curiosity. Her would-be suitors should have followed the first of our Ten Mack Commandments: 'Flee and they will follow, follow and they will flee.'

This principle applies equally to men and women, for **just as a bad boy turns women on by being independent and aloof, a bad girl can attract men by the same means – or keep their current partner faithful.** When you're constantly available to a man, and he knows you're at his beck and call, he'll begin to take you for granted. On the other hand, when you remind him that you're a hot commodity, that you've got a life outside of him and other options should he ever stray, he's going to work that much harder to hold on to you.

This is important advice for women who want their men to commit to them exclusively, as a boyfriend or as a husband. For a lot of guys, it's only when faced with the prospect of *losing* you that they'll commit themselves fully.

This principle can also be used by married women who feel they're being taken for granted by their husbands. When a man knows that you're available to him twenty-four/seven, that your entire world revolves around him, it's easy for him to lose sight of how precious you are. What's his motivation to buy you gifts and flowers, or make elaborate plans for Valentine's Day, when he knows you're sticking with him no matter what? If he thinks you're content staying home with him every night and cooking his dinner, why should he bother taking you out to a nice restaurant? If he doesn't feel any outside threat – in other words, he doesn't think other men are interested in you – he's not going to be motivated to treat you with the care and attention that you deserve.

By nature, men are competitive, but also lazy in relationships. They lose interest when a relationship with a woman no longer provides any challenges. As discussed previously, this is when some men will seek this stimulation elsewhere, by pursuing relationships with other women.

So how can you add a bad-girl edge to your persona that's going to tweak his competitive instincts? If he has a tendency to call you every day, ignoring a call occasionally can work wonders. Blow off his call, and you'll be at the forefront of his mind until you get back to him. If you're in the dating stage of the relationship, don't be available to see him any night of the week at his convenience. (Give him a vague reason, such as: 'I'm really busy this week, I've totally booked up . . . Let's talk on Monday.') There's no question that the next time he sees you, he'll be completely and utterly focused on you. You've made him understand that your time is valuable, and he'll appreciate the opportunity to spend time with you.

If you're in a committed relationship, remember this: **if your man worked hard to win your heart, it's up to you to make him work equally hard to keep you.** A woman named Cindy complained to us that her husband, Tim, no longer seemed sexually interested in her. Yet Cindy knew she was still desired by men; at 43, she was in terrific shape and frequently received looks and smiles from guys, especially at her workplace and at the gym. On occasion, men would approach her and try to chat her up. As a married woman, she never gave any of these guys the time of day, but she did admit to us that the attention was flattering. At least *someone* was reminding her of how attractive she was.

We gave Cindy some advice. We encouraged her to tell her husband about some of the guys who attempted to flirt with her. Naturally, Tim got jealous and annoyed, but it instantly shocked him out of his complacency. The sex that night was the best they'd had in months. The thought of other men coveting his wife got his blood pumping, and reminded him of how lucky he was to have her.

Since then, Cindy makes the occasional, offhand comment to Tim about how some guy tried to hit on her, or complimented her on her appearance. She laughs about it, telling Tim how she blows these guys off, making it clear that she would never cheat on him. But these comments have a powerful effect. Just knowing that she is desired by other guys never fails to grab Tim's attention and focus it on his wife, where it belongs.

Another story, from a guy named Robert, shows how some 'strategic jealousy' can work wonders.

ROBERT, 30: 'I'd been going out with a girl named Sara for a few months. She was talking about moving in with me, but I was reluctant. I had strong feelings for her but I was hesitant about making that type of commitment. I've always done pretty well with women, and I knew I had other options; I wasn't sure that I was ready to settle down.

'Well, one night I took her to my company Christmas party. She bought a sexy red dress for the occasion and she looked incredible. As soon as we walked in the door, I could sense the other guys in the room checking her out.

'I don't dance, but Sara loves to. When her favourite song came on, I stayed at our table and let her go on the dance floor. Within 30 seconds, this buff guy approached her and started dancing with her. They were really getting into it. I was shocked when he put his arms around her and started grinding with her – and she was into it! It's like she had forgotten I was there.

'When the song ended, I went on the dance floor, grabbed her hand, and led her away. I felt angry and jealous but I have to admit, I was also completely turned on. I was seeing her in a new light – it was like the first night I met her, when I knew I was competing against every other guy in the room. All of sudden, she wasn't just this sweet girl that I knew was devoted to me; she was a sexy, desirable woman who had options, just like me.

'Right then and there, I told her I wanted her to move in with me. She did, and we've been living together now for six months. I just bought an engagement ring and I'll be proposing to her shortly.'

Now, we don't want you to send your man into a jealous frenzy just to make him show you he cares. Some guys will fly off the handle when they feel threatened by another man, and you don't want to instigate a fight. But you can tweak his competitive nature *just enough* to get the results you want. Maybe this means mentioning to him that you've been getting flirty looks from other men. You might tell him that a male friend of yours complimented you on the outfit you wore today. You could head out onto the dance floor the next time you're at a club together, and let him watch the other men checking you out. *You* know what will do the trick.

While you don't want him to think that you're in any way interested in cheating, it always helps to remind him why he fell for you in the first place: you're an attractive, desirable woman that other guys would love to be with. The message you're sending is that if he blows his chance with you, you've got other options. If you always make sure that he values you, and realises he's fortunate to have you in his life, he won't want to risk the consequences of cheating.

CUPID'S AMMO: PASSION PARTIES

Any couple's sex life, no matter how often they're doing it, can grow stale if they're going through the same motions every time. Many women are curious about ways to add a new spark to their sex lives with their partners, but aren't sure where to begin. Other women want to learn more about how to pleasure their men, but are too shy or conservative to ask anyone they know for advice. The good news is that there's a new form of sex education taking place in homes around the world, one that's guaranteed to teach *any* woman a few new tricks.

A friend of mine, Becky, recently told me that she'd invited her girlfriends over for a 'Passion Party'. Immediately, my thoughts flashed to some wild lesbian free-for-all. She laughed and explained that it was something completely different: she'd asked a company called Passion Parties to host a gathering in her home. It turned out to be an evening that she and her friends would never forget, and injected an unexpected turbo-boost into all of their sex lives.

Just call Passion Parties, or your local equivalent, and tell them you'd like to host an event, and they'll send over one of their friendly female consultants. While you and your girlfriends kick back with cocktails, the consultant gives a talk about improving the sex in your relationship and understanding your own erogenous zones. She then shows off the company's line of products – which includes feathers, chocolate-flavoured 'body pudding', 'sensory enhancement gels', erotic board games and dozens of different toys designed for maximum stimulation.

The vibe of these get-togethers is fun and casual. Even the most uptight women tend to loosen up and get a little wild in this environment. Becky told us that when the consultant started showing off her products, some of her friends turned red with embarrassment and wanted to leave; by the end of the party, these same women were giddy with delight. They wound up purchasing hundreds of dollars' worth of products, then went home to their husbands and boyfriends and had the best sex they'd had since they could remember.

Passion Parties is one of the leading companies in this growing industry, providing an ideal way for women to learn more about their own sexuality and have their questions answered, while doing so in a comfortable, confidential environment. We paid a visit to the Las Vegas headquarters of Passion Parties, which has received rave write-ups in publications such as Oprah's O! magazine, the *New York Times* and *Time* magazine. Created in 1994, the company has over 10,000 consultants nationwide at the time of writing. At least 10,000 parties are held each month in homes across the country, making the company an extremely lucrative enterprise.

Women of all ages and backgrounds have been attending these gatherings; at one, the guests included a grandmother, her daughter and her granddaughter. And companies like Passion Parties aren't just helping couples achieve a spicier sex life; in many cases they're rescuing marriages. The company is currently operating in the United Kingdom also – surely it's only a matter of time before Passion Parties comes to a town near you.

Between approving new products and overseeing her rapidly growing staff, Pat Davis, the president of Passion Parties, sat down with us for a discussion. We weren't expecting this acclaimed sex guru to be a grandmother in her early sixties who could pass for a Sunday school teacher. But her own 44-year marriage provides the ultimate testimonial about the power of her product; clearly, this is a woman who knows a thing or two about maintaining a healthy relationship in and out of the bedroom.

'I forgot to wear my pheromones today,' she joked as we settled in for our chat. She claims to always wear a pheromone fragrance when she has meetings with men. 'They really do work,' she laughed. 'One time I got pulled over for speeding, and they got me out of a ticket.'

Pat, the biggest complaint we hear from men in long-term relationships is that they get bored and want something new. What's the secret of your own marital success?
You've got to keep it interesting. You can't have the same menu day in and day out. You have to add new spices, new flavours. Otherwise, you'll get bored of it, no matter how much you love the person.

What inspired you to create Passion Parties?
Women were seeking more information and educa-tion. They've started to understand that they need to

take control of their sex lives, but there wasn't a forum for women to go to, to chat among themselves – like Tupperware or Mary Kay, where they get together in a woman's home. It creates something confidential, where it's safe. [Before Passion Parties], when women wanted something to spice up their relationship they would have to go to one of those adult toy stores, and that wasn't always comfortable. I know myself, I wouldn't go in. A lot of them are run by men.

Tell us about your consultants.
We train and educate our consultants. They teach women about their body parts. I'm amazed at how many women don't know their body parts and what works. If you don't know what works, how are you going to teach him what works?

What are the typical reasons why a woman would want to attend a Passion Party?
Our research has shown that women come for three reasons. One is being curious. The second is social – women love being social. And the biggest reason is that they leave with an education. People are hungry and looking for answers . . . and sometimes they're just looking for fun. The 30-year-olds are really tired. They have the children, they've got work and there isn't enough time [for a great sex life]. They're climbing their career ladder and don't have time for the relationship. We also have women who have never had an orgasm. They're coming to find out how to have one. We even have women who are trying to learn how to have multiples.

What's the age range of your customers?
Eighteen to 80, but we usually deal with the 30 to 40 group.

What's a typical Passion Party like?
After refreshments, usually wine or margaritas, the consultant will display the products and go through them. Then she'll give an 'education party'. I think one of the biggest problems today is how to go from the 'stressed out' to the 'make out'. How do you go from all the demands of your day to being a sex goddess at night? How do you come home and then let go? We teach how to attract all five senses, and how all of these senses can add to lovemaking. Sixty per cent of our product line is lotions and potions and foreplay. Forty per cent of our product line needs batteries. Of those, 17 per cent are phallic. Women buy products based on their touch and feel.

Our motto is 'Where every day is Valentine's Day'. First-time visitors are called 'virgins'. They go home with [a product], and they have fun with it. This encourages them to come back and try more. We have hundreds and hundreds of products.

Do you think women need to get more proactive about improving their sex lives with their husbands?
If the woman is not taking some responsibility, she can't blame him for all the failure in the relationship. Some women are 'oohing' and 'ahhhing' and moaning, just to get through [sex], because they're tired. He thinks it was great, but you're really not happy because you weren't honest to begin with. So we talk about communication, too. That's where

our games (sexual board games) come in, to make you communicate. It's about being honest with each other.

We say in our book that men respect it when they know their mate is making an effort, whether it's trying out a new look or trying new things in the bedroom . . .

It's interesting that you're talking about 'the effort', because I really believe that foreplay starts in the morning. It's how you speak to each other, it's the wink, it's that long look or smile or a note in his lunch box . . . you're setting a tone for that night. You have to do the flirting. You have to do the same things you did when you dated. I've realised that so many people don't put that little bit of effort, or care, or flirting into the relationship. You also have to make time for the relationship. My husband and I have a date every week. We've done it for 44 years. We don't talk about work, we don't talk about kids. It's just about us – even though life is ten times busier than it used to be.

How do you select your products?

We do several things. The consultants tell us what people want. We go to trade shows. And, I'm always listening to what people are looking for.

Do you solicit input from men?

Absolutely. It's 50–50. The biggest trend right now is toys designed for the female anatomy. Before, it was just phallic toys. Not any more. Now they're made to hit the clitoral and the G spot.

How does someone become a consultant?

They buy a demonstration kit, and then we train them. Our consultants are all passionate about the products because they've used them. They want to help other women. If it takes a new product or technique to bring the romance back, you have a responsibility to do that. There was a woman that attended a party – she was about 50. She said, 'Oh, you guys can't do anything for me. We're too old to change.' She ended up buying a sexually oriented board game. She went home and was too embarrassed to show it to her husband, so she hid it in the closet. A few weeks later he was looking for something and found the game. He confronted her about it and she confessed her trip to the Passion Party. He invited her to play. They didn't even get to the end of the game! Most people don't finish [before they have sex]. She called me and told me the next day she got roses. It was the first time in the 30-year marriage that she received roses.

Chapter 13
Manhaters

Men should be like Kleenex... soft, strong, disposable.

Cher

On the internet, we uncovered countless websites devoted to the subject of infidelity. One of the most popular (and controversial) is www.manhaters.com, which has evolved into a vast online community with members from around the globe. The heart of the website is its extensive message boards, where women are invited to vent about the men who've cheated on them, solicit advice from other members, and riff on a wide range of relationship topics.

Another area of the site – guaranteed to strike fear into the hearts of habitual cheaters – allows women to post the names and details of the men who've done them wrong. Before you agree to a first date with that smooth talker you met at the gym (or accept a wedding proposal, for that matter), you might want to enter his name into the Manhaters database and see if his exes have anything to say about him. You never know, he may have forgotten to mention the wife and four kids in Kansas, or those years he spent in a federal penitentiary.

The creator and web mistress of the site goes by the moniker 'Little Miss Manhater'. While she prefers to keep her identity a secret – operating the site from her home base in Costa Rica – she shared with us the reasons why she created her site, how it's providing a form of online therapy for women, and why cheating men have more reasons than ever to watch their step.

Why did you create Manhaters.com, and why do you think the site has become so popular?
I started Manhaters.com in early 2003 but didn't start working full-time on it until 2004. I started the website because I was saddened to hear stories from my acquaintances, family and friends about the abusive men they'd been involved with, or were involved with. My sister and best girlfriend are social workers and their daily stories of abuse left me shocked and angry. The intention behind Manhaters.com was to help women not only avoid abusive partners, but to help them heal from abusive relationships.

The website has become the second largest abused women's support group on the internet. It's a snowball that keeps getting bigger by the month. I created it for the people, and it's the people who will decide how large and popular it becomes. From the moment I thought of the idea, I knew I was on to something and that it would be a success. The afternoon I thought of the idea, I was walking down a street in midtown Manhattan. I literally felt like I was struck by lightning, and had difficulty catching my breath. That's when I knew I would soon be doing something that nobody on this Earth had tried before.

'Manhaters' is an awfully strong way to put it. Do you really hate men?
No, of course I don't hate half the world's population. There are some wonderful men in the world. I chose the name 'Manhaters.com' for shock value and marketing purposes. It's a name that people don't forget and I attract many visitors just because they're curious about the name. My slogan is 'We don't hate ALL men, just the jerks.' This website may provide the ability for the truly nice guys to finally finish first.

What has your romantic history with men been like? Did a failed relationship lead you to create this site, and are you in a relationship with a man currently?
I'm friends with all my ex-boyfriends and have never been cheated on, that I know of. Thus far, I have chosen not to get married. However, I have experienced physical and emotional abuse caused by men. I purchased the domain name for Manhaters.com when I was happily involved with a man residing in New York City. After our break-up, I had the necessary energy I needed to pursue my idea. I was bitter and angry when I started the site, and I vented and dealt with my pain by taking my negative energy and unleashing it in a creative endeavour. As I heal, grow and learn, the website evolves and continues to change.

What do you feel are the top five most common reasons why men cheat?

One, as [US comedian] Bill Maher would say, 'Men are only as faithful as their options.' I agree.

Two, men who travel frequently are more likely to cheat because they become lonely on the road and are less likely to be caught.

Three, some men tire of having steak for dinner every night [the same woman]. They seek variety.

Four, some men cheat to feed their egos. It makes them feel attractive and wanted.

And five, some men cheat for the thrill and sheer pleasure of sexual gratification with a different woman.

Do you feel a relationship can be salvaged after the man is caught cheating?

If a man has a history of repeated cheating, chances are slim that he will change his ways. He merely becomes sneakier if he is caught. If it was a one-night stand with no emotional ties to the other woman, there is a better chance the relationship will survive. With communication, love, and perhaps some therapy, many couples are able to overcome this type of infidelity.

What's your take on the women who post on your website, who seem obsessed with catching their men cheating? (Monitoring his internet usage, spying on him, trying to set traps to see if he'll remain faithful, etc.) Do you support this type of behaviour, or do you think it becomes a waste of time and energy?

A woman's gut instinct is usually correct. Cheating is something she can pick up on, even though her partner may not be exhibiting any signs. If a woman feels her partner is cheating, she needs concrete proof to ease her mind. By checking emails, internet usage, cell-phone history and making surprise visits, a woman can relax and feel at ease if she doesn't find anything. The thought of a partner cheating can literally drive a woman crazy. She needs to do whatever it takes to find out the truth so she can be at peace.

Are there any particularly crazy or outrageous cheating stories that you've heard, that stand out in your mind?

There are many crazy and outrageous stories I've heard and read. One particular story of revenge is when a wife with three children discovered her husband's affair with his secretary. She proceeded to gather all their emails, text messages, etc., and forwarded them by email and postal mail to his acquaintances, friends, family, company co-workers and boss. He lost his job shortly thereafter and his life was destroyed.

Another time, two women discovered they had been played by the same man. The mistress invited the wife over for a glass of wine and let her sit in the bedroom. As the husband was swearing in the adjoining room that he wasn't married and professing his love to the mistress, the wife walked into the room. The man tried to shift blame and ran out of the house yelling.

Many women create entire websites about their experiences, with details of the abuse and photos to warn the world. I've heard stories about sugar in the gas tank, slashing tyres and throwing all their partner's items in the dumpster. However, many women are able to get closure by venting and posting their stories on the Manhaters.com message board. They also feel a sense of relief when they add his name to the database. I feel this is a much safer way to seek revenge than trashing someone's belongings or attacking them physically.

Percentage-wise, it's been said that the numbers of women who cheat, and men who cheat, is growing closer. Do you believe this to be true?

Yes, women are definitely cheating more. With the invention of birth control and more women in the workplace, the opportunity for women to cheat has increased. I think this trend will continue to increase. People don't value the institution of marriage or even serious relationships like in the past. I think many people are always looking to trade up, or think the grass is greener on the other side of the relationship fence.

When we hear about women installing spyware on the computer to try to expose their husband's cyber-affairs, or following him around trying to catch him in the act, the relationship might as well be over already. What advice do you have for women so that their relationships don't get to this point? What pre-emptive actions can women take to make their relationships stronger and more honest?

Once in a relationship, communication between partners is obviously the number-one most crucial aspect. After that, I think common interests and hobbies can bond a relationship together strongly. If you don't enjoy doing the same activities, you won't be spending much time together. A couple who plays together in and out of the bedroom will have a much better chance of staying together because of their mutual respect for their friendship.

What's your take on why women cheat, vs why men cheat?
Women cheat because their emotional (and sometimes sexual) needs are not being met in the home. Perhaps their partner doesn't spend enough time with them, or the time they are together isn't quality time. If a woman is not getting attention at home, she may seek it elsewhere.

Men cheat for sexual gratification. They are after a release. When men say, 'But honey, it didn't mean anything', sadly they are usually telling the truth. Men also cheat if they are in an unhappy relationship and seeking an escape.

What do you think of the institution of marriage these days?
I think more and more couples are foregoing marriage and cohabiting. A marriage is much more complicated now than it was 40–50 years ago. Roles have changed and three out of every five marriages end in divorce. Many couples stay together for the sake of the children and/or finances. I have posed this question to hundreds of couples, and so many of them admit this to be true. That's why there are a large number of divorces that happen as soon as the kids are in school or become teenagers. If I had a

crystal ball and could predict the future of marriage, I'd say the institution of marriage will continue to decline in popularity. It's a tradition that will never disappear entirely, but the rules are definitely going to change.

Tell us about the part of your website where women can rate their ex-boyfriends or ex-husbands. Has this been useful for women? Do you feel it's unfair towards the men, since we're only hearing one side of the story?

The dating game is difficult at best. I think women networking with women, listing their experiences with men, can be very helpful for them. It can be the difference between a woman going full force into a relationship with all her heart, or proceeding with caution because of a few red flags she has been made aware of.

Many men self-post their names into the database. It's usually obvious because they always rank themselves quite high in the sexual performance category. Women tend to write things like 'He slept with my best friend', 'He has illegitimate children everywhere' or 'He's still married and playing as a single.' No information on the website can be verified or guaranteed. It would be humanly impossible to verify millions of opinions and statements. If a man wishes to post a rebuttal, he is free to do so at no charge.

Do you think the popularity of your website has caused any men to think twice before they cheat?

The owner of overstock.com once said to me that he

thought my idea may have the ability to change the behaviour of certain men. The internet is a medium where both men and women can be held accountable for their actions.

What do you think is the most common mistake that women make, when they enter into relationships with men who wind up cheating on them?
Women need to screen out players by not having sexual relations with a man for a few months. Most male players will not wait that long to get laid, so they proceed on to their next target. A woman needs to ask a lot of questions about why the partner's past relationships failed. She should also do an in-depth search for his name on the internet or any sex-offender lists. Ideally, a woman should have a friendly conversation with one of his exes and/or family members.

In addition, a woman should *always* request a home telephone number and address. A married man will make up every excuse under the sun to not give out that information. Surprise visits are also a wonderful way to make sure your partner is truly single.

How would you describe the underlying message of your site? Is it anti-men? Pro-woman? Is it about female empowerment?
I created the site to help women avoid potentially abusive relationships and to have a place where they can anonymously seek help for their problems. Many women do not have a family member or friend they feel comfortable confiding in, and others

don't have the finances to pay for a professional therapist. My message board offers women (and men) free, anonymous advice from many members.

I don't think the site is anti-men. My members are frequently accused of being fat, ugly lesbians. Nothing could be further from the truth. However, we all have one thing in common: we've all experienced a form of abuse from a man and recovered. I have taken a very sensitive subject, one that most people don't want to deal with, and tried to present it with a sense of humour. I created man-bashing jokes, e-cards and games that allow a woman to laugh, if only for a moment, about serious situations. It's also very empowering for women to realise how many thousands of other women in the world have experienced the same thing they have. It's a form of bonding, and women helping women. We do have a few, very special male members, who take time each day to give a man's opinion to women in need.

Note: Since conducting this interview with Little Miss Manhater, she decided to change her site to www.womansavers.com. She told me that some people 'just couldn't get past the negativity of the [original] name.' The content of the site remains the same, however, and typing in the old URL will direct you to the new one.

Chapter 14
The Twelve Types of Cheating Men

Marriage must constantly fight against a monster which devours everything: routine.

Honoré de Balzac

Christopher and I were having drinks at a casino on the Las Vegas Strip and discussing the subject of fidelity with a cute 25-year-old blonde named Veronica. Sipping her third cosmopolitan, she was spilling the details of her current relationship.

Veronica was visiting Vegas for the weekend with her live-in boyfriend, Brad, who'd left her at the bar to go pump more money into the slot machines. The young couple, who drove out from California, had been dating for a little over a year. In the course of our chat, Veronica had already declared twice that the two of them were 'totally in love'. She stressed that Brad was a 'hottie' and showed us the picture of him that she carried in her wallet. He had chiselled looks but was unshaven and greasy-looking, wearing a singlet and a baseball cap flipped to the side. His arms were adorned with tattoos, including one on his shoulder that bore another woman's name. Imagine Kevin Federline, but with less of a clothing budget.

Veronica told us that Brad did have a certain reputation. His buddies described him as a 'pimp' because of the way women had always flocked around him. The women he'd dated in the past were more likely to call him a player or a dog. At the age of 25, Brad already had two kids from two different previous relationships. The first woman was his ex-wife, to whom he was married for a tumultuous six months. He had the other child with a girl he dated briefly. Both relationships ended because of Brad's inability to be faithful.

I told Veronica that such a history of infidelity would normally be seen as a giant warning sign. She was quick to defend him: 'People don't understand what Brad is really like. He's a sweet guy. He never loved any of the girlfriends that he cheated on in the past, but he loves me.'

'You really believe that?' I asked.

'Well, 90 per cent of me does, but there's 10 per cent that still isn't sure,' she admitted. 'I check his cell phone whenever I get the chance, to see who's been calling him. When he comes home late, I'll check his pants pockets while he's sleeping to see if he got any phone numbers from girls. A couple of times when he's gone out at night, saying he's going to the bar, I've followed him in my car to make sure he's not going to see another girl.'

'Have you ever found any evidence that he's cheated?'

'I busted him once. He came home drunk, and when he got into bed with me I could smell another girl's perfume all over him.'

'So what did you do?'

'I freaked out. He admitted he'd made out with some girl at a party, but he said he was drunk and he was sorry and it didn't mean anything. I just wanted to know why – I'm waiting for him at home, why does he need to make out with some skank at a party?'

Then Brad came walking over to us, in a foul mood after blowing his money on the slots. He yanked Veronica away before we had a chance to offer our opinion. It was probably for the best, since she wouldn't have wanted to hear what we had to say.

We know from experience that relationships like theirs can only end one way. It was just a matter of time before Veronica caught Brad cheating again or he ditched her for another woman. Leopards don't change their spots, and 'dogs' don't change their cheating ways.

If you're aware that your man has a history of cheating on his significant others, don't fool yourself into thinking that you're 'the one' who is going to cause him to behave. When we enter into a new relationship, we don't want to think about the other person's exes. We'd rather not even know they exist. We want to believe that *we're* the one the other person has been waiting on, that *our* relationship is the most important one they've ever had. It's like we want to believe that their previous relationships didn't count. But guess what: in regards to cheating, they *do* count. If your man admits to you that he cheated on his ex, it doesn't matter what justifications he gives – and men will always offer a justification ('We didn't love each other any more', 'We were growing apart', 'She'd already cheated on me', etc.). If he cheated, then he's a cheater.

Veronica's story also made an interesting point about how men and women view cheating. When a man finds out his woman has been cheating, the first thing he usually wants to know is *who* it was with. When a woman finds out her man has been cheating, the first thing she usually wants to know is *why*. (Finding out the identity of the 'tramp' or 'slut' is normally the follow-up question.)

Why is this? It's because, with men, knowing they've been cheated on is a blow to their ego and male pride. They immediately wonder, *What guy was able to steal my woman out from under me?* The visceral reaction of women, on the other hand, is to ask themselves what *they* did wrong, or where they fell short. Interesting indeed.

THE TWELVE TYPES OF CHEATERS
We've found that practically all unfaithful men fall under one of twelve categories. If you can imagine your man offering one of these justifications or fitting one of the descriptions then you'll need to start addressing certain issues in your relationship. Otherwise, he may take it as a licence to cheat.

'I need the ego boost'
As you know, the male ego is fragile. It's also hungry, requiring constant validation. Cheating can be a quick fix for men who need to boost their self-esteem. This is even more true for men who've been married for many years, who might begin to wonder if women still find them sexually attractive (especially if their wife henpecks them and makes them feel emasculated). Some guys will cheat just to prove to themselves that they've still 'got it'. Going out and buying a sports car

isn't the only way men battle their insecurities during a mid-life crisis.

'I'm not getting enough at home'

Men require sex on a regular basis, some more than others. As we explained in the 'Let's Talk About Sex' chapter, you know how much he needed at the beginning of the relationship and it should be obvious if your sex life is now suffering. It's natural for men (and women) to 'cool off' over time; if you were screwing each other's brains out three or four times a day at first, it's highly doubtful you'll sustain this pace two years into the relationship. But he's still going to need it regularly. If you find yourself not wanting as much sex as he does, it's going to create problems, and it's unfair for you to start faulting him for wanting sex if his appetite has remained the same. It's also going to create problems if you no longer want to have sex in the ways that he's grown accustomed to.

Most married men enter into affairs with women who remind them of how their spouse looked, or behaved, back when they first met. If his spouse is no longer young, he may desire a younger 'version' of her. If she's put on weight, he may desire a thinner version. If the stresses of life and raising children have made her a more 'serious' person, he's going to seek a woman who's care-free and spontaneous. And if his spouse is withholding sex or has lost interest in sex, he's going to look for a woman who can excite him in the bedroom the way his spouse used to.

'I know I can get away with it'

Some men are very adept at covering their tracks, or have

trusting (or naive) spouses who are easy to deceive. The more times these guys cheat and get away with it, the less of a risk it begins to feel like. Then there are men who are married to insecure or overly dependent spouses. These guys realise their spouses need them so much or are so attached to them, that even if they get caught they're not going to get dumped. Guys in this position can be terribly arrogant.

'She'd never leave me. I know it and she knows it,' says Danny, 44. 'She caught me cheating once and I fessed up. She was furious but I knew she would take me back. Now I'm extra careful about my affairs, but in the back of my head I know that if I get caught again, the worst she'll do is make me sleep on the couch for a while.'

'I need the variety'
Again, this is about the thrill of the hunt that instinctually motivates men. We're reminded here of a guy we know named Harry. After a night out drinking with the boys, he'll drive halfway across the state for a booty call instead of going home to his wife. None of the other women he sleeps with is nearly as attractive as she is and, according to Harry, his sex life with his wife is still going strong. But because he's grown bored with their relationship in other areas, he craves the rush of new women and new experiences.

'I'm a guy – it's inevitable'
Some guys take the attitude that monogamy is a losing battle for any man. They say you can either be faithful and eternally frustrated, or do what men are wired to do and sleep around. A man's father is often an indicator

of how much he respects monogamy. If his dad was (or is) a womaniser, with a string of ex-wives and illegitimate kids all over the place, there's a good chance the apple didn't fall far from the tree. No matter how much he claims to love his spouse, this guy says he 'can't help' himself.

Unfortunately, these men are often so needy and selfish that they wind up getting married anyway, knowing full well that they're going to cheat. We'll warn you once more: **a man's past history as a cheater is a clear indicator of whether he's going to cheat on you.** Remember the saying about old dogs and new tricks.

The relationship saboteur

Other guys cheat because they feel stuck in relationships they want out of. They're intimidated by their mates or feel guilty about wanting to end it. They know if they try to have 'the break-up talk', she's going to put up a huge fight. By cheating, the relationship saboteur is secretly (or not so secretly) hoping to get caught, so that she'll have no choice but to break up with *him*.

Another type of relationship saboteur is the guy who cheats in order to figure out whether he truly loves his partner. (At least, this is what they tell themselves.) This story from a friend of ours provides an example.

EDDIE, 35: 'I'd been dating Samantha for three years and it had reached the point where we were discussing marriage. I honestly thought this was the woman I wanted to spend the rest of my life with. I'm a very social guy and have always had lots of female friends, and I got plenty of other offers during my years with Samantha – but I never strayed, and was proud of this.

'Things started going downhill when I left my corporate job to start my own business. It has always been my dream to be an entrepreneur. Initially, Samantha said she supported my decision, but her attitude changed when it became clear that I wouldn't be bringing in the bucks like I used to, at least not until my business got up and running. This meant scaling back on the restaurants and our nights out on the town, and cancelling our annual vacation. This bothered her, and I began to see her as a materialistic person who didn't truly support my goals. I still loved her, but seeing this side of her definitely made me think twice about whether we belonged together.

'I decided to test my feelings for her by starting a fling on the side with a girl I'd known socially for some time. I didn't consider myself to be "officially" cheating, because my relationship with Samantha was deteriorating at this point. I wanted to see how it would make me feel to indulge in a fling. Would I feel guilty and be scared of losing Samantha, or would I enjoy entering into a fresh relationship?

'As it turned out, the fling only made me realise that I was happier being single and not having to deal with any woman's expectations at this point in my life. I ended up breaking off the fling after about a month. Even though Samantha was never aware of my fling, and wanted to continue our march towards the aisle, I broke things off with her a short time later. I'm single now, my business is picking up, and I feel I made the right choice.'

Obviously, Eddie was kidding himself by conducting this test. He knew he didn't want to get married to Samantha and was looking for a way out. What if, by cheating, Eddie had realised that he really did love Samantha and wanted to spend the rest of his life with her? He would've had to either admit his infidelity or enter into a marriage with her knowing that he'd betrayed her. Cheating is never a test. It's the fulfillment of a selfish desire.

The dog

These types of philanderers are the serial cheaters – 'dogs', as ladies are fond of calling them. Ironically, while these guys fancy themselves as studs, they're usually anything but. While it may appear they're obsessed with sex, they actually chase other women because they need constant reassurance that they're still desirable. They also feel threatened by women. They're insecure about their masculinity or their sense of self-worth, and crave these hook-ups because it makes them feel 'in control' over women.

Dogs are usually very smooth with the opposite sex, at least on first impression. They're able to rack up conquests because they know what women want to hear. Even though they act cocky, many women mistake this for confidence and find it a turn-on. They're all too willing to succumb to the dog's charms.

Deep down, dogs don't like women. And they absolutely hate it when women try to control their behaviour. Many dogs have steady girlfriends since they want the constant reassurance of having a woman around. They choose to date women who are insecure and would rather turn a blind eye than confront them about their cheating.

We know a lot of dogs, and here's the interesting thing: it's not really about sex for them. In fact, sex isn't their primary goal. It's the thrill of the chase and the smug satisfaction of knowing they've 'conquered' yet another woman. By the time they've got a woman to agree to sex, the battle has already been won.

Kirk, a good-looking buddy of ours, has a hopelessly devoted girlfriend yet he prowls the nightclubs and hooks up with at least one new woman every week. Rarely will Kirk even exchange phone numbers with these girls afterwards, because once he's had his orgasm, she's served her purpose and it's on to the next. And Kirk makes no secret of the fact that he's a lousy lover; he actually jokes about it. 'I'm a five-minute man – max,' he smiles. 'All I care about is winning them over and getting them home with me. Once we're in the sack, I just want to finish and be done with it.'

Don't confuse dogs with sex addicts. These are two very different types. Dogs behave the way they do out of narcissism, insecurity and a deep dislike of women. Usually, this attitude is a product of their upbringing. A lot of dogs had philandering fathers and were raised by weak mothers who never had their respect.

The accidental cheater

This is the guy who says 'It just happened', much to his wife or girlfriend's infuriation. He's unable to come up with any logical explanation for his behaviour. He's not in love with the other woman. He probably didn't have any feelings for her whatsoever, apart from temporary lust.

While this type of cheater might feel that 'accidental' infidelity isn't as bad as having a premeditated, drawn-out affair, even accidental cheating is usually somewhat premeditated because of the situation he chose to place himself in. Remember the third type of man, outlined in this book's Introduction: the one who will cheat if placed in certain circumstances. This means a guy who hangs out in singles bars, meets up with ex-girlfriends for drinks or even allows a conversation with another woman to veer into flirtatious territory. Trust us, he knew what he was doing and made a series of conscious decisions that led to him cheating. Never buy the 'It just happened' excuse: **men who are truly committed to being faithful don't place themselves in situations where they *know* they're going to be dangerously tempted.**

The fool in love

The most disastrous form of infidelity often occurs when the cheater 'falls in love' with a new woman within a short time of meeting her. He gushes to his friends that he's finally found 'the one', as if they were destined to be together, even when he's a 55-year-old executive and she's a 22-year-old cocktail waitress.

The rush of leaping into a new relationship, especially for someone who's been suffering in an unhappy relationship for years, can be more mind-blowing than any drug. Having sex with another woman – or even getting flirtatious vibes from one – can cause normal, logical guys to become hooked and throw all common sense out the window. As discussed in the feature box on the next page, powerful biochemical reactions occur when a guy cheats with another woman.

The 'rush' of cheating can be even more powerful when the affair is with a younger woman, or a woman who is struggling with her own problems and is in need of rescuing. We call this the 'damsel in distress' syndrome.

PEA and sex addiction

Researchers have begun to discover exactly how sexual attraction and feelings of love affect the brain's internal chemistry. They've even identified a specific chemical in the brain, called phenylethylamine, or PEA, which they believe is connected to the euphoria we experience when we first fall in love. Feelings of infatuation cause these chemical levels to soar. Meanwhile, sexual arousal triggers the same areas of the brain and central nervous system — causing hormone levels to skyrocket and boost heart rate and blood pressure. PEA is the brain's built-in 'love drug' and is a stimulant not unlike cocaine or amphetamine.

These studies also help to explain the reasons behind sex addiction. Sex addicts aren't simply guys out to screw anything that moves; in a sense, they're junkies that crave a constant fix of PEA. They're permanently seeking that euphoric rush, just as drug addicts do.

So why isn't everyone who enjoys sex a sex addict? Well, for the same reasons that not everybody who drinks is an alcoholic, and not everybody who smokes the occasional joint is a drug fiend: every human brain is wired differently, and each of us is shaped (or damaged) by our experiences early in life. For instance, people who've been abused may suffer self-esteem problems as adults. This, in turn, might cause them to crave love and attention in the form of constant sexual affairs.

We've seen successful married men, with high-powered jobs and families that depend on them, hurl themselves into toxic relationships with dysfunctional, much younger women. These men usually don't feel needed by their partners and aren't allowed to play the masculine role in their relationship. Younger, troubled women can make these men feel masculine and heroic, even if in reality these women are using them and playing them for fools.

We know a guy named Paul who was very successful in his career but miserable in his marriage. He'd had a string of younger girlfriends, whom he would shower with expensive gifts. By the end of the first date, it was customary for him to offer to pay their bills and take care of them. He didn't do this out of generosity. He did it because he felt neglected and taken for granted by his wife. He was desperate to feel needed, to feel like he was playing the hero. (Inevitably, these other women would wind up taking Paul for granted, too.)

Alternatively, a man will plunge into this type of affair because he's trying to escape from reality: perhaps he's facing a life-changing event that demands that he change his ways and grow up. It might be a health scare, the death of a parent or close friend, the birth of a first child, or a sudden change in his financial situation; it could be the loss of a job, or a break-through to a new level of success.

'I knew that on one level, it was crazy,' says Paul, a 52-year-old executive who had a brief, torrid affair with a 26-year-old waitress he met in a Las Vegas casino. 'But I hadn't felt that alive in years. All the hours I worked, all the money I made . . . my wife took it all for granted and none of it brought me any happiness. But with this new girl, she was so excited every time she saw me. I'd buy her gifts and she'd be ecstatic. She made me feel twenty years younger.'

The fire that fuels these infatuations burns at a white-hot temperature, but burns out fast. We've never heard of one that led to a happy, healthy long-term marriage. Paul's latest fling came to an abrupt halt when his mistress's ex-boyfriend came back into the picture. Here was a guy, Paul, who had 100 people working under him at his company and had spent at least $50,000 on gifts for her, yet she wound up dumping him for a 25-year-old mechanic. Even worse, Paul had confessed the affair to his wife because he was convinced that he would marry the other girl. His wife divorced him and won a huge settlement, leaving him alone and shattered. But even Paul got off easy compared to many fools in love. Other stories end with suicide, bankruptcy, heart attacks and even murder.

Unlike their female counterparts (whom we'll discuss in the next chapter), male fools in love are more likely to put on blinders. The infatuation and the thrill of the sex will cause them to take foolish risks and damn the consequences. They eventually get careless . . . and this is why they get busted.

'Cheating keeps us together'

Sometimes a man will love his wife, and sincerely want to stay married to her forever, yet will feel the need to sleep with other women in order to keep the relationship intact. It's usually men with kids who adopt this mentality.

In other scenarios it's a financial consideration. He knows he stands to lose half of his assets (or more) in a divorce. Bear in mind, this doesn't only apply to wealthy men who stand to lose millions. It's also relevant to the guy who makes $30,000 a year and would be forced to move back in with Mum as a result of a divorce.

We know one woman whose husband moved out of their house over a decade ago, yet they remain legally married. She doesn't want to lose the insurance coverage that his job provides for her and their children, and he doesn't want to lose a big chunk of his assets in a divorce court. They split up and they've each been in relationships with other people for years, but neither wants to terminate the legal contract that binds them. Personally, I wouldn't want this hanging over my head – I'd prefer a clean break, if only for my peace of mind – but in their case, they seem to have made the situation work.

Children are often a major factor. Some men cheat but stay married for fear of splitting up their family and traumatising their children. I can tell you from personal experience, in this situation you're not doing your kids any favours. Kids are better off splitting their time between divorced parents than living in a tense, hostile household with two parents who can't stand being around each other. (And it's not like a ton of kids at their school aren't living in single-parent households.)

Finally, there are cases within the 'cheating keeps us together' category where a man genuinely loves his wife and wants to remain married to her, but feels that an extramarital affair is the only way to satisfy his needs. He's unfulfilled emotionally or sexually (or both), and feels that by cheating he can replace what's missing in his marriage without having to end it.

'My wife just doesn't like sex the way she used to,' says Rico, 37. 'But I love her, she's my best friend, and I would never want to subject our kids to a divorce. So I made a decision. I could either obsess about the sex problem and resent my wife for it, or I could find a girl-friend on the side who could satisfy those urges. Now, when I'm home with my wife, I don't worry about sex. I can focus on my family and on the good aspects of our marriage.'

Aside from those that find themselves in the 'fools in love' category, married men who cheat seem to be better than women at mentally defining the emotional boundaries of their affairs. They create an arrangement that works for them, and want to keep it within those limits: they have their wife, they have their mistress (or mistresses), and that's how they want it to remain. Just as they have no desire to leave their families, they have no desire to marry the other woman and build a new life with her. And if the other woman starts making waves about wanting to be with him exclusively, then, like a typical husband hunter, that's when they know they have to terminate the relationship.

'The key is to be upfront with them,' says Michael, 33, of his extramarital paramours. 'Don't mislead them and give them hope that you're going to leave your wife. That's a dangerous game to start playing. They'll hold you to it, and if they eventually realise you're full of crap, they might try to sabotage your marriage. That's when things get ugly.'

Another guy we spoke to, who cheated in order to 'save' his marriage, speaks for a lot of men when he relates this story . . .

RON, 38: 'If you told me five years ago that I would end up cheating on my wife, I would have called you crazy. Tina is everything I thought I ever wanted in a woman: beautiful, caring, patient and an amazing mother. But over the last few years I've strayed. The simple fact is that while Tina is everything that I wanted in a wife, she lacks what I want in a lover. We always have sex the same way: turn off the lights, crawl under the covers, and as soon as she climaxes she wants me to hurry up and finish. I guess for a lot of guys this is adequate, but I want more.

'One day about two years ago I posted a personals ad in a newspaper, saying I was a married man looking to rediscover my wild side. I wanted to see if there were any attractive women out there who would actually respond. I didn't really expect any to. Well, you can imagine how surprised I was when I received three responses the first week the ad was posted.

'I've had sexual relationships with a number of women over the past two years, and it has saved my marriage. Now that I'm satisfied sexually, I can love Tina for her good qualities and not worry about what's missing. These other women are aware that I'm married and have no problem with it. They know I want to stay married. Despite our problems, I love my wife and I would never put my children through a divorce.

'Of the women I see on the side, Brenda is my "steady". She told me once that if I was single, she wouldn't even consider me as a mate. She likes our relationship just the way it is: great sex, no expectations, no lies. Maybe more guys should fish from the pool that I do. The women are out there.'

'I'm not the same guy I was before'
This is a challenge faced by many couples who marry at a young age. After years of marriage, the husband finds himself in a very different position in life. When

he married in his twenties, he had little money, lacked self-confidence and had few options with women. He was probably sexually inexperienced and felt lucky to find a steady partner. But now, ten or twenty years later, he's got a booming career and his confidence level has risen commensurately. He realises that other women now find him attractive, and that if he was single he'd be quite a catch. He has options he never had before, and the temptations are gnawing away at him.

WILLIAM, 37: 'When I got married at age 22, I felt blessed. I was broke, overweight, and had no direction in my life – yet Julie loved and supported me. Now, fifteen years and three kids later, the situation has changed quite a bit. I got my act together, landed a great job, and now earn a six-figure income. I have a beautiful home, I drive a brand-new Mercedes, and I've even lost over 20 kilos and am in great shape. I'm noticing that attractive, younger women are checking me out, which is an ego trip.

'Julie is the only woman I've ever been with. I never had the urge to cheat on her before. But now I want to explore what it's like to be with other women, and I have opportunities that are hard to pass up. Maybe there's another woman out there who I'm truly meant to be with. What did I know about love when I was 22?

'I don't want to cheat on Julie or sneak around, so I'm wondering if I should just level with her and try to end our marriage amicably. As much as I love and respect her, you only live once.'

It's a tough situation. You want to encourage and support your man and help him achieve his goals, but do you risk getting dumped if he breaks through to a new level of success? We see it all the time in Hollywood, on a more exaggerated scale – the actor whose first wife stood by him through the lean, early years, only to get left in the dust once he becomes a star making millions of dollars.

But there are occasional, inspiring exceptions. **Denzel Washington** has been married to his wife Pauletta since 1983 and they have four children. **Paul Newman**, the sex-symbol equivalent of Brad Pitt back in his heyday, has been married to his wife, Joanne Woodward, since 1958. (She once said of Newman, 'Sexiness wears thin after a while and beauty fades, but to be married to a man who makes you laugh every day, ah, now that's a real treat.') Obviously, these marriages have a rock-solid foundation and they've communicated with each other every step of the way. If Denzel can pull down $20 million a film and be a sex symbol to women of all ages and races, and *still* stand by his woman, then there's hope for any couple.

'I feel trapped'

Men who feel 'locked down' by their women are going to react in one of two ways: they're either going to submit and resent it, or they're going to fight back – often by cheating. When a guy feels trapped by a woman his sense of masculinity becomes threatened. This can result in the first category outlined in this chapter, the cheater looking for the ego boost.

Even worse is when a woman tries to force her man to commit to her by getting pregnant. For guys, there's no greater feeling of 'entrapment', as this story from Peter shows.

PETER, 31: 'I've been married to Amanda for a few months. We had dated for several years and she'd been increasing the pressure on me to pop the question. Her friends were all married and starting families, and she was throwing out constant reminders: her biological clock was ticking, we weren't getting any younger, if I loved her I'd marry her, etc. But I wasn't sure I ever wanted to get married – not just to Amanda, but to anyone. Why couldn't we just live together as boyfriend and girlfriend? I kept telling her that half the couples who marry wind up getting divorced. As for kids, I told her maybe down the line. I was focused on my career and it definitely wasn't the right time for me to be a dad.

'Then one day she announced she was pregnant. We'd always been careful about using birth control, so this came as a huge shock. Though she wouldn't admit it, I suspected that she went off her birth control without telling me and got pregnant intentionally, in order to force me into marriage. (She knew my parents would freak out if I had a child out of wedlock.)

'So we got married. She's now four months pregnant and I've been cheating, with women from my job and others I meet at bars. I'd pretty much been faithful to Amanda during our years of dating, and used to feel guilty on the rare occasions that I messed around. But now, since the marriage, I don't feel that guilt any more. To be honest, I feel like she deserves it and brought it on herself.'

We know a lot of guys who've been through similar situations, and here's the bottom line: **women who get pregnant in an attempt to hang on to their man are kidding themselves.** When a relationship is crumbling, the last thing you need to add to the mix is a child. No man is going to suddenly switch from a fear of commitment to being a doting husband *and* dad. He might step up and be a loving and supportive father (which is what he should do), but he's not going to be both. He's going to feel too much resentment towards you for putting him in this position. Even if he agrees to get married, as Peter did, the relationship is severely damaged. He's likely to cheat out of revenge, to feel like he's getting back at the woman who put him in this spot.

There are two options for a man who finds himself thrust into this difficult and awkward position. He's either going to get angry and panicked and terminate the relationship, or do the honourable thing and marry her – in which case he'll feel trapped and deeply resentful. Both options are going to result in nothing but pain for the woman, the man and, eventually, the child.

In hindsight, Peter and Amanda should have ended their relationship when it became obvious that they wanted completely different things. She was pressing for marriage and a family; he wasn't interested in any of that. But they were too insecure to let each other go. Peter wanted a girlfriend without having to make any further commitments, and Amanda probably felt that she'd invested years in the relationship and wasn't about to chalk it up as wasted time.

As for the child, the effects of living in a household with two parents who don't love each other can be far more detrimental than being raised in a single-parent household. We don't advocate having kids out of wedlock; there's far too much of that going around. Having your children with a loving, committed husband is the ideal scenario, and one that is worth holding out for. But if your man is gun-shy about marriage and kids, don't think that a baby is going to suddenly make him come around. It's more likely that you'll wind up joining the ranks of frustrated single mothers, chasing down your ex for financial help and bitterly complaining to your friends about your situation. And as a single mum, it's that much harder for you to find a great man to marry.

Chapter 15
Why Women Cheat Too

When a man steals your wife, there is no better revenge than to let him keep her.

Sacha Guitry

We were at a house party hosted by a friend of ours, chatting with a guy called Nate as we refilled our beers from the keg. Nate was the type of guy who might as well have had the word 'PLAYER' tattooed across his chest: hair gelled and impeccably styled, biceps bulging against a T-shirt two sizes too small, laser-whitened teeth. His eyes were constantly scanning the room for prospects.

The three of us simultaneously noticed a blonde woman strolling past. Her face suggested she was in her mid-forties but her body was taut and toned, no doubt sculpted by an expensive personal trainer and an even pricier plastic surgeon.

As soon as she was out of earshot, Nate flashed us a sneaky grin. 'I was chatting with that MILF earlier,' he said, identifying her as a 'Mother I'd Like to F***'. 'I'll bet you twenty bucks I end up taking her home.'

'Is she single?' I asked.

Nate smirked. 'Even better. She's *married*. Check the rock on her finger.'

'Is her husband here?'

'No, she came alone,' he grinned. 'And when the cat's away . . . the mouse will play.'

We'd met women who had a thing for married guys, who had reasons why they actually preferred to go this route (as explained in the 'Husband Hunters' chapter). But guys who preferred to chase married women? We were curious to know more about Nate's thought process.

'The great lie about men is that *we're* the only ones who go out looking to cheat,' he explained. 'The truth is, women are just as bad as we are. If I meet a girl at the bar and find out she's been married for more than three years, I know I've got a good shot at hooking up. In fact, a lot of times it's *easier* for me to score with her than if she was single. I just need to play it more aggressive than I normally would. If something's going to happen, it needs to happen that night. The chances of us hooking up right then are a lot better than the chances of her ever calling me.'

For women, being branded an adulterer is no longer the awful disgrace it once was. The literary classic *Madame Bovary* tells the story of a doctor, Charles Bovary, who marries a beautiful farm girl named Emma. An avid reader of romantic novels, Emma begins to desire a life of luxury and romance that her dull but well-meaning husband cannot provide. She embarks on a series of affairs, seeking the 'finer life' with a string of men. But when the townspeople begin to suspect that she's been cheating on her husband, she fears becoming a social outcast. She is so consumed with shame that she commits suicide by swallowing arsenic. Her husband, Charles, is devastated – even more so when he finds a collection of love letters sent to her by one of her lovers. He dies soon after, leaving their daughter an orphan.

Spend five minutes in a typical nightclub and you'll see a very different story. It's not unusual to find married women flirting and partying up a storm. While there are plenty of wives out there simply looking for a quick thrill – making them candidates for an evening with a player like Nate – most married women who cheat do so for different reasons from the ones that spur married men. The sex isn't as important as their desire for emotional attachment and intimacy.

Pop quiz

Your friend tells you she cheated on her husband last night. It was a one-night stand with a guy she met at a bar: no strings attached, they didn't even exchange phone numbers. She says her husband deserved it because she caught him cheating last year. Although her husband has been faithful since then, she says she's always wanted to pay him back for what he did. She says she now feels satisfied and that they'll both be faithful from now on. Do you think what she did was fair?

The GEWIS social research institute, based in Hamburg, Germany, polled 1427 men and women between the ages of 25 and 35. The results, published in *Woman* magazine, found that 53 per cent of women admitted they'd been unfaithful to their partner, compared with 59 per cent of men. The survey also showed that non-sexual desires, such as the need for understanding and reassurance, were a chief motive among women who strayed.

Certainly, there are more opportunities these days for married women to meet men to have affairs with. Today, nearly 60 per cent of American women work outside the home, up from about 40 per cent in 1964. There are far more opportunities and temptations when you're at the workplace every day surrounded by guys, as opposed to staying at home tending the kids and the house. In fact, the workplace is where women most commonly find their other lovers. One of the chief reasons why is that women bring their 'best selves' to work: they're nicely dressed, their self-esteem is high, and they're removed from the stresses and problems of home. It's the same with the men. In an office environment, a corporate guy wearing a suit and commanding respect from his staff carries himself with confidence. He *feels* much more desirable to women, especially the ones he works with, than he would while shopping for groceries in a T-shirt and jeans.

Virtually all of the adulterous women interviewed in a recent survey said they cheat because they deserve all of the pleasure and thrills associated with a secret affair. The *New York Post* reported that Susan Shapiro Barash, an author and professor, interviewed 120 random women from diverse professional back-grounds. She found that 90 per cent of the cheating wives said they suffered absolutely 'no guilt' and felt 'entitled' to the good feelings they got. (Her research also showed that six in ten women will cheat on their husband at least once during their marriages.) The actual numbers might be even higher. It's been found that men, when polled about cheating, tend to exaggerate their number of sexual experiences while women are more likely to downplay them.

Scott, a 40-year-old personal trainer, says he's slept with over twenty married women as a direct result of his job. 'I can't imagine a job that's more conducive to having affairs with your married clients,' he says. 'It's a very hands-on job, and I'm motivating these women, inspiring them, and helping them to shed their stress. They talk to me about their problems at home and the things they want to achieve, and I listen. It creates a very strong physical and emotional connection. Recently, though, I made a vow to stop screwing around with married women. The last one I was with, her husband called me at home, sobbing. He begged me to stay away from his wife.'

There are female philanderers too, and they too are usually the daughters or ex-wives of philanderers. They often have deep feelings of resentment towards men, because they believe all men screw around as their father or ex-husband did. A female philanderer is not likely to stay married for very long, since that would require her to make peace with a man, and as a woman to carry more than her share of the burden of marriage. Marriage grounds people in reality rather than transporting them into fantasy, so marriage is too loving, too demanding, too realistic and not romantic enough for them.

While straying wives tend to look for a long-term partner to cheat with, single women who mess around with married men are quite likely to sleep with a large number of them. These women prefer to raid other people's marriages, breaking up relationships and then dancing off to their next tryst. Like male philanderers, female philanderers put their victims through all of this just to give themselves a sense of gender power.

THE DIFFERENCES BETWEEN MALE AND FEMALE CHEATERS

As you know by now, adultery is by no means an exclusively male activity. Many female cheaters fall into one of the twelve categories we used to describe the types of cheating men – particularly the category of 'cheating keeps us together'. But while men and women may share similar motivations, they tend to conduct their affairs in a different manner and have different expectations.

'Back when I was dating Robert, he was a rock star in bed,' says Donna, 28. 'Every time we had sex there was a lot of foreplay first. He loved going down on me. But after three years of marriage, our sex life has burned out. Maybe once a week, five minutes and he's done. I guess that's enough for him, but it's definitely not enough for me. Otherwise, he's still the same wonderful guy that I married. I love him and I don't want to end our marriage just because we've lost our spark in bed.

'Well, I found the answer. There was this cute guy at my gym who was always talking to me and flirting. I agreed to meet him for a drink after work and we wound up going back to his place and having sex. Now we get together about once a week, at his place during the day, and screw each other's brains out for an hour. It's actually improved my relationship with my husband, Robert. I go home to him and I feel happy with him. I'm no longer frustrated about our sex life.'

Plenty of married women make similar choices.

They're unfulfilled by a relationship that lost its passion years ago, they're financially dependent on their man (as are the kids), or they genuinely love their husbands but aren't getting the romantic attention they need. So they start seeing a guy on the side. The difference, usually, is that the cheating wife will seek a long-term affair rather than quick flings, and in many cases the affair can go on for years. In a sense, she seeks to become monogamous with the man she's cheating with – and will consider it cheating if her lover sleeps with other women.

Like male 'fools in love', married women also get swept up in the crazy euphoria of affairs. There is one interesting difference, though: women tend to proceed with far more discretion and caution. They may be in love with their guy-on-the-side, but they tend to remain aware of what's at stake. They understand that leaving their husband, or getting caught, will cause great turmoil in their lives and could break up their families. And in another contrast to cheating husbands, these women will often romanticise their affairs and harbour the idea that one day they'll wind up remarried to this other man. (It rarely works out this way.)

For the past six months, Michelle, a 35-year-old married woman, has been involved with a married man named Kyle, whom she met online. It started out as steamy sessions in hotel rooms, no strings attached. But things progressed to another level when Kyle brought her along with him on a business trip to New York. (Michelle told her husband she was going to visit her sister.) They spent four romantic days together. Michelle has now developed strong feelings for Kyle and wants to know if their relationship has a future.

She's tired of being ignored by her husband and is ready to leave him, if only Kyle will agree to leave his wife. She's worried, however, that he will stay with his wife because they have two kids together. When she tries to bring up the topic of their 'future' together, he shuts down and changes the subject.

Michelle's story illustrates another important principle about how men and women differ in the way they approach affairs. Women, by nature, fail to understand that men are rarely capable of living up to their romantic fantasies. While women may be okay at first with no-strings-attached sex, it's often only a matter of time before they form a romantic attachment and start to consider a future with this 'other man'.

'I've had to stop seeing several women because they started asking questions about us getting serious,' says Tom, a married 28-year-old. 'They know the deal: I love my wife and my family and I'm just looking for some fun on the side. But it keeps happening, usually after a couple of months. They start asking questions about my marriage, trying to scope out whether I'm ready to ditch my wife. I'm honest with them – I tell them I have no intention of getting involved in a messy divorce and losing my kids. If they can't accept that, then it's time for me to move on.'

Like Kyle and Tom perhaps, cheating men will often justify their behaviour by telling themselves they don't love the other woman. These men will assure themselves that the affair 'means nothing', that they still love their families and are committed to them. On the other hand, most married women who fall in the 'cheating keeps us together' camp will tell themselves that they *don't* love their husbands. They justify their affairs in a different way, by telling themselves that because they don't love their husband, or their husband doesn't love them, they deserve to have someone else.

Interestingly, in the end, men tend to be as forgiving as women of their spouses' affairs. Married guys declare that they would *never* tolerate their wife cheating; it's a macho thing, a matter of pride. They say if it ever happened, they'd divorce her in an instant. But when it comes down to it, if they love their wives, they're just as likely as a cheated-on woman to try to keep the marriage together and do what it takes to work things out.

We'll end this chapter with the words of a married woman whose brand of cheating best belongs in the 'I feel trapped' category. She wanted to become pregnant – and was willing to do it by any means necessary.

TARI, 37: 'I'd been married to my husband for three-and-a-half years and had my heart set on having children, but it just wasn't happening. He'd had a vasectomy prior to our marriage, after having a child with his ex-wife, and even after undergoing a reverse vasectomy we were unable to conceive. Making matters worse, his ex-wife was a constant nuisance, always calling our house to ask for more money to cover their child's expenses. She was always a complete bitch to me on the phone, and it was very painful for me knowing that he'd given her a child and couldn't give me the same.

'We decided to go the sperm-donor route. We selected a donor, but just before my scheduled in vitro procedure, my doctor informed me that I would need minor surgery to remove fibroids from my uterus. This would set back our plans a while.

'Then the company my husband worked for sent him overseas to head up a new division. I would only be seeing him one weekend a month, at most, so now he wanted to postpone our plans for a child indefinitely. The final straw came when I learned his ex-wife was having another child with her boyfriend. It killed me to know that this bitch was having *another* child and I couldn't even have one. During a phone conversation with my husband, while I was telling him how frustrated and upset I was, he snapped at me that I should just go "do what I needed to do".

'I decided to take matters into my own hands and seek another man to impregnate me. I started going out at night with my girlfriends and I met a great guy named Joe. We started dating. I didn't tell him about my intent to have a child and told him we didn't need to use protection because I was on the pill (which I wasn't). After two months of dating him, I was pregnant. I didn't tell Joe about the pregnancy until I began to show. When I told him, he was upset at first but then became supportive. When I found out I was actually pregnant with twins, I was twice as thrilled.

'My husband never knew. I told him that I'd gone ahead and gotten the in vitro procedure done, and that the twins had been fathered by a clinic sperm donor. The only person who knew the truth all along was my aunt, who's in her fifties and never had kids despite three in vitro attempts. I felt confident in my decision when she told me that if she could go back in time, she would have also had an affair to get pregnant. (Yes, motherhood is that important to some women.) I eventually told my mother the truth – when the twins were a year old – and even though she wasn't happy about being deceived, she told me she understood.

'My adorable twin girls are now seventeen months old, I'm in the process of finalising my divorce, and Joe is still in the picture. We plan to raise the twins together, and though we're no longer a couple, we remain very close and there's a chance that we'll have a romantic future together.

'Yes, I cheated. I'm not proud of the course I chose. But I felt that it was my only option because I desperately wanted to start a family. Sometimes the end justifies the means.'

Chapter 16
Private Dancers:
What Every Woman Needs to Know About Strippers

Strippers fill a void ignored by many wives. And, they typically have bigger hooters.

from an internet message board

Five in the morning on a Monday finds Christopher and me ensconced at a table in a dark corner of Cheetahs, one of Las Vegas's more infamous strip joints. In the name of research, we'd decided to hunker down at this den of debauchery to gain a deeper understanding of one of the most powerful male fantasies: the stripper.

Earlier in the night, we'd formulated a game plan. Spend an hour, and a hundred dollars each, to buy enough time with a few dancers to ask some questions. Since it was a ridiculously late hour on a 'school' night, there weren't too many other customers for the girls to fleece; they'd be willing to hang out and have drinks with us.

Of course, me in a strip club trying to remain sober and professional is like sending Paris Hilton into a shopping mall and expecting her to keep her credit cards in her purse. Sure enough, once the booze started flowing and a succession of G-string divas started grinding on our laps, common sense went out the window. I did manage to scribble a few notes on a cocktail napkin, although it was difficult to compose my thoughts with gigantic fake breasts jammed in my face.

I'll admit the evening's research wasn't entirely necessary, since I was already a seasoned veteran of these establishments. My first year in Las Vegas, I'd burned through thousands of dollars on these silicone-enhanced hustlers. Packed to the gills with gorgeous women – all of whom seem oh-so-happy to see you – the strip-club experience can be addictive.

To these girls, 'regulars' are money in the bank. These are customers who visit the club on a regular basis to see a particular girl, and monopolise her time by purchasing numerous lap dances. These men come to view their favourite strippers as confidantes, and are intoxicated by the attention and affection their girls lavish on them. At home, they might feel taken for granted by their wives; here in the strip club, they get to feel like heroes and generous benefactors, helping their young damsels in distress with a steady stream of $20 bills. And when their wallets run dry, their damsel will gladly accompany them to the ATM machine to make a withdrawal. The machine's transaction fee may be an outrageous $8, but at this point, who's counting?

In the end, the strippers laugh all the way to the bank. While some high-rolling customers have more money than they know what to do with, others are blowing their kid's college tuition while their favourite dancer drives home in an $80,000 sports car. Whatever the case may be, these guys feel it's worth it to spend a few hours living the fantasy – believing that these sexy, nubile young women find them handsome and generous and fascinating. Pay for a few dances, and they'll sit on your lap and make you feel like your job selling insurance is more interesting than being a Hollywood superstar.

'You just need to be a good listener,' says Sharon, a 30-year-old veteran with the streetwise demeanour of a natural-born hustler. 'Let them tell you about their problems at home, and at their job, and build up their ego.'

When it comes to the fragile male ego, strippers are masters of manipulation. Some guys will literally kill for their phony affection. Back in 1997, a 34-year-old Philadelphia shlub named Craig Rabinowitz became infatuated with a stripper named Shannon Reinert. She used the stage name 'Summer' while working the pole at a high-class jiggle joint called Delilah's Den.

It was lust at first sight for Rabinowitz, a struggling entrepreneur with a wife and baby at home. He began showering money on Shannon that he could ill afford, spending at least $100,000 over the course of a year on cash gifts, furniture and a Tiffany & Co. necklace for Valentine's Day. To finance his obsession, he scammed friends and family members into investing in his phony businesses, then took the cash straight to the strip club. Rabinowitz was the ultimate 'regular'. Summer never slept with him; chances are, she didn't even like him much. But she sure knew how to play him.

Eventually, Rabinowitz's sleazy double life spiralled out of control. Drowning in debt, his investors demanding to know where their money went, he saw only one way out: his 29-year-old wife's life insurance policy, worth $1.8 million. One night, Rabinowitz slipped a sleeping pill into her drink and strangled her in the bathtub. He called 911, doing his best to sound distraught, and claimed that she'd drowned while taking a bath. But the autopsy results, and the strangulation marks, told a different story. Rabinowitz wound up pleading guilty. He's now doing life in prison without the possibility of parole.

'One of my regulars always comes to see me after he's had a fight with his wife,' says Keilani, a stunning 22-year-old Asian dancer. 'He just wants a woman to take his side. I agree with him and tell him his wife is being unfair. He pays me for dances – $100 for every three songs in the VIP room – but the time we spend together isn't about turning him on. He just wants a woman who will listen to him and agree.'

Keilani is currently dating a guy she met in the club. He bought a few dances that first night, then returned a week later for some more. He kept coming back. On his fourth visit, he made her a straight-up proposition: he'd buy her a house and a car if she agreed to be his girl-friend. Keilani negotiated the details (she'd had her eye on a hot new Mercedes convertible) and agreed to the arrangement. He's twenty years older than she is, and has a wife and three children. Who says you can't buy love?

Another young dancer, Shauna, regularly goes on dates with married customers. But it's always strictly business – no sex, not even a kiss, just a flat $200 per hour for her time. These schmucks take her to the fanciest restaurants in town and wine and dine her. Some of them are hoping to get lucky, but they never do; others are willing to pay just for the companionship, or to be able to tell their buddies about their 'date' with a stripper.

'They're losers that couldn't get a date otherwise,' Shauna chuckles. But she doesn't feel guilty for a second about taking their hard-earned cash: she's got kids to feed and car payments to make. And as long as there are desperate married men willing to shell out the bucks, she's willing to listen and act interested.

Interestingly, we've never heard of a strip bar that features male strippers all the time. Instead, some strip clubs feature male strippers on certain nights of the week. It would be hard to imagine an all-male strip club doing strong business every night of the week, since women (with rare exceptions) wouldn't patronise such a place with any regularity. Women go for special occasions, such as a bachelorette party or a girls' night out. For them, it usually has nothing to do with sex or fulfilling fantasies; it's about getting silly with their girlfriends. A lot of men, on the other hand, hang out at strip clubs regularly – and as we've noted, spend money on their favourite dancers for more than entertainment purposes.

The majority of men visit strip clubs simply to have a good time and check out beautiful women. But men who visit the same club regularly are going to develop 'friendships' with certain dancers. As long as they're willing to shell out money, they can have a sexy woman to chat with, to provide a sympathetic ear, and to stroke their ego. If a man feels he's lacking these things in his relationship with you, then strip clubs offer yet another form of temptation. And even if your man doesn't visit these places, every woman should be aware of what draws men to strippers, beyond the obvious titillation factor. It's to have an attractive woman reaffirm their masculinity, to rub their back and make them feel desirable, to *listen* when they talk. You might say it's a guy's version of going to a therapist. The fact that men are willing to spend hundreds of dollars on this form of therapy shows just how important it is to them.

While for most strippers it's just a job – they want to make their money and go home – it's not uncommon for them to meet customers that they wind up dating. A guy who is normally successful with women can get a phone number from a stripper just as easily as he would from a girl at a regular bar (we've done it ourselves on many occasions). For the average married guy, it's highly unlikely that he'll end up sleeping with a stripper; but the experiences he has in these clubs, if he's hanging out regularly, can seriously damage his relationship with his wife.

We've seen it happen. The more time a guy spends around strippers, having them falsely build up his ego and taking his side whenever he complains about problems at home, the more inadequate his mate seems in his eyes – and the greater the chance that he'll wind up cheating. While he probably can't afford to maintain a stripper girlfriend, there's always a bar down the street where relationships can be had for cheaper.

Christopher Curtis says . . .

There was always a different energy in the locker room on 'Third Fridays'. My fellow cops would laugh and joke while changing into their uniforms, acting unusually excited and energised. You'd think a new pay raise was just approved. But for a lot of these guys, the third Friday of the month was even more important than extra cash. It meant freedom — the chance to leave their wives at home and spend a night out with the boys. It always involved boozing at a bar. It definitely involved flirting. And sometimes, it meant cheating.

Back when I was a young cop, this was a ritual with my squad. For me, as the only single guy among them, it was more amusing than anything. Third Friday was like a glimmer of hope that kept them going. They all professed to love their wives and treasure their families, but for this one night a month they were like a pack of frat boys.

I remember a cop in my squad named Mitch and how, several days after a Third Friday, I went to the christening of his baby girl. Our whole squad was there, as well as his and his wife's families and all of their friends.

Angela, Mitch's wife, was beaming. After the service I wound up chatting with her away from everyone else. She couldn't have seemed happier with her marriage. 'Mitch has been so amazing,' she said. 'It was a difficult pregnancy but he's been everything I could have hoped for in a husband.' I glanced over at Mitch. Standing there in his black suit, cradling his infant daughter in his arms, he was the picture-perfect husband.

I couldn't help flashing back to the previous Friday night. Mitch had been a completely different guy. We were at a strip club, which among my married buddies seemed to be their best friend next to the remote control. Usually, these nights out were fairly harmless: a table full of guys and several dancers sharing drinks and stories. This night was a little different. Mitch was spending a lot of time with one girl in particular. At first I thought nothing of it, but then I glanced over to check on them . . . and they were gone.

Mitch returned a half-hour later. He told us that the dancer had finished her shift and he'd walked her out to her car. A goodnight kiss turned into a passionate high school-style romp in the back of his SUV. 'You should have seen me with this chick, doing acrobatics over the babyseat,' he said, as our crew burst into laughter.

I snapped out of the flashback, half-heartedly listening to Angela as she told me about the new extension they'd put on their house so the baby would have a playroom. I hoped that my uneasiness wasn't showing on my face. I wished her all the best, then slipped away and joined the guys. I couldn't help but feel sorry for Angela. If only she knew . . .

Chapter 17

Paying the Piper: The Legal Consequences of Cheating and Divorce

The difference between divorce and legal separation is that a legal separation gives a husband time to hide his money.

Johnny Carson

Mike, 44, sits slumped at the bar with a shot of tequila in front of him. He takes a drag of his cigarette and exhales with the deep sigh of a broken man. He's just shared his tale of woe, a fate that awaits many guys whose marriage falls apart: a divorce so financially devastating that he'll forever rue the day he said 'I do.' He admits he cheated, but he wasn't the only one at fault. His wife also slept around, and the marriage became a miserable mess for both parties.

Mike was married to his ex-wife Melissa for nineteen years. They didn't have any kids. When she filed for divorce his business was thriving and he was worth several million dollars. They both wanted out of the marriage. He wanted to do the right thing and make sure she was fairly compensated, but more than anything, he just wanted it to be over with.

Unfortunately for Mike, her idea of fair compensation was very different to what he had in mind. She was ready for war. Their divorce dragged through court for four agonising years, during which he was ordered to pay her $100,000 in alimony and give her all of the equity in the marital home so that she would have a place to live. He also gave her a vehicle and all of the home furnishings, which totalled in excess of $50,000. The stress of the divorce caused Mike's business to suffer, and he was eventually forced to declare bankruptcy – as a result of which, Melissa was awarded over $500,000 worth of his assets. On top of that, he was ordered to pay her $1000 a month in alimony for the rest of her life, which, after his bankruptcy, equalled about half of his take-home pay. As Mike struggled to make ends meet, his ex-wife moved her new boyfriend into the house he'd paid for, *and* he was forced to continue supporting her.

Cheat Sheet stat

In the United States, the median age for first marriages is 26.7 years for men and 25.1 for women. According to Martin O'Connell, chief of the Census Bureau's fertility and family statistics branch, these median ages are roughly a year older than they were a decade ago. In every state, men are waiting longer than women to tie the knot; the youngest median ages are found in Utah, where it's 21.9 for women and 23.9 for men. Men and women in Washington, DC, hold out the longest, where they wait until about age 30.

When kids are involved, the financial and emotional strain can be far worse for a man. We've heard stories of men struggling to get by on 20 per cent of their salary after child support, alimony and a chunk of their pensions are deducted from their pay cheques. Instead of divorce allowing a fresh start for both parties, it can often be a crushing financial blow for men that impacts on them for the rest of their lives.

Stories like Mike's underscore a harsh reality that married men face: no matter which party was in the wrong, the odds are stacked against them in a divorce court. This is another reason why men go to extreme lengths to conceal their extramarital affairs. The fact of the matter is, divorce laws in the United States cause a lot of guys to remain in an unhappy marriage, and cheat like crazy.

If you suspect your husband is cheating on you, you might wish that he'd just come clean and admit it, so that you both can agree to end the marriage and move on with your lives. But the nature of divorce laws makes it more complicated than that. For men, the stakes are higher than ever.

FROM HOOKS-UPS TO PRENUPS

It's stories like Mike's that cause many men these days to insist on **prenuptial agreements,** or to at least seriously consider the idea. Simply put, these are legal documents that specify how assets will be divided up in the event of death or divorce. Prenups need to be signed by both parties but don't need to be filed in court. They can legally determine how virtually anything the couple shares will be distributed. Without a prenup, in most US states (including California, where most of the big celebrity marriages occur), anything that is earned or bought after the wedding is considered community property. During a divorce, this property will then be divided equally.

Prenups, however, are an extremely sensitive and emotional topic for most women (who typically earn less than their men). Most view the mere suggestion of a prenup as a grievous insult, one that reduces the sacred vows of marriage to a business transaction. They take it as a sign that their spouse lacks trust in the relationship – or, even worse, views them as a gold digger – and is already planning for an eventual split.

Men, on the other hand, are more inclined to look at the situation in practical terms. After all, they're the ones who stand to get taken to the cleaners; and, they may argue, marriage is just as much a legal contract as a prenup is. The key difference is that marriage has the potential to ruin him financially, while a prenup ensures that the marital assets will be divided fairly if things fall apart for any reason.

Real estate mogul turned reality TV star Donald Trump, now on his third marriage, is an outspoken advocate of prenuptial agreements. 'The Donald' has issued advice on this subject to a number of young celebrities who are planning to walk down the aisle. Sure, a tycoon like Trump is always looking at the bottom line, but a lot of guys (and a growing number of women) are now thinking along these same lines. **In this day and age, is it wise to risk your financial future on a relationship that could end for any number of unforeseen reasons?**

'Every time celebrities get ready to walk down the aisle – and, believe me, I know all about that – I continuously caution them to get a pre-nuptial agreement,' Trump said. He publicly warned pop princess Britney

Spears to protect her assets from her husband, Kevin Federline, who entered into the marriage with next to nothing and two kids from a previous relationship. He also warned Paris Hilton about her engagement to Paris Latsis – heir to an even greater fortune than hers – who proposed to her after a few months of dating. (To the surprise of absolutely no one, the engagement was called off within weeks.)

Raoul Felder, known as 'the divorce attorney to the stars', once said a celebrity who doesn't insist on a prenup needs a psychiatrist, not a lawyer. Celebrity prenups have included some of the following incredible clauses:

- The husband's mother-in-law is not allowed to sleep over at the house, and he is not required to go on vacations with her.
- The husband may only watch one football game per Sunday.
- If the husband cheats, he relinquishes all his frequent-flyer miles to his wife.
- If the wife's weight surpasses 120 pounds (55 kilos), she must relinquish $100,000 of her separate property.
- The wife gets to perform random drug tests on her husband, with financial penalties for positive results.
- The husband must pay $10,000 each time he is rude to his wife's parents.

If both parties sign the papers, these clauses are all legal and enforceable. (Incidentally, issues dealing with custody of children or child support can't be determined by a prenup.)

Filthy-rich female celebrities have as much reason to be concerned as male ones. Jessica Simpson, who is in the process of divorcing Nick Lachey at the time of writing, didn't have a prenup. Ironically, it was Nick who wanted a prenup when they decided to get married three years ago; as a member of the boy band 98 Degrees, he was the wealthier of the two at the time. Simpson, however, reportedly refused to sign. This may now come back to haunt her, since her career has exploded since then and she earned around $35 million in 2004 alone. As noted above, California law says that earnings amassed during the marriage must be split evenly, which means Lachey may never have to work again. (If this means he'll never record another solo album, that can't be a bad thing.)

When Roseanne Barr was at the height of her success, she was so head over heels for Tom Arnold that she fired her attorney for suggesting she draw up a prenup. The couple married in 1990 and split four years later, allowing Arnold to walk away with a $50 million settlement.

Britney Spears didn't think she would need one with K-Fed, but her mum and business managers were able to talk some sense into her. Now that their marriage is reportedly on the rocks, this could prove to be the smartest move she's made in years. Walking out of a Vegas casino, K-Fed reportedly told a reporter from *In Touch* magazine that he would seek a $125 million settlement if the marriage were to end.

It gets a bit trickier for bad-boy extraordinaire Charlie Sheen, whose prenup with Denise Richards calls for her to get a minimum settlement of $4 million if he gets caught cheating. In March 2005, Richards, six months pregnant with their second child, filed for divorce, citing 'irreconcilable differences.' After a brief reconciliation, she refiled the divorce papers in January 2006. Catherine Zeta-Jones also reportedly stands to receive additional millions from her husband, Michael Douglas, who has a history of infidelity, if he cheats. The rumour is that she'll receive $2.8 million for every year they've been married; if she's able to prove he cheated on her, she's entitled to $5 million. 'Anybody in my position or Michael's who doesn't sign [a prenup] is dumb,' she told *USA Today*. 'I'd want my daughter to sign one.'

When basketball superstar Kobe Bryant married Vanessa Laine, he reportedly became estranged from his family over his refusal to follow their advice and make his wife-to-be sign a prenup. (He was 22 at the time; she was only eighteen.) Then, when Bryant was later accused of raping a hotel clerk, he went on TV to refute the criminal allegations but did admit that he'd committed adultery. Days later, he bought his wife a $4 million diamond ring. It was an expensive way to say 'I'm sorry', but with his Los Angeles Lakers contract worth more than $136 million, he stood to lose a lot more than that in a divorce court.

Tom Cruise didn't have a prenup with Nicole Kidman, but when he decided he wanted out of the marriage he made sure to file divorce papers right before their tenth wedding anniversary. In California, when a couple splits before the ten-year mark, the wealthier half only has to pay alimony for half the length of the marriage.

Regardless of how much financial sense they might make, the average woman still loathes the concept of prenups. 'As a matter of principle, I would never sign one,' says Cindy, 27. 'Marriage needs to be about trust, and handing me a prenup to sign is like saying you lack faith in me, and in our future together.' Jim, a 42-year-old who was forced to declare bankruptcy after losing half his assets and being saddled with alimony payments – even after his ex-wife remarried – begs to differ. 'Look, I believe in true love as much as anyone. But what sane guy would enter into a legally binding contract where he could lose 50 per cent of his investment just because the other person decides to call off the deal?'

As much as you may despise the idea of prenups, the reality is that you've got to consider the man's perspective if he wants you to sign one (provided that the terms of the prenup are fair and reasonable to both parties, of course). Bear in mind that if a woman decides one day that she's bored with the marriage, or even ditches him for another guy, she can still take half of his assets. This can include his business, even if he started it years before the marriage and she had no involvement with it. And prenups cover more than just money; they also include the assets that both parties brought with them into the marriage, whether it's his favourite piece of furniture, or money that she inherited from her parents.

One thing that's for certain is that prenuptial agreements are no longer just for rich old geezers looking to protect their fortunes from their latest trophy wife. A lot of younger couples about to marry for the first time are signing prenups, or at least weighing up the option. As are men who have children from a previous relationship and plan to remarry, but want to make sure that if they die, or the marriage dissolves, their children will be provided for. 'I would never get married again without a prenup,' says Gary, 40. 'Women might complain that it shows a lack of trust on my part, but what's *her* agenda if she insists on getting half my money even if she winds up leaving me?'

The bottom line is this: **when a man is reluctant about marriage, sometimes it's about more than the idea of committing to one woman for the rest of his life.** With the laws set up the way they are, marriage can be a huge financial risk that is tilted heavily in the woman's favour.

For guys who've been through a hellish divorce, the most bitter bill to swallow is when they're required to pay alimony – to continue supporting their ex-wife in the manner she grew accustomed to during the marriage. Unfortunately for men, the things *they've* grown accustomed to don't count. As comedian Chris Rock said, imitating a guy standing before the divorce court judge: 'If she's accustomed to a way of living, what about me? Your honour, I'm accustomed to f***ing her four times a week!'

To give you a sense of just how expensive divorce can get for the modern man, here is a list of some of the biggest divorce settlements of all time. In most cases, these are just the lump-sum payments that were forked over – and don't even take into account monthly alimony payments.

TAKEN TO THE CLEANERS

In 1976, movie star **Harrison Ford** met screenwriter Melissa Mathison on the set of the Vietnam war epic *Apocalypse Now*. Ford went on to become one of Hollywood's most bankable stars, commanding over

$25 million per film. (Mathison had some pretty impressive earning power as well; among her screen-writing credits was Steven Spielberg's *E.T.*) Their eighteen-year marriage collapsed in 2001. The terms of the divorce broke new ground: not only was he required to divide up his assets with her, but Mathison was also entitled to future video and DVD royalties from the films he had made during their marriage, which included two of the massively successful *Indiana Jones* movies.

But old Han Solo wasn't exactly forced to return to carpentry (which is how he paid the rent before George Lucas cast him in *Star Wars*). He remained at their $47.4 million Wyoming ranch after paying Mathison half its value, and held on to his collection of motor-cycles and cars, and his six aircraft – although Mathison did win the right to use the jet any time she wanted to.

Michael Douglas, Academy Award-winning actor and producer (and alleged sex addict), gave up a reported $45 million to ex-wife Diandra when they divorced in 1999. They had married in 1977 when Douglas's movie career was just beginning to take shape. He's now married to Catherine Zeta-Jones, who, as we mentioned, insisted on a rock-solid prenup.

Tending bar on the classic TV sitcom *Cheers* earned handsome **Ted Danson** enough loot to buy a Third World country. After fifteen years of marriage and raising two children with his wife Casey – who was ten years his senior, and had suffered a paralysing stroke while giving birth to their first child – the marriage crumbled and Danson started seeing Whoopi Goldberg on the side. Danson divorced in 1992 and was forced to hand over a cool $30 million.

Film director **James Cameron**, who helmed blockbusters such as *Terminator*, *Terminator 2*, *Aliens*, *True Lies* and *Titanic*, married actress Linda Hamilton in 1997 (whom he'd long before cast in the role of Sarah Connor in the *Terminator* movies). The doomed union lasted a mere seventeen months, out of which they were separated for eight. Cameron was ordered to hand over more than half his revenues from *Titanic*, totalling over $50 million.

Country music star **Kenny Rogers**, singer of the immortal lyrics 'You gotta know when to hold 'em, know when to fold 'em', amassed an estimated fortune of $250 million from his records and restaurant chain. In 1977 'the Gambler' took his fourth trip down the aisle, with Marianne Gordon, an actress whom he'd met while taping an appearance on the show *Hee Haw*. When they split in 1993, Rogers willingly surrendered $60 million and claimed that she deserved it.

Actor **Kevin Costner**, famed for hit movies such as *Dances with Wolves*, *The Untouchables* and *JFK*, married Cindy Silva in 1978 while attending college. After three kids and sixteen years of marriage, they split in 1994. The divorce was settled privately, and Cindy left with an estimated $80 million.

In the 1970s, easy-listening hitmaker **Neil Diamond** shattered world records with his stratospheric album sales and sold-out concerts. During his four-decade career, he has sold over 100 million records. In 1969, Diamond was already married when he met TV producer Marcia Murphey; as the story goes, Diamond stepped out for cigarettes and never returned. Within three weeks the Rhinestone Cowboy had divorced wife number one and married Murphey. They stayed married for 25 years, until they divorced in 1994 amid rumours of Diamond's extramarital dalliances. Diamond forked over half of his $300 million fortune and has claimed that he did so willingly, calling his ex-wife 'worth every penny' for bearing their two children.

Craig McCaw might not be an A-list name, but this guy's bank account would put any Hollywood celebrity to shame. He inherited a struggling TV cable service from his father and transformed it into a successful business, which he eventually sold for a staggering $755 million. And that was just for starters – in the early 1980s, he made the prescient move of acquiring cellular phone licences as that industry was starting to heat up. He later sold this company to telecommunications behemoth AT&T for around $12 billion.

McCaw had been married to his wife, Wendy, since 1974; they met as students at Stanford University, where she was his tutor. Divorce papers were filed in 1995, with Wendy insisting that he continue to support her $200,000-per-month lifestyle. In the end, she walked off into the sunset with a whopping $460 million, most of it in Nextel stock.

Saudi billionaire **Adnan Khashoggi** made his fortune as an international arms dealer, then launched a Switzerland-based business that bought up banks, hotels and real estate around the globe. He and his wife Soraya, whom he'd married in 1961, were one of the world's great jet-setting couples, and both reportedly engaged in adulterous affairs. They split in 1982, with Soraya's out-of-court settlement earning her a reported $874 million.

In 2002, **Robert Johnson**, founder of BET (Black Entertainment Television), divorced his wife Sheila after 33 years of marriage. She was awarded half of his $3 billion fortune, which he amassed when Viacom bought BET, making her America's first black female billionaire. (Soon after, Oprah Winfrey was certified as the second one.) She went on to marry the judge who presided over her divorce case.

Australian-born media baron **Rupert Murdoch**, one of the richest men on Earth, married his wife Anna in the 1960s and remained with her for 32 years as she bore him three children. Their 1999 divorce reportedly netted her $1.7 billion worth of Murdoch's assets, including $110 million in cash. Murdoch remarried seventeen days later.

Indeed, Hollywood lore is rife with blockbuster divorce payouts. In 1983, Johnny Carson's divorce from wife Joanna netted her $20 million in cash and property, a sum that sent shockwaves through the Hollywood community. Those numbers look meagre compared to the $90 million that Demi Moore was awarded in her split from Bruce Willis, or the $109 million that Tom Cruise handed over to Nicole Kidman. Perhaps the largest divorce settlement in Tinseltown history was surrendered by **Steven Spielberg**, who married actress Amy Irving in 1985. After bearing him a son, Max, they called it quits and Irving walked away with $100 million. (Factoring in inflation, that settlement would be worth $148 million today.)

It's hard to feel too sympathetic towards anyone worth hundreds of millions of dollars; these money-making machines can fork over half and still never need to work another day in their pampered lives. But the same division-of-asset rules apply to the average working stiff who makes $40,000 a year. For him, handing over half could mean moving back in with Mum.

The moral of the story? However deeply in love you are with each other, no matter how committed you both are to making it work, you can't blame a guy for at least considering the financial consequences of divorce. However strongly you feel about prenuptial agreements, it may be worth exploring if it's going to guarantee him peace of mind – or your own, since it's not uncommon these days for women to earn more than their husbands. If one of you winds up wanting out, but the financial stakes of divorce are too high, cheating could be the next step.

Chapter 18
Paying to Play: Married Men and Prostitutes

Behind every successful man is a woman. Behind her is his wife.

Groucho Marx

No discussion on cheating would be complete without examining 'the world's oldest profession'. Far more married men than you would suspect visit prostitutes. You'd probably imagine these men to be old or ugly, or trapped in horrible, loveless marriages. But the reality is that plenty of normal, attractive husbands regularly pay for action on the side. And it doesn't require a business trip to Bangkok: prostitutes are readily available in every town and every city. They can be found in the phone book, on the internet, in the newspaper classified ads or at the massage parlour down the block.

We talked to 'working girls', we talked to their 'johns' (the clients who hire them), and we drew some interesting conclusions. This aspect of cheating shows a fundamental difference between how men and women value sex. For most women, the concepts of love and monogamy go hand in hand – there cannot be one without the other. Men, however, can make the distinction between their need for sex and the role they fulfill as a husband and head of the household. As crazy as it may sound, many men claim that visiting prostitutes helps to keep their marriage together.

And as with husbands who indulge in 'meaningless' affairs outside their marriage, a lot of these guys don't even consider it to be cheating. (Similar to someone we know who follows the 'zip code' rule – if it happened in another zip code, it doesn't count.) To these guys, though, there's an important difference between paying for sex with a prostitute and engaging in an affair with a 'normal' woman. The majority of them have never cheated in the traditional sense; they may worry about getting caught, or believe that affairs are morally wrong, or simply lack the ability to date women outside of their marriage. But a quick romp with a prostitute? To them, it doesn't *really* count as infidelity.

'Going to a prostitute is like going to a restaurant,' read one message we came across on an internet site dedicated to brothels. 'It's fast, comfortable, different, and you don't have to wash the dishes after your meal.'

Cheat Sheet fact
One of the richest men in the world today, the Sultan of Brunei, has over 100 wives. (Just imagine the fights over the remote control in that house.)

In the early 1990s, actor Charlie Sheen was on top of Hollywood. He had it all: looks, youth, fame and a ton of money. He could've had his pick of world-class women. Yet over a two-year period, he spent more than $50,000 on prostitutes. (This came to light during the trial of Heidi Fleiss, the infamous 'Hollywood Madam' who supplied hookers to Sheen and many other members of Tinseltown's elite.)

When asked why he would pay for sex, Sheen replied with an oft-quoted truism: 'You don't pay hookers to sleep with you, you pay them to leave.' This is the basic mindset of most men who visit prostitutes: it's immediate sexual gratification with no strings attached, no expectations (besides the man having an orgasm), and no hurt feelings in the morning.

THE WAGES OF SIN

Seeing as we've penned this book in Las Vegas, which richly deserves its reputation as 'Sin City', we've got a keen perspective on the situation. Nevada is the only state in America where prostitution is legal (though it's only condoned in counties with populations of less than 400,000, because the bigger cities fear that open prostitution might scare off tourists and detract from their primary business, which is gambling).

While hooking is illegal in Las Vegas, prostitution is advertised everywhere with a nudge and a wink. Gigantic billboards loom over the roads, advertising 'Strippers direct to your hotel room in 30 minutes or less!' (Once they arrive, the 'private dance' will progress into something else for an added fee.) You can't walk down the Vegas Strip without people pressing flyers and glossy cards into your palm, hawking nubile young women only a phone call away, ready to entertain you in the privacy of your room.

Massage parlours can be found on practically every block, where the house special is a 'happy ending' that concludes your full-body rubdown. And the *Yellow*

Pages contains literally hundreds of pages of ads for stripper services, erotic 'entertainers', and in-room masseuses of every imaginable colour and variety. If you're seeking the companionship of a transsexual Korean midget, just pick up the phone book and let your fingers do the walking.

At night, hordes of hookers descend on the casinos and sit at the bars – nursing their drinks, idly playing the video poker machines and trying to catch the eye of prospective customers. Some of these working girls are strikingly pretty, not the type you'd expect to be free-lancing at a casino bar at five in the morning. Las Vegas is a magnet for legions of these girls, for one simple reason: fast money. Every day of the week brings an endless stream of horny married (or soon-to-be married) guys with pockets full of chips and cash, intoxicated by the never-ending flow of casino booze. 'What happens in Vegas, stays in Vegas' – that is, until you get busted by an undercover vice cop and have to call your wife at four in the morning to arrange bail.

Then there are Nevada's full-service brothels, many of which are called 'ranches', which pay taxes and are licensed and regulated by the state. They're open 24 hours a day, 365 days a year. They're a major source of revenue for the rural counties they're based in, and a major draw for married guys looking for a thrill. They range from hovels that resemble large trailer homes to sprawling sex ranches with spas, swimming pools, private bondage rooms and themed environments such as 'African Safari' or 'Ancient Rome' (the ideal setting for indulging your inner Caligula).

Customers ring a buzzer at the front door and are then buzzed inside. As they step into the front parlour, the house madam calls for a 'line-up'. Every girl that isn't currently with a customer reports to the front parlour and lines up in front of the customer. Going from left to right, each girl says her name and gives a polite smile. There is a strict protocol with these verbal introductions: no girl is allowed to say or do anything flirtatious to win the guy's favour. (That would be known as 'dirty hustling'.)

The girls that work in these brothels are independent contractors. They set their own prices and are required to live on the premises as long as they're working there (usually a period of several weeks). Each girl is given her own bedroom, in which they entertain their clients. They're not allowed to leave the premises unless it's been approved by management, and never for more than a day. This is so that girls can't arrange dates with their customers on the outside, where they wouldn't be required to pay the 50 per cent commission to the house for every transaction.

House rules are strict and the brothel has a language of its own. All customers are referred to as 'gentlemen' and a sex session is called a 'party'. The girl (or girls), duration of the party and the specific sex acts required will determine the price. A gentleman can pick a girl from the line-up and retire to her room to negotiate the price; or he can take a seat at the bar, order a drink and chat up various women until he makes a decision. Money is never discussed out in the open; all negotiations take place in the room, with prices typically ranging from $150 for oral sex to thousands of dollars for a few hours of rock-star hedonism. Each room is wired with an intercom system that allows the women manning the front desk to hear what's going on in the rooms, and if a customer starts any trouble there is a hidden 'panic button' so that the girl can alert security.

Unlike out in the real world, guys can't be turned down, as long as they've got the necessary cash. If you're willing to pay the house minimum and play by the rules, the girl generally must accept your business. If wives can take any comfort at all in the idea of these brothels, the sex *is* quite safe – Nevada law mandates condom usage for all sex acts, and the girls are inspected by a house doctor and tested for STDs on a regular basis. Websites devoted to the topic claim that not a single case of STD transmission has ever been reported in a Nevada brothel.

WHY PAY FOR IT?

'Every time I have sex with my wife, she wants it to feel romantic and special,' laments Jeff, 38. 'But I'm a guy. We're *not* romantic all the time. Sometimes we just want to get our rocks off without any conditions or strings attached. My wife insists on a lot of foreplay and wants me to pleasure her until she climaxes. Not that there's anything wrong with that, but sometimes I just want to screw and be done with it. She won't stand for that, and if I don't satisfy her, then she's pissed off at me the next day. Or, I can go to the brothel, get what I need, and avoid causing myself and my wife all that aggravation.'

Late one night at a casino on the Vegas Strip, I struck up a conversation with a particularly pretty working girl named Rachel. She could have passed for a young Hollywood starlet with her classy cocktail dress and perfectly styled hair. But any illusions of glamour were stripped away once I noticed the fat, greasy-haired tourists milling around her, waiting to make their approach and strike a deal. This ain't *Pretty Woman*, and the average customer sure ain't Richard Gere.

'The sex usually only lasts a couple of minutes – if that,' she told me. 'Usually they're so nervous and excited, it's over real quick. Once they cum, that's it. I get dressed and I'm outta there. I always get the money upfront. Two or three hundred bucks for a few minutes . . . if you do the math, I charge a higher rate than most surgeons.'

With escorts who have 'regular' customers, it's often a different story. Eva, a beautiful 24-year-old Latina who works for an escort agency, said the majority of her clients are married. She sees some of them up to twice a week. 'I have several regulars who don't even really care about sex,' she says. 'They want companionship and physical affection. They want someone to listen. Having an attractive woman care about what you have to say, and make you feel like a desirable man . . . that can be more powerful than sex. Sometimes I feel more like a therapist. Either way, I earn every penny.'

For other men, the main appeal of prostitutes is that they're willing to do things their wife won't – or things they'd be embarrassed to ask their wife to do. 'As much as I love blowjobs, I can't allow my wife to do it,' says Jerry, 44. 'She kisses our children with those lips.'

Men get off on the power-trip aspect as well. In their marriages, their wives might call the shots; when paying for sex, they're the ones in charge. There might also be a revenge factor. Having sex with a prostitute is a way for him to 'get back' at his wife for the problems in their marriage.

Another brothel enthusiast posted on the internet: 'If you're married, you're always paying for sex in one way or another – and if you get a divorce, you end up forking over a fortune. I like my way: pay as you go.'

In no way are we trying to excuse the behaviour of men who visit prostitutes behind their wives' backs. If this is the only way a man feels he can prevent his marriage from disintegrating, then clearly there are major problems with the relationship that need to be addressed. Guys can spin it any way they want to, but it's still cheating.

For women, it's important to understand the reasons why men behave this way and adopt this mentality. File this knowledge in your mental archives. Prostitutes are an option for men on the prowl, one that exists beyond the usual threats (his female co-workers, girls he meets at bars, or ex-girlfriends). In many ways, they provide an easier form of infidelity, and one he's more likely to get away with.

Many of the men who visit prostitutes are the type you would never expect to do so – they're clean-cut, professional and certainly attractive enough to find companionship with 'regular' women. But if you find their behaviour shocking, just wait until you hear about this next category of cheaters and the type of thrills they're looking to purchase.

SEX ON THE DOWN LOW

At first glance, it would appear to be your typical Las Vegas dive bar. Early in the evening it's dimly lit, stinks of stale smoke, and is vaguely depressing. A handful of guys are bellied up to the bar with their beers and packs of cigarettes, idly playing the video poker machines implanted in the bartop, occasionally looking up to check the score of the ball game. Other patrons are scattered around the red banquette booths in the rear of the room. The jukebox plays the latest MTV hits, while a bored-looking – but strikingly voluptuous – female bartender replenishes drinks.

Among the dozen or so customers is a blond surfer-dude wearing a T-shirt and baggy shorts. A stoic Asian guy in his fifties. Two Mexicans murmuring to each other. A couple of middle-management types wearing suits, loosened ties, and nametags from some convention. A few blue-collar average joes, making a pitstop on the way home from work to knock back a few brews. At the end of the bar are a pair of big black dudes wearing basketball jerseys and diamond studs in their ears, acting too cool for the room.

But stick around as the hour grows late, and you'll realise the Sin City Lounge is anything but typical. Women dressed in skimpy outfits begin to filter in off the streets, arriving alone or in groups. All of them are done up as if they were strolling into a hot nightclub on the Vegas Strip, not a crummy bar in an area notorious for its sex clubs and hardcore gay bars. Their make-up and nails look immaculate. There are skinny ones, chubby ones, petite ones and tall ones. Some of them are *really* tall, in fact – over six feet in their stiletto heels.

Then you realise that some of them have shoulders befitting an NFL linebacker. And their voices . . . let's just say something is *off*. Though they giggle and chat like girly-girls, it sounds like they're trying to speak an octave higher than their normal tone.

As these new arrivals enter, taking seats at the tables or sidling up to the bar to order drinks, the male customers take notice. Stealing glances at their curves, eyeing this parade of silicone breasts and long legs. The bolder customers approach girls and start chatting them up. Other girls identify the guys in the room who look like they've got cash to spend, and start dancing provocatively while shooting them flirtatious looks. Then a customer leaves with one of the girls and drives off in his car; she returns alone half an hour later, and is soon chatting and flirting with another patron.

It's just another evening at the Sin City Lounge. Open 24 hours a day, seven days a week, this is where men go in Las Vegas to pick up transsexual prostitutes.

You see, every one of these 'ladies' was born a man. Some are transvestites, men who dress in drag (and perhaps tape their bulges between their legs). Others are transsexuals who have undergone gender re-assignment surgery, got breast implants and are taking hormone injections to physically resemble females in every sense. The most feminine-looking ones strip down to G-strings and high heels and stroll around the bar bare-breasted, or climb up onto the stage to perform stripper routines. If you weren't aware of this place's reputation, you'd never suspect these aren't natural-born females.

For a couple of hundred bucks – maybe less – any one of them can be yours for an hour of sex, or however long it takes you to get off. You can do it back at your house, in your hotel room or in the back seat of your Toyota. Of course, most customers don't opt to bring their 'dates' back home, since that's where their wives are.

Christopher had clued me into the place. He was on patrol with another officer one night, during which they were assigned to walk through some of the seedier establishments in this stretch of town and make sure nothing *too* shady was going on. Poking his head into the Sin City Lounge, he was shocked to see topless women stripping and grinding on guys. The place wasn't known to be a strip club, and didn't have the necessary permits to be one. It took him a few minutes to realise that these weren't actually women, at least not in the biological sense. In an interesting legal loophole, because they're technically males, there's no law against them walking around or dancing in a bar topless. (Prostitution *is* illegal, but the sex they have with customers doesn't take place on the premises.)

When Christopher told me about the joint, I had to investigate. What kind of guys would frequent a transsexual bar? I wondered. If you were gay, you had bars right next door that catered to that clientele. If you were straight, there were sex clubs and regular hookers around the corner. Who went out cruising for a 'she-male'? The answer, according to the bartender, Lola, is a whole lot of married men. She pegged the percentage of married patrons at over 90 per cent.

I spoke with a number of customers, most of whom were understandably reluctant to discuss their reasons for visiting. Then I met Lenny from California, who'd been partying all night and was in a loquacious mood. He told me he was in Vegas for the weekend with his buddies. While his pals were back at the hotel, gambling and trying to pick up chicks, Lenny had slipped off to check out the Sin City Lounge. He'd read about it online, and had apparently found it promising.

Back home, Lenny worked for a software firm. He had a wife, two kids, a dog and a mortgage. Here in

Las Vegas, he got to indulge what he called his 'wild side'. He'd already taken two of the trannies from the bar to a nearby motel and had sex with them, now he was back for round three. I joked that the bartender must've been spiking his gin and tonics with Viagra.

I asked Lenny whether this behaviour made him gay, or at least bisexual. He looked mildly offended by the question. 'I'm not a fag,' he said matter-of-factly. 'It's just that once in a while, I want to suck some dick. It's something different.'

Different, indeed. I'd noticed that a number of the guys sitting at the bar wore wedding bands. Surely some of them had children, like Lenny. Yet here they were, scanning the trannies and looking for a gender-bending thrill. Some of them were making laughable attempts to be incognito, wearing baseball caps pulled down low and acting as if they'd come here just to drink beer and watch the ball game. Who did they think they were fooling? In Vegas, there's a bar on every corner, open twenty-four/seven. There was a reason why they chose this dive, the only joint in town where topless trannies ask you to light their cigarettes.

In fact, all of the guys I spoke with declared themselves to be straight. They didn't believe that hooking up with a she-male fell under the category of homosexuality – or at least that's what they told themselves. I resisted the urge to correct them: sorry, bub, but in my book wanting to give someone a blowjob is *not* a heterosexual impulse . . . I guess it was the wrapping on the package that allowed them to justify what they were doing. And in this dim lighting, with enough booze in you, the lines could get a bit blurry . . .

Speaking with the 'working girls', I heard more tales of married men and secret lives. Many of the girls told me they had boyfriends who were married. Lola the bartender, giggling like a schoolgirl with a crush on the captain of the football team, told me about the cute young businessman from Seattle, Scott, who flew to Vegas once a month to see her. He'd rent a hotel suite on the Vegas Strip and they would hole up for a weekend of kinky sex. The problem was that Lola was beginning to seriously fall for this guy, but he had a wife and a young child back home. Scott had been promising for months to leave his family to be with Lola exclusively. She believed him, but I knew he was talking typical married-guy crap. The chances of a married man abandoning his home and family to be with another woman are slim; when that woman is a transsexual Las Vegas bartender, those odds diminish exponentially.

Infidelity comes in many shapes and forms – and in the case of the Sin City Lounge, a mix of genders. Sitting there and watching these men in various states of denial, I was reminded of the stories I'd heard about guys living on the DL, or '**the down low**'. This sexual practice sent shockwaves through the African-American community when the news reports started surfacing about a year ago. The DL is the practice of seemingly straight black men (many of whom are married) having covert sex with other men. Writers came up with a number of sociological reasons for why black men, in particular, choose to indulge in this secret lifestyle while maintaining relationships or marriages with women. Some say it's because of deep-rooted homophobia in the black community, which makes black men more likely than whites to conceal their homosexual desires. Black men living on the DL aren't outwardly effeminate or flamboyant; in fact, they're quite the opposite. They take extra measures to project a macho, masculine image. On the New York City gay club scene, the term 'homo thugs' is used to describe tough-acting gangstas, dressed in hip-hop gear, who are actually looking for other brothers to get down with.

The media, always eager to exploit a new story guaranteed to scare the hell out of people, ran with it. J.L. King, author of *On the Down Low: A Journey into the Lives of 'Straight' Black Men Who Sleep With Men*, appeared on *Oprah* to discuss the phenomenon. (When King's wife caught him sleeping with other dudes, he spun it into a career as an author and activist.) The TV drama *Law and Order: SVU*, which frequently rips its storylines from news headlines, devoted an episode to the subject.

The most frightening aspect of the DL is that most participants refuse to practise safe sex. The psychological explanation is that slipping on a condom would force these men to acknowledge what they're doing. By keeping the sex mostly random and anonymous, they can justify in their minds that they're just getting off and not actually living a gay lifestyle. This dangerous form of denial is resulting in a lot of unwitting wives and girlfriends being infected with sexually transmitted diseases, brought home by their man's down low adventures.

While these types of cheaters may be a fringe group, women need to be aware of them. **The more information you're armed with, the better equipped you'll be to spot a cheating boyfriend or husband before it's**

too late. And if he's ever in Vegas and tells you he's going to the Sin City Lounge to watch a football game . . . consider yourself warned.

Chapter 19
Swinging or Sinning?

A successful marriage requires falling in love many times, and always with the same person.

Mignon McLaughlin

Swinging puts a whole different spin on the concept of fidelity. Simply put, **swinging** is the practice of introducing other people into your sexual relationship with your partner. Veteran swingers refer to it as 'the lifestyle', and for many that try this route, it indeed becomes a new way of life. They consider themselves to be the antithesis of cheaters, since everything they do sexually is with the consent of their spouse, and with them present – and usually directly involved.

If you're like most people and have never actually known any swingers, you've probably got some erroneous assumptions about what the lifestyle is all about. Serious swingers pride themselves on the fact that they've discovered a way to enjoy an exciting sex life with a variety of partners, while sharing these experiences with their spouse and maintaining honesty and trust. While some are in it for the thrill of anonymous hook-ups – and there are swingers' clubs that exist strictly for this purpose – many swingers are members of a larger community and enjoy long-term friendships and sexual relationships with other couples. They believe that by shedding the hang-ups that leave most couples feeling unfulfilled, swinging allows them to connect with their partners, and with other couples, on a deeper level. They also believe that spending time in these environments – where you can watch others getting it on, or have them watch you – results in a much hotter sex life when you and your partner are alone.

Those in the lifestyle attend special parties and events where they can relax and hook up with like-minded couples. They have barbecues, go on boat trips and spend weekends at special retreats where you can lounge on the beach or play volleyball in the nude. They come from all walks of life. There are soccer mums and businessmen, whose neighbours would never suspect in a million years that they 'swung' on weekends. There are parents and grandparents. There are beautiful people, and ones who you *really* wish would put some clothes on.

We checked out some swingers' clubs, chatted with some of the folks, and respected how some couples approached the whole scene and the trust they had in their partners. But we're not endorsing it; we're just laying out the realities for you to form your own opinion. As enthusiastic as swingers are about the lifestyle, we've also heard of couples who dabbled in it with disastrous results. It might seem like fun and games, up until the moment when one of you sees their partner actually screwing around with someone else.

We know one guy who took his wife to a swingers'

club simply because he wanted to be allowed to have sex with other women – as if being in the club was supposed to make it acceptable. But the moment he turned around and saw his wife being touched by another man, he freaked out. They wound up getting into a huge fight over it, even though he'd been the one who pushed for them to visit the club in the first place.

So, is swinging really about sexual enlightenment and strengthening your bond with your partner, or is it just a way for people to indulge their urges without technically cheating? As swingers are fond of saying, it's all about going into it for the right reasons. But is there ever a right reason for you and your partner to have sex with other people, even if you tell each other it's okay?

However you feel about the subject, it's one that *The Cheat Sheet* needed to explore. We paid a visit to the Lifestyles Convention, held annually in Las Vegas, where thousands of couples and singles come to strike up new friendships and attend 'play parties' at night, where you check your inhibitions – and your clothes – at the door. It was here that we met Nicholas Olevsky, 51. Along with his wife Judy, 46, they've been swinging for thirteen years.

Nicholas serves as a relationship counsellor for people engaged in 'alternative lifestyles', and runs a company with Judy called Hideaway Couples, which provides swingers with a retreat in the mountains of San Bernardino, California. Members are invited to enjoy a private, secluded 15-acre estate, which he describes as a 'safe, clean, classy environment', allowing couples (and sometimes single guys as well) to get to know each other in a casual, laid-back way.

Nicholas was introduced to the world of swinging through Judy, whose work as an erotic photographer led to her being hired by Lifestyles to photograph their events. He began accompanying her to the events she was working, and eventually they decided to take the plunge for themselves. After more than a decade in the scene, they feel it has done wonders for their relationship, yet Nicholas is quick to warn that the lifestyle is not for everyone.

To help explain the lifestyle to newcomers, he created a handy chart that explains the eight levels of swinging and identifies them by colour. At the Lifestyles Convention, attendees wore coloured badges which signified which level they 'swung' at, so that individuals and couples with similar proclivities could identify each other.

As he explained it, they're called 'TP' levels, based on the idea that relationships between swingers are similar to the teepee tents once lived in by Indians – flexible, easily accessible, with no locks on the doors to prevent you from coming or going. Nicholas says, 'The nice thing is that you can be in one particular "teepee" for a while and be totally comfortable, but then you might feel you want to graduate and go to a different one . . . It's about finding the right circle of friends, but being able to leave and join new and different circles.'

Here's how the chart breaks it down:

- **TP-1.** This is a couple that enjoys sharing sexual fantasies from a safe distance, such as over the phone or via email. They most likely enjoy being in the company of open-minded adults.

- **TP-2.** This couple enjoys watching or being watched while performing sexual acts. Maybe they will share a hotel room with another couple or individual with two queen-size beds right next to each other.

- **TP-3.** This couple has preset rules and limitations as to how far they will go sexually with another couple or individual. This may include sexual massage, licking and kissing, but never penetration (other than with their primary partner). Usually at this level, a bond or friendship is the goal of all and the encounter is not intended as a one-night stand.

- **TP-4.** This couple usually has preset rules and limitations as to how far they will go sexually with another couple or individual. This may include sexual massage, licking, kissing and even intercourse beyond their primary partner. They usually have a common bond and an ongoing friendship.

- **TP-5.** This is a couple that shares sexuality with another couple or individual. They generally do not have limitations other than 'safe sex'. They enjoy the presence and participation of their primary partner. There is no expectation or obligation for long-term friendships . . . just fun sex. This level, as with any of the levels, does not rule out the possibility of a long-term friendship between any or all of the parties involved.

- **TP-6.** At this level, a couple enjoys meeting people who want to have sex, plain and simple. Safety from disease is usually their only rule . . . however, primary partners are still part of these encounters and even though they may have all the fun they want, the primaries always go home to bed (or sleep) together.

- **TP-7.** This is no longer considered elementary swinging. This is the hard-core swap – 'You take mine and I'll take yours.' We find this a lot with 'open relationships'. However, there usually is still the desire to be somewhat attracted to the other individuals involved.
- **TP-8.** This is easy . . . any time, anywhere with (almost) anyone.

We discussed swinging at length with Nicholas, who was able to shed light on the subject and answer a lot of the questions that us non-swingers are curious about. It's an interesting scene, to say the least. Most couples aren't cut out for it, and swinging certainly shouldn't be necessary in order to enjoy a gratifying sex life with your mate. But it does put an intriguing twist on the concept of fidelity – and there's something to be said for *any* couple that is able to express their sexuality to each other with complete openness and honesty.

Nicholas, for you and your wife, what was your first experience as a swinging couple?
We were invited to a dance in Anaheim [California], through Lifestyles. When we walked in, we felt totally awkward. We were one of the youngest couples in the room. Then the host and hostess introduced us to another young couple, and we got to talking and became friends. We went over to their house one time, and they were all 'playing'. It was pretty nice . . .

And that was it? You embraced the lifestyle and never looked back?
Yes. To this day we've never had a bad experience.

What advice would you have for a couple that is curious about trying the lifestyle, but have their doubts about whether it's right for them?

The most important thing is that you have to be doing it for the right reason. Any time you're in an alternative lifestyle, everything is okay as long as you're doing it to enhance your relationship instead of trying to distract from it. It doesn't really matter what your rules are, or whether you're a TP-1 or a TP-8. The question is whether you're doing it to enhance your relationship, or because something's lacking. You need a strong relationship before you get into it.

What's the biggest misconception that the general public has about swingers?

Most people think swingers are people that swap wives. That's [rarely] the case. It's a fairly low percentage of people who are into 'You take my wife, I'll take yours.' Swinging is any time that you bring somebody into your sexual relationship with your primary partner. This is with both people aware of it, obviously – if both people aren't aware of it, it's called cheating. It doesn't mean you need to have to have sex with [the other person], or touch them, or talk to them for that matter. It can enhance your own love life even if you never touch another individual. The reason that porn videos are the number-one selling videos in the world is that most happily married couples fantasise about the same thing: either seeing someone else having sex, or someone else seeing you having sex. That's the excitement of having sex in an elevator, or in a parking lot, or the back seat of a car: *What if someone else sees us?* That's why people will have sex while watching porn videos. With swinging, they can take that to the next level and actually have friends seeing it happen, live. It's that much more erotic.

I can't tell you how many times I've talked to people about this, and I wind up saying to them, 'You're already a swinger.' They say, 'No way, I would never swap wives!' Then I explain the simple fact that if you would enjoy watching another couple having sex, if that turns you on, then that makes you a swinger because you're involving an outside person, beyond your primary partner, in your sexuality. Once people understand that, they're more comfortable with [the idea of] swinging, because they know it wouldn't hurt their relationship to watch someone having sex.

It's hard for some people to imagine that having extramarital sex can actually make for a healthier marriage.

In actuality, one of the lowest divorce rates in the United States and Canada is among swingers. That blows people away. Think about it: if you're a good Christian and things aren't right at home, what do you do? You go out and cheat, then go to church on Sunday and do your Hail Marys, and you're okay for the next week. With swingers, there's no lying, no cheating, no deceit. You always know what's on each other's mind. That makes for a much healthier relationship. With cheating, it's not the sex act that destroys the relationship. It's the lying and the deceit. Among swingers, you don't have that.

Do you and your wife have any ground rules when it comes to swinging?
We don't swing with single people because that can threaten or weaken the relationship if the single person falls in love [with one of us]. We also agree that when it comes to intercourse, we both have to agree on the couple . . . If we both agree that we're comfortable with the couple, if we feel like they're going to be around for a while and they're friends, then we wouldn't have any limits.

What if your wife was having mindblowing sex with some young, handsome guy, or you were with some gorgeous younger woman? Neither of you would feel any resentment?
No. It all depends on how secure the individual is. I'm very secure in myself. I don't care if she's with some young stud or some bombshell woman. And I feel that if Judy did decide she wanted to be with somebody else, then I believe in unconditional love – my feeling is that she should then be with somebody else. I wouldn't hold her back. I just need to be the best possible husband I can be to her. Most people in the lifestyle do have fairly high self-esteem and are secure in who they are.

Is it mostly couples hooking up with other couples?
There are all types of people. There are a lot of couples that would just as soon have a single guy to help fuck the wife's brains out. That's okay, there's nothing wrong with it. Does that work for Judy and I? Not necessarily. But would it bother me if she was totally turned on by some guy and wanted to [hook

up] with him? No, because I know she's going home with me.

What's your take on monogamy? Is it a losing battle for most men?
Not only for most men, but for most women. In this society, marriages don't last. Women have as much power as the man. Before, the woman would just roll over and do whatever the man said. If he said he was going out to go fuck around, the woman would be pissed and throw pots and pans, but would she leave him? No, because the man was their security. It's not that way any more. No one has their security. Either person can easily walk. People are going to do what they're going to do. It's amazing how many men and women cheat on their spouses, when if they were in a swinging lifestyle, there wouldn't be any of that. Monogamy really doesn't work for the majority of the population. And they feel something's wrong with swinging, but they don't really understand what it is.

Have you seen swinging save a lot of marriages?
I can't tell you how many relationships it's saved. Let's say the kids are grown and out of the house. They've been together for fifteen or twenty years. They're curious but they just don't know how to broach the subject. Who's going to bring it up first? The husband thinks, *I don't want to say anything because she'll explode [if I propose swinging].* The wife thinks, *I don't want to say anything because he'll divorce me.* A lot of times when these couples come to me for counselling, I try to help them open up their

minds. They may think swinging is wrong, but once they hear somebody professional say it's okay, we take baby steps.

Usually I'll have them go to a site called www.heartsincommon.com, which is sort of a 'soft swing' website. You can set up a profile but you don't need to put up a picture. You can be incognito and just talk to other people, email with people. It allows them to realise there's a whole world out there that can add all sorts of excitement to a relationship. When they realise, *Wow, we can do something we aren't supposed to do* – that's like having sex in the living room when Mum's asleep in the other room. When you think, *We're not supposed to do this, we might get caught* – well, that's the best sex you'll ever have.

Tell us about a couple you've seen swinging do wonders for.
We used to take people out on 'fantasy cruises' on a 64-foot sailboat. This one couple from Canada had accidentally signed up for the wrong cruise; they thought they were going on a 'scenic' cruise. We had 22 couples onboard and we were sailing out to a reef. So the Canadian couple is sitting there and all of a sudden, everyone's getting naked. They're still in their bathing suits. Judy said to me, 'Something's wrong here.' She went over to them and told them it was a nude cruise. We told them we could turn around and take them back to the resort. They said: 'Well, if no one minds we'll just stay in the back. It's a beautiful day, so we'll just look backwards and let everyone else do their thing.'

Pretty soon we're about to get to the reef. We turn back around and, lo and behold, they're naked – in public, for the first time in their entire lives. They had their arms around each other. They ended up going swimming and snorkelling and having the time of their life. Meanwhile, everyone's fucking and sucking, there's music and drinks, and we're all having a really good time. So at the end of the afternoon, we're heading back and everyone is getting dressed. We look up, and the Canadian couple is up there [on the top deck] fucking each other's brains out. Having the best sex of their entire lives. We got a letter from them afterwards that they sent from Canada, saying we'd literally changed their lives. They're happier than they've ever been, communicating better, getting involved with the lifestyle. This was a couple that went on vacation for their thirtieth anniversary and had never dreamed of doing something like this. They always thought it was disgusting and bad. It's all perception.

Chapter 20
The Dirty Dozen: Twelve Signs of a Cheating Man

Even a paranoid has some real enemies.

Henry Kissinger

If your man is cheating, there are always going to be clues. Sometimes these clues are obvious; other times he's what we call a **sex ninja** – so stealthy and crafty that his affairs are nearly undetectable. A lot of women insist they'd catch on immediately if their man was cheating because he's a 'lousy liar'. They assume *they would know* if their man was having an affair, that there's no way he could pull it off without her noticing.

Well, a lot of women assume wrong. When it comes to getting sex on the side, you'd be surprised at how sneaky and resourceful the average joe can be. But there are always clues. Even when dealing with a seasoned philanderer who knows every trick in the book, there are going to be signs that you can pick up on.

Many relationship experts and authors who've penned books on adultery say the primary sign is when your spouse starts exhibiting behaviour that is outside the norm of the relationship. In many instances, unusual behaviour is indeed an indicator, especially if you've been with him for years and you know his routine inside and out.

But we say be careful about rushing to any judgments. Remember that relationships suffer, and end up fizzling out, when they remain completely inside the norm – that is to say, when they never change or evolve in any way. If your man decides to change his routine (for instance, taking more care with his appearance), there could be positive, constructive reasons why. Explore those reasons first before assuming the worst or interrogating him. Talk to him about his change in behaviour, but don't take an accusatory tone. The way he answers, filtered through your female intuition, is usually going to make it pretty clear whether he's being honest or evasive.

Almost all evidence of cheating is circumstantial. Short of catching your man in the act, there are very few ways for you to be absolutely certain that he's been cheating. It's when the circumstantial evidence begins to pile up, and your female intuition is telling you something's wrong, that you can form the conclusion that he's being unfaithful. You can't rely on getting a confession, nor can you expect him to confess. You can yell at him, accuse him and throw evidence at him until you're blue in the face, and most men will still deny they did anything wrong. They figure that without a confession, you'll eventually have no choice but to give him the benefit of the doubt. A lot of women, unable to extract a confession, will give up and do just that.

Usually, the only time a man *will* confess is when he

was planning on leaving you anyway. Even then, he'll rarely admit his true motivations. He'll make up other reasons in order to deflect the blame away from himself, to downplay his actions, or to avoid making you even more angry. He might admit his guilt, but he won't confess the reality of why he did it.

To give you the real scoop, from a couple of guys who are intimately familiar with the mentality of cheating boyfriends and husbands, we created 'the Dirty Dozen': twelve signs that your man is up to no good. Bear in mind that many of these signs, on their own, can be innocent or even positive. But when your intuition is telling you something's amiss, and these signs begin to add up one after the other . . . that's when it might be time for you to confront him. Just assume that he's going to deny everything. If he does, you need to be prepared to make some hard decisions and do what's best for you.

THE DIRTY DOZEN

1. He suddenly begins to work a lot of overtime, or has frequent over- or under-explained absences

When a man cheats, he needs more than a willing woman; he also needs time for the rendezvous. One of the biggest indicators of cheating is when he suddenly becomes unavailable to you during certain days or nights of the week. Usually, he'll say it's because of work. An ambitious guy who puts in a lot of overtime can be a good thing, but this can also be a cover story for spending time with another lover.

If he makes an hourly wage, overtime brings in extra money. If you're married to him, you should see this reflected in his pay cheque. If he earns a flat annual salary and says his company needs him to put in more time, talk to him about it and find out more. Without seeming like you're probing, express curiosity about his situation at work, and get details.

Ask what this extra work entails. Men usually aren't the greatest liars, and in many cases they'll *over-*explain instead of under-explain. You know his personality. You know how he feels about his job, and whether he's the type who's eager to work extra hours to get ahead. If he normally doesn't like to discuss his job with you, but now offers some long, rambling explanation as to why it's absolutely necessary for him to work late these days, it's a red flag – especially if he's not gunning for a promotion, or isn't being paid any extra.

2. He gives you gifts for no reason

As with many of the Dirty Dozen, this one can be completely innocent, but coupled with other indicators, an unexpected gift can signal that your man feels guilty about cheating and is trying to assuage his conscience. Most cheating guys do have feelings of remorse. Because they're unable to express these feelings to their partners, though, they use gifts to mitigate their guilt. We've heard of cheating men purchasing new cars for their wives, out of the blue – and guys who come straight home after having sex with their mistresses, bearing flowers and candy for their wives. These gifts aren't given out of true generosity. Men do this for their own selfish reasons, to make themselves feel better about their sleazy behaviour.

As mentioned earlier, Kobe Bryant was a famous example of this. After being publicly accused of raping another woman (and claiming it was consensual), he bought his wife a gigantic diamond ring worth millions. He'd already been forced to admit his infidelity, but the principle is the same: a man clings to the notion that gifts, especially expensive ones, can make a woman happy and cause her to forget his misbehaviour.

Furthermore, when a cheater thinks he's got a good thing going – a loving wife and family at home, and a mistress on the side – he'll do whatever it takes to maintain the status quo. He wants to keep this arrangement for as long as possible.

So how do you know if a sudden gift is a gesture of love, or if he's a cheating dog looking to throw you off his scent? As with the first sign in this list, you should talk to him about it. Thank him, tell him how much you love the gift, but then ask him (in the most innocent way possible) what prompted him to purchase it. Again, look out for over-explanations.

3. Weird phone behaviour
The three most common scenarios are:

- Your house starts receiving a lot of hang-up calls when you're the one answering the phone.
- He gets touchy if you go near his cell phone.
- He starts going into the other room to take calls.

People in relationships must communicate. This includes a cheating man and his mistress. Prior to mobile phones, wives would complain of hang-up phone calls on their house phones. Nowadays, no cheating guy with half a brain would ever give a woman his home phone number; they operate strictly on cellular. But mobile phones contain a feature that has tripped up many adulterers: they keep track of incoming and outgoing calls. This is why a cheating man is going to be extraordinarily sensitive about his partner touching his phone. He knows that if she checks his phone's call log, even by accident, it could expose him.

A basic protective measure is to have caller ID on your home phone, and set it so that it won't accept blocked calls. (Besides shutting out any potential mistresses, it will assist you with dealing with pesky telemarketers.) But knowing that if he *is* lining up dates he'll do it by mobile phone, gauge his behaviour when you pick up his mobile and tell him you need to use it for a minute. Even better, say that you need to find the phone number of a mutual friend and start scrolling through his address book. If he practically leaps off the couch to grab the phone out of your hands, you can be fairly sure that there are names and numbers in there he does *not* want you to see.

On a more positive note, the other day we ran into one of our old buddies, Dave, who used to hang out with us on the bar scene. We hadn't seen him out in months. The reason why, he told us, was that he'd met the 'woman of his dreams' and was getting married. We asked him what was up with his cell phone – we'd been trying to call him to invite him to hang out with us, but the number seemed to be disconnected. Dave said he'd got rid of it for the time being. 'It is a cheating man's tool,' he told us. We laughed, but his words rang true.

4. He begins a new exercise routine, shows a strong, sudden desire to lose weight or starts dressing better

So your man decides to get off the couch and get his sorry butt into shape. According to many so-called experts who've written about cheating, this is a sign that he's trying to tone up for his romps with other women.

Consider the best-case scenarios first: maybe he wants to look better for you, or feel better about himself. It's all about your understanding of his personality. If he's a fairly athletic guy, or has been expressing his desire to get in better shape, then you should encourage him to do so.

If his sudden interest in working out seems to come out of nowhere, the reasons are more sinister in many cases. If this sign is coupled with others, there's a good chance that he's found someone new and is trying to look his best for her. Men who are settled into long-term relationships usually doesn't feel a sudden urge to look more attractive to their mates. As we've already explained, a man will often feel that he's already 'won' you and therefore doesn't need to exert any extra effort. This extends to the way he dresses. The normal time for him to cut his hair and dress more fashionably is when he's courting you – not when he's been married to you for years. If he suddenly replaces his eyeglasses with contact lenses (without telling you first) or starts putting on cologne before he leaves the house without you, there's a chance that he's trying to look his best for someone else. Or, that a new woman in his life is giving him style tips.

A woman we know, Sharon, suspected her boyfriend Martin was cheating because of his sudden interest in having six-pack abs at 45. He also went out and had his hair dyed, from grey to black, and started reading fitness magazines.

Sharon spent three months wondering and investigating. Ultimately, her suspicions proved true: Martin had been sleeping with a woman he met through his job. When she confronted him with the evidence of his affair, he admitted it. When she demanded to know why, he explained that he'd lost his physical attraction to her some time ago.

Sharon was furious and broke up with him. But once she'd got over the shock and anger, she realised that she'd been neglecting herself ever since they'd started dating two years before. She'd stopped exercising and watching her diet, which resulted in a steady weight gain. Ironically, over the past three months of playing detective and stressing out about whether Martin was cheating, she'd put on another 10 kilos.

Always take care of yourself. You should look and feel confident, sexy and secure. It's important for *everyone* to be at their mental, physical and sexual best – not just for their partner, but for their own well-being. And who knows, you may find yourself back in the dating scene one day.

5. He suddenly uses new sex techniques in the bedroom

Mark isn't one of the brightest light bulbs we know, but he's always good for some comic relief. He's been living with his girlfriend for several years. She's caught him cheating several times but has always been willing to take him back.

Mark's latest fling turned out to be a kinky one:

she enjoyed being choked during sex. At first he was shocked when she asked him to wrap his hands around her throat while they were in the throes of passion. But her orgasms were explosive this way, and after a few sessions of 'rough sex', Mark started to get into it.

One night, while having sex at home with his girl-friend, Nicole, he got lost in the heat of passion and tried the choke move with her. She freaked out and practically kicked him across the room. Unable to come up with an excuse for his actions, he admitted that he'd learned it from another woman.

This sign of cheating is hard to nail down, because your man might have good intentions. As for what inspired him to try something new, most guys watch porn – probably more of it than he'll ever admit to you – and all kinds of kinky moves can be learned from those sexual acrobats. For instance, anal sex is some-thing that guys love seeing in porn movies, but are often reticent to try with their partners.

When he pulls a sudden new move in bed, or tries something sexually that is totally out of character, it's a sign of one of three things:

- **He has sexual desires that he's never discussed with you.** Now is the time to discuss them. Are these desires going to enhance your sex life perhaps, or do they freak you out? Either way, talk about it and get it out in the open.
- **He's trying something he heard about, or saw in a video, to see if it gives the sex with you an extra spark.** Again, as long as you're okay with trying it, some experimentation can't hurt. If his idea doesn't

turn you on, there are other new twists you can try in the bedroom that are mutually enjoyable.

- **He's cheating.** Another woman is doing things with him that he normally doesn't feel comfortable trying with you. By attempting it with you, he's testing you, to see if you can be as exciting as the other woman.

As long as you're comfortable with giving something new a try in the bedroom, go with it, see if you enjoy it, and save the questions for afterwards. That's when you can delicately ask him what inspired him to try it, and why it turns him on. This conversation can lead to some fun revelations that can make the relationship grow. Or, in a worst-case scenario, it will reveal infidelity.

6. Loss of sex drive

This is a huge indicator of infidelity, or the chances of him cheating in the near future. When a man loses his interest in having sex with you, there are really only three reasons: either he has some type of medical condition, or his needs are being satisfied elsewhere, or he no longer enjoys sex with you. (Under the category of medical conditions, we would include work-related fatigue. After a very long and stressful day at work, some guys will quite genuinely lose their libido.)

But there is a tell-tale sign that his loss of sex drive could stem from cheating. This may strike you as a bit crude, but it's a biological reality: men can only produce a certain amount of semen in a given time span; and, if he doesn't use condoms with you, you should have some idea of how much he ejaculates each time. Now, if you notice a sharp drop-off in the amount of semen he produces, and his general behaviour has given you cause to be suspicious, chances are he's already had sex that day with someone else.

For our friend Vicki, this was the third warning sign that caused her to confront her boyfriend, Dennis, and demand to know the deal. He'd been 'working late' and offering lame explanations; he'd suddenly become concerned with his outfits and appearance, waking up early to go to the gym; and now, when they had sex, it took him an unusually long time to climax and he produced a mere trickle of semen when he did.

After one especially minuscule spurt, they both knew he was busted. Vicki and Dennis used to have sex several times a day, and would joke about how his semen barely dribbled out by the third round. After a few moments of uncomfortable silence, Dennis admitted he was still seeing his ex-girlfriend. Vicki dumped him. Case closed.

7. He doesn't wear his wedding ring

It always looks a bit strange to us when married men don't wear their wedding rings. Usually, it's the guys in their twenties and thirties, and they don't feel it's any big deal. Some men say they don't like to wear rings, that it's a nuisance. Others claim that wearing the ring is an old-fashioned custom that really doesn't mean anything; they know they're married, and that should be enough. The ring is a powerful symbol, however – and one we feel should be respected. It's a constant reminder to a man that he has a wife at home, and it's a sign to other women (husband hunters excluded) that he is off the market.

One guy we know, Charlie, always removes his ring during social outings with 'the boys'. As he explains it, it's not because he's looking to cheat. In fact, he never has cheated. He says he takes it off because he doesn't want women to blow him off just because he's married. He feels that if he's going to hang out at a bar with his friends, he doesn't see any harm in appearing to be single, since he has fun meeting girls and chatting with them.

For guys like Charlie, it's a slippery slope. We'd set the Vegas odds of him cheating within the next year at 2–1. When a man removes his ring because he doesn't want to be perceived as being married, it's a sign that he's looking for something outside of his relationship.

8. Unexplained credit card purchases

This sign of cheating has tripped up thousands of men and resulted in countless break-ups. In marriages, there should be no reason for secrecy when it comes to banking and credit accounts. Yet cheating men tend to be careless with their plastic, whipping out a card to pay for their outings with other women.

In this day and age, both people in a relationship should periodically check for unexplained purchases – not necessarily to sniff out cheating, but to ensure that you haven't been a victim of identity theft. If you find that he's made suspicious purchases, you should pull out a calendar and draw up a simple timeline. Is there a legitimate reason why he made a purchase at the mall last Sunday, for instance, when he said he was out golfing with his buddies all day?

On a credit card statement, mysterious expenditures that are billed to a generic-sounding company can often mean something sex-related. These types of businesses bill their customers under a different company name in an attempt to make the transaction appear quite innocent. Whether it's subscribing to a porn website, paying a bar tab at a strip club or using a phone sex service, it will often show up on the credit card statement under a bland but somewhat suspicious-sounding name. A $200 charge to 'Leisure Concepts, Inc.', processed at 3 am, probably has a story behind it that he doesn't want you to know.

9. He smells of perfume, alcohol or 'foreign substances'

The nose doesn't lie. Some scientists say that it's the strongest of all our senses. Cheating guys aren't going to appreciate us telling you this, but one of the best ways to 'sniff out' a cheater is to approach him as soon as he walks in the door. Give him a hug and a kiss, like you're happy to have him home.

If he's returning from a rendezvous with someone else, having you this close is going to make him highly uncomfortable, which will be evident from his body language. Even if he showered after sex, he'll be worried that you're going to pick up the other woman's perfume or scent. He's going to want to shower or change clothes before getting close to you. As with when you're investigating the other signs listed in this chapter, the key is to act natural and not make him feel that you're checking him for evidence.

10. Excessive use of the home computer

One recent survey showed that over 70 per cent of cheaters communicate with their lovers through the internet, and over 40 per cent of those relationships started on the net. If he's spending excessive amounts of time on the computer and insists on having privacy while doing so, you should view this as a major red flag. If you have a healthy relationship, there should be no reason why you can't come into the room while he's surfing the net. When you do enter the room unannounced, notice whether he minimises the screen to hide whatever website he's on.

11. He's spending less and less time with you

Guys have a finite amount of emotional and physical energy. Just as a man who's sleeping around is going to have a diminished sex drive when he comes home, he's also going to have less energy and patience for engaging in other activities with you. Perhaps he used to accompany you on weekends to run errands, shop or go to the movies; now, he's constantly telling you that he's tired and wants to stay at home. Maybe you used to hit the bars or clubs together on a regular basis; now, he just wants to chill out and watch TV. This can be a strong sign that he's been spending time, money and energy on someone else.

If he's falling in love with this other woman, he might also feel a twisted sense of loyalty towards her. He still shares a home with you, but she's the one in whom he's now emotionally invested. When he's with you, he's just biding his time until he can be with her again. And if he's got a guilty conscience, being around you is only going to make him feel more uncomfortable; therefore, he's going to bow out of spending one-on-one time with you whenever he can.

12. He's restless at home

For a man engaged in a secret, passionate affair, the home he shares with his wife can begin to feel like a cage. Picture him as a couped-up tiger, and his mistress as a juicy steak lying just outside the front door. A tiger in this situation would pace, growl and exhibit other forms of restless behaviour. A man with a mistress on his mind – and if it's a new relationship, he's probably obsessing over her – is going to act in a similar fashion around the house. He's likely to be grouchy, irritable or downright hostile. The stronger his attraction to the other woman, the more he'll begin to view you as the warden that's keeping him locked up.

If he's been acting restless lately, or unusually irritable, you need to get to the bottom of it. Don't be confrontational; your tone of voice should imply that you're concerned and want to help him with whatever he's going through. Encourage him to tell you what's wrong. Watch how he reacts when you try to engage him in this discussion. Maybe he's got a genuine problem, something he hasn't told you about, and could use your support. Then again, he might indeed have another woman on his mind – in which case he'll refuse to explain or make up an excuse.

If he leaves the house whenever the two of you have an argument, it's a bad sign. Many times a cheater will start arguments on purpose in order to give him an excuse to go and see his other woman.

A GUILTY VERDICT

With the Dirty Dozen (or any other signs that make you suspect he's cheating), remember that no sign on its own can ever provide 100 per cent certainty. It's when they begin to add up that you have serious cause for concern. And there's no substitute for female intuition, and your understanding of his personality. You, more than anyone, know when he's acting out of character.

Also remember what we said before, about cheating men being more devious and cunning than you'd suspect. When it comes to getting away with an affair, even the most inept, disorganised guy can manage to come up with airtight alibis and cover every possible base. You can demand the truth and hurl accusations, but as long as there's no smoking gun, there's really no reason for him to admit his guilt. If you lack tangible proof, he's likely to flip it around and accuse you of being insecure and paranoid.

So don't waste your time and energy obsessing about finding the 'proof'. In a court of law, the smoking gun isn't necessary to win a conviction – probable cause is enough. If the signs are adding up and your intuition says something's definitely wrong, then consider him a cheater until he proves otherwise.

Cheat Sheet history lesson: The divorce ranch

Nowadays, Nevada's economy is fuelled by its glittering mega-casinos (particularly the endless procession of suckers who come and blow the mortgage payments on slot machines). But early in the century, before the legalisation of gambling, the state sought to solve its economic woes by establishing the country's most liberal divorce laws. You simply had to check into a Nevada hotel for a period of several weeks in order to establish residency, and you were then eligible to have your divorce granted with a quick signature from a local judge. (Even today, you can establish residency in Nevada and get your marriage terminated in around six weeks, provided that both parties agree to it.)

Back in those days, a string of 'divorce ranches' sprang up to cater to this crowd. Reno became famous as the world's divorce capital, as celebrities such as actress Rita Hayworth, boxer Jack Dempsey and social scion Gloria Vanderbilt all moved to Reno to await their divorce hearings – and explore other romantic options in the meantime. The ranches were one big non-stop party, as singles of both sexes came to fish from the same pool.

As other states eased up their divorce laws, 'the Biggest Little City in the World' (as Reno is otherwise known) lost its reputation as Splitsville, USA. Since then, its casinos have more than picked up the financial slack.

Chapter 21
101 Ways to Make Your Relationship Cheat-Proof

We have the greatest prenuptial agreement in the world. It's called love.

Gene Perret

By this point in *The Cheat Sheet*, the prognosis for your love life may seem grim. The chances of maintaining a monogamous relationship for the next 40 years may appear to be as unlikely as you strolling down the aisle with George Clooney next week, with Brad Pitt on hand as best man. But we're not trying to discourage you from committing your heart to someone. We're not saying that honest guys aren't out there, ready to respect and adore you. What we are saying is that keeping a man faithful requires more work than most women realise, or are willing to put in.

We've shown that men are compelled to cheat for all kinds of reasons. We've explained how they do it with far greater frequency – and shrewdness – than women want to believe. Give him a reason, or an excuse, and there's always the chance that he'll capitalise on the next opportunity that comes along in a tight pair of jeans. It doesn't matter whether you've been dating for two months or married twenty years.

At the same time, though, the chapters that precede this one have armed you with enough strategies to be able to challenge what, on one hand, might seem to be a depressing inevitability. For, as promised in the Introduction, there are ways that women can protect themselves from adultery and reinforce their relationships so that your man doesn't view cheating as an option. And it's that *good* news that we'll be concentrating on in this penultimate chapter.

THE CHEAT SHEET 101

After conducting our undercover *Cheat Sheet* research – examining relationships that have crashed and burned, as well as ones that have remained rock solid over the years – we've boiled down the steps you can take to a list of 101 snippets of advice and requests, delivered from the male perspective. This is a viewpoint that women need to become more familiar with, because us guys are more complicated and sensitive (yes, *sensitive*!) than most women give us credit for.

These aren't the lame, clichéd tips that you've heard before. This is the real deal, gathered from bar-stool conversations and locker-room confessions; from guys from all walks of life and the women who've loved them; from loyal wives and the mistresses who've stolen their husbands from under their noses.

Mostly, this list is about having the courage and awareness to take pre-emptive actions. You've got to take steps to reinforce the bond between you and your man so that it grows strong enough to resist any threat. When it comes to preventing cheating, the best defence is a good offence. Instead of dwelling on the problems and obsessing over your suspicions, it's time to get proactive.

Remember that during the courtship phase, it's the guy who steps up his game to win the woman's affections. As the relationship settles into a familiar routine, if he's a man worth keeping, you mustn't hesitate to step up *your* game in order to keep him focused on you.

You might already do some of the things on this list. In fact, you might practise many of them. But adding even one new element into your routine can surprise him, impress him and inject an adrenalin boost into your relationship and sex life. **Never forget that the greatest enemy of any romance is complacency.** If your relationship has settled into a monotonous routine, take it upon yourself to add some spice to the mix. You'll both reap the rewards.

We should also note that every relationship contains its own unique dynamics. When it comes to matters of the heart, few situations are cut and dry, and the advice that works for one couple might not work for the next. This list is meant to express the most common challenges faced by couples, and to offer solutions which you may use – or modify to fit your own set of circumstances.

And so, without further ado, we present the Cheat Sheet 101.

101. 'Don't sweat my bachelor party'

Seeing as we, the authors, live in Las Vegas – the undisputed capital of the notorious male bonding ritual known as the bachelor party – we'll tackle this one first. Many of my friends have come to Sin City to commemorate their final days as single men, and I've been called upon to help coordinate the festivities.

With some wives-to-be, the words 'bachelor party' elicit overblown reactions, ranging from disgust, to fear, to red-faced fury. But in 99 out of 100 cases, it's a lot of suspicion and angst over nothing. What you need to understand is that these events are basically harmless. They're an occasion for a bunch of friends to reunite, booze themselves into oblivion and 'bond'.

The bachelor party from hell

The worst thing is when a buddy's fiancée feels the need to get involved with planning the bachelor party. Ladies, do everyone a favour and stick with the wedding details. Pick out the china. Work out the seating arrangements. Choose a band that plays your favourite Journey song. But do not, I repeat, *do not* attempt to plan or in any way influence the bachelor party.

One time a friend of mine named Derek was getting married to this girl, Vicki, who he'd been dating since they were teenagers. He was completely faithful to her and she kept him on a short leash. Derek was the kind of guy who had to 'check in' with his girlfriend three times a night on his cell phone on the rare occasions that she parolled him from the house to meet his friends for a beer.

Naturally, she was freaked out by the idea of him having a bachelor party. She managed to find out that a stripper had been hired for the event and decided she was going to turn the tables on us. She called the stripper's agency and cancelled the gig; next she called another agency that specialised in 'novelty' strippers.

Cut to the big night. About 30 of us are all partying at a house, looking forward to the arrival of the 'entertainment'. Derek's having a great time with all his best friends, some of whom flew cross-country for the occasion. We've got the living room arranged with a bunch of chairs in a circle, with a chair for Derek in the middle so the stripper can give him a lap dance. Routine, PG-13 stuff.

Then the doorbell rings and in waddles this monstrosity, sucking on a Marlboro and looking like she applied her make-up with a paint roller. She must've been 50 years old and weighed 400 pounds. When she shed her robe to reveal a garter belt and thong ... to this day, I sometimes wake up in a cold sweat just thinking about it.

Then, in walks Vicki with a bunch of her giggling girlfriends. She was supposed to be out having her bachelorette party; instead, the girls decided to spend their evening making sure our fun got trampled on. Derek tried to be a good sport and play along, allowing the she-beast to bump and grind on him, but it was painfully embarrassing with Vicki and her friends cheering it on. The party was ruined and Derek looked like a complete wuss in front of his closest pals.

Two years later, they're still married but Derek is a miserable, henpecked shell of his former self. Ever since that fiasco, I've said that if a woman can't trust her fiancé at his own bachelor party, neither of them should go anywhere near an altar. And you know what? My female friends, some of whom are happily married, agree with that philosophy 100 per cent.

If his friends hire a stripper for the festivities or take your man to a strip club, don't get bent out of shape. It's as much a part of the tradition as the morning hangover. If you're sincerely worried that this get-together is going to transform the future father of your children into a coke-snorting, hooker-banging maniac, then you need to re-evaluate how much you really trust him. If you don't trust him implicitly, forget about marrying him. The temptations are always going to be there.

A final word of advice on the subject: view his bachelor party as an opportunity for you to be the *cool* wife. Your relationship with your husband should be the one his henpecked buddies envy. When it's time for the bachelor party, don't lay down ground rules. Don't interrogate him afterwards. Let the boys be boys. He knows where the line is. A good man isn't going to cross it – and even if he gets so hammered on Jägermeister that he tries to do something regrettable, good friends are going to put him in check.

100. 'Stroke my ego'

Men can be every bit as insecure and sensitive about their appearance as women. (How else do you explain the billion-dollar hair replacement industry, or the frightening concept of penile implants?) You expect him to pay you compliments when you change your hairstyle or wear a new outfit, well, he wants his props, too. It can be as simple as looking at him and telling him he's as hot/cute/sexy as when the two of you first met.

99. 'Understand the touch balance'

Every guy has a different level of appreciation for physical affection. Some guys want to hold your hand whenever you're in public together, and expect you to snuggle up during a movie; others prefer to have their personal space, and would rather save the touching for the bedroom. It's important that you learn where your man falls on this scale, and understand the specific types of touching that he likes and dislikes. If neither of you expresses much physical affection outside of having sex, but you desire more, try upping the ante. Put more passion into your kisses. Give him a little neck massage when you're sitting together. If he's not an especially affectionate guy, this may feel awkward to him at first, but he may start enjoying it. Make him miss your touch, and he'll miss *you* twice as much when you're apart.

'I might be a big macho-looking guy, but I'm a junkie for affection,' says Rick, 27. 'It's one of my criteria for dating someone. If she doesn't like to hold hands, if she doesn't enjoy cuddling on the couch, then I grow tired of being around her pretty quickly. I don't know how you're supposed to sustain a relationship if you don't enjoy holding each other.'

98. 'Handle a typical man's task'

Instead of presenting him with things that need to be fixed as soon as he walks in the door, do what you can to handle them on your own. Men don't expect women to be able to build a patio, but if the toilet is broken, call a plumber. If the cable TV isn't working, call the cable company and see what you can do.

'My girlfriend came by my house one day while I was at work, to use my computer,' says Simon, 30. 'She noticed that a couple of light bulbs were out, so she went to the store, picked some up and changed them. It was a small gesture but I appreciated the fact that she took the initiative. Other girls would've just pointed out the problem the second I got home.'

97. 'Spring small surprises on me'

Men often say they hate surprises. This isn't true, though; they just don't always appreciate the over-the-top surprises that women plan for them, even if it's done with the best intentions.

'One time I got a promotion at my law firm, but I was exhausted from all the hours I'd been putting in,' says Robert, 33. 'That Friday night, all I wanted was to spend a quiet evening at home with my girl. When I came home with a bottle of wine, ready for some loving, I walked into a massive surprise party. Most of my family was there, including some relatives I really didn't want to deal with. When I complained to her about it during a private moment, she was hurt and offended that I didn't appreciate her efforts. The whole night was a mess.'

Men prefer the small surprises: you're preparing his favourite dinner, you've picked up his favourite ice cream or beer at the supermarket, or the two of you are going to spend an extra-romantic evening at home. He knows you love the big, dramatic, romantic gestures; he'd just rather receive his on a smaller scale.

96. 'Compliment other women in my presence'

Insecurity is never sexy, and it's never more obvious to a man than when a woman tears down other women in front of him. 'I hated going to parties with my ex,' says Tommy, 28. 'She was constantly making snipy comments about other girls, pointing out their outfits, their hair, whatever. I guess it was her way of trying to point out how good *she* looked, but it just sounded stupid and immature.'

Brooks, 31, tells a different story: 'My girlfriend is

into fashion. Sometimes when we're out together she'll see another girl wearing an outfit she really likes. She'll walk up to her, tell her how cute it looks, ask her where she got it, etc. It's actually quite an endearing quality – she's a confident, outgoing person and she's not intimidated about telling another woman how good she looks.'

95. 'Encourage a silly moment'

To illustrate this point, we refer to an episode of *The Sopranos*. Our man Tony is taking a shower after having sex with his mistress. She sneaks into the shower and douses him with cold water. His initial anger gives way to laughter; that simple act of silly spontaneity was a turn-on, since it was something his wife, Carmela, never would have done. Later, at home, Tony does the same to Carmela while she's in the shower. She screams at him and it sparks a furious argument. Needless to say, Tony is soon back in bed with his playful girlfriend.

Men enjoy a silly moment every once in a while. Try sparking one when he's not expecting it, and lighten up the mood.

94. 'Make out with me unexpectedly'

Steamy make-out sessions are one of the hottest things about new relationships; why should they cease once you've been together a while? At an unexpected moment, walk up to him with a seductive look in your eye, plant your lips on his, and rock his world. 'My boyfriend, who was older and married, was really into kissing,' says Tina, 23. 'He told me his wife and him never made out any more, and he missed it. That was all he needed to tell me . . . we would go to the movies just so we could sit in the back row and French kiss.'

93. 'Only be my mum in the kitchen'

He's not your child, and he'll resent being treated like one. If you're going to straighten up his clothes and fix his hair, act like you're making a helpful suggestion, not correcting a mistake. This is part of establishing your role as his partner and lover, not his mother. If he expects to be mothered – as some men do – it's especially important that you establish this.

92. 'Make decisions'

Don't always defer to him and expect him to choose which restaurant you're going to eat at, which movie you're going to see, where you're going to go on vacation, etc. Have your own opinions and express them. Guys grow bored with women who constantly defer to them. 'My wife has broadened my horizons in so many ways,' says James, 45. 'My idea of a vacation, ever since I was a teenager, was driving to the Jersey shore. She insisted on us checking out Europe one year, which I was reluctant to do. She booked the tickets and made the arrangements. Since then, we've gone there every couple of years – and I love it now even more than she does.'

91. 'Be punctual'

Men who have mistresses will tell you: their 'chippies' don't keep them waiting. Being on time for someone means you respect them and their time. If you've planned an evening out with your man, don't leave him pacing the living room while you change outfits ten times and talk on the phone. If you were meeting him for a first date, you wouldn't keep him waiting for an hour. Maintain the same attitude even when you're living together. In return, your man should give you the same respect.

90. 'Go out sometimes without me'

It's important to show him that you have a life outside of the relationship. The day after you've enjoyed a night out with your girlfriends, chances are he'll be more attentive. You've shown him that your entire social life doesn't revolve around him, and that you've got options besides hanging out with him.

'When my girlfriend started her new bartending job, she made some new girlfriends at work and they started going out together a couple of times a week,' says Joe, 32. 'I have to be at work early, so I couldn't join them. I was a little bothered by it at first, but I noticed something interesting: while she was out with her friends, I missed her. I couldn't stop thinking about her. I would even straighten up the house so it looked good when she got home. Now I actually like letting her go out and do her thing. It makes for awesome sex when she gets home, because I can't wait to get my hands on her.'

89. 'Write me sexy notes and stash them at my place or the place we share'

A note that you've tucked away, and he hasn't found yet, is like money in the bank collecting interest. A playful, erotic little note demonstrates imagination and creativity. Show him you're a live wire and keep him on his toes. 'My girlfriend used to put Post-It notes inside my briefcase sometimes, before I left for work,' says John, 30. 'I'd reach in my briefcase during a meeting, and see a note about how she couldn't wait for me to screw her brains out when I got home. I'd be thinking about it the rest of the day . . . and rushing home as soon as I got done.'

88. 'Always be growing'

Make it a point to develop new interests, friends and hobbies. The more you evolve as a person, the more you bring to the relationship – and the more you show him that you have a life outside of him. Again, it's going to make him work harder to keep you.

87. 'Oprah and Dr Phil don't know everything!'

In our television-obsessed culture, too many women get their relationship advice from the boob tube and accept it as gospel. While Dr Phil seems to fix even the most dysfunctional relationships in 60 minutes (minus commercials), the reality is much more complicated. Don't buy into the quick fixes that you see on television, or measure your relationship against the 'flawless' celebrity couple sitting on Oprah's couch. (Besides, behind closed doors, those gorgeous Hollywood couples are usually more screwed up than a guest panel on *Jerry Springer*.)

86. 'If we have kids, put me first during intimate moments'

Obviously, children have certain needs that must be attended to right away. When you're enjoying intimate time with your spouse, however, make him feel that he comes first. 'One time on our anniversary, my ex-wife and I had a romantic evening planned at home,' says Dean, 37. 'Just when things were heating up, our five-year-old daughter came into our bedroom saying she couldn't sleep and wanted to sleep with us. My wife told her to hop into bed with us. I know she was being a good mum, but she could have tucked our daughter into her own bed and told her that Mummy and Daddy wanted their time alone. It bothered me that she ignored my needs without a second thought.'

85. 'Let me acknowledge other beautiful women'

It's awkward when an attractive woman walks into the room and a man feels forbidden to even look in her direction, for fear of his wife or girlfriend jumping down his throat. Don't be offended if he acknowledges the fact that she's attractive, as long as he does it in a respectful fashion. If you cultivate this attitude in your relationship – that he can occasionally look, as long as he never touches – you demonstrate that you're not threatened by other women because you know he's *yours*. As a bonus, you'll gain a better understanding of what type of women catch his eye. Maybe it's a different hair colour, or outfit, that you can surprise him with.

84. 'Tell me how you feel'

If you're upset with him about something, talk it out. Don't use the silent treatment and make him try to figure out why you're upset. This tactic is a waste of time and energy for you, and it drives men up the wall. It's counterproductive in every way.

83. 'Never freak out on me in public'

If an argument is necessary, have it behind closed doors. Women who start loud arguments in public places look out of control, and cause their men to cringe in embarrassment. And even more importantly . . .

82. 'Never argue in front of friends and family'

If you're trying to win an argument, there's no way your man is going to concede ground in front of his friends or family. You're fighting a battle you can't possibly win. It's only going to create more animosity and possibly turn his friends and family against you. Again, save the showdown for behind closed doors.

81. 'Make me miss you'

The saying 'Absence makes the heart grow fonder' is one of the truest statements about relationships ever made. Here's another *Cheat Sheet* fact for you: compared to the general population, airline attendants have an extremely low divorce rate. Why? Because all that travelling makes their spouse miss them, and it makes them miss their spouse. This makes their time together that much more important . . . and passionate.

If you've been seeing a guy on a regular basis and want to stimulate his interest in you, don't hesitate to leave town for a weekend to visit family or friends. Turn down a couple of his invites. Don't be available twenty-four/seven. If he's into you, watch how he showers you with attention as soon as you return from your time apart. By making yourself constantly available, you risk him taking you for granted.

80. 'Be independent enough to be able to handle life without me'

This breeds respect, admiration, and lets him know you're capable of making it on your own if he ever betrays you. We've heard guys say with a grin, 'Sure I cheat, but my girl won't leave me because everything is in my name.' If everything *is* in his name – the house you live in, the car you drive, your insurance, etc. – he knows he holds all the cards and will act accordingly.

In a relationship, as in poker, the cards should be dealt out fairly. Sometimes men will intentionally hold all the cards, since it gives them a licence to behave however they want to. Do what you can do to prevent this. Maintain a degree of dependence, emotionally *and* financially.

79. 'Form bonds through music, scents and sights'

One of the most important breakthroughs in modern psychology was achieved by a behaviourist named Pavlov (1849–1936). He proved that dogs could be conditioned to associate a reward with a sound. Every time he fed them, he would ring a bell. After a while, all he had to do was ring the bell and the dogs would start salivating in anticipation of food. He termed this a 'conditioned reflex', meaning it was one that had to be learned (as opposed to an 'innate reflex', an automatic response such as pulling your hand away from a flame).

Play 'Pavlov' with your man. Condition him to associate specific visuals, music or scents with the great sex you've shared. If he likes a certain perfume that you wear, wear it whenever the two of you spend a romantic evening together. If you're spending the night away from him, put a dash of that perfume on his pillow, so that it's the last thing he smells before he sleeps. Or, whenever you've got an evening of incredible sex in store for him, wear a certain outfit or colour. (Red seems to be especially effective.) Soon, simply seeing that dress is going to rev up his engines because of what his brain associates it with.

78. 'Teach me new things'

The key to keeping a job is to become indispensable – when your company needs to lay people off, you should be the last person they can afford to cut loose. This same principle applies to relationships. The more you teach your man, whether it's straightening out his finances or turning him on to new books and hobbies, the more valuable he'll consider you to his life. He'll know that ending the relationship will cause him to lose much more than he could possibly gain.

77. 'Don't scream unless the house is on fire'

Our home should be a peaceful place where we can both unwind away from the stresses of work. Make it a habit never to be loud or hysterical when at home. From a guy's point of view, it's not cute when a woman screams at the sight of a cockroach or shrieks at the top of her lungs when her girlfriend relates some gossip over the phone. Please, take the volume down a notch.

76. 'Raise my sex-pectations'

Relationships are about an equal give-and-take, and this extends to your activities between the sheets. 'I loved issuing little challenges to my boyfriend when he wanted sex,' says Suzanne, 26. 'If he wanted it but I was trying to sleep, or I was busy doing something, I wouldn't turn him down . . . but I'd tell him that it had better be *good*. I made him step up his game. Instead of just trying to get off, he would take it as a challenge and do all the things I liked. Not only was the sex much better for me this way, but he loved knowing that he'd risen to the occasion. It was like the more he stroked me, the more it stroked his ego.'

75. 'You don't need to be a fitness freak, but do make an effort to stay fit'

Some women will never be a size 10. Your man understands that, and he wouldn't be with you if that was a major concern. But by at least making the effort to stay healthy and get some exercise, you're going to strengthen your relationship in numerous ways.

SCOTT, 35: 'My wife has always been on the larger side, which I don't mind at all. What was weird was that she would barely eat in front of me, but she would binge on junk food when I wasn't around. When I found out she was doing this, I confronted her about it. I wasn't angry, I was more confused and hurt that she felt she had to hide this from me. She explained to me that she was embarrassed to eat in front of me; she'd been going on and off diets for years and was miserable about the way she looked.

'The good news is, this ended up bringing us closer. I asked her to let me help her. I started taking her with me to the gym a few times a week, and we researched different new diets and got her on a sensible one. For me, it isn't about how much weight she loses, it's about her feeling better about herself. Now she's in a much healthier mood, which makes our relationship stronger. And it also makes the sex a lot more fun, since she's not so ashamed of her body any more.'

74. 'Be a financial helper, not a liability'

Men tend to be less responsible than women when it comes to balancing a chequebook and staying on top of their finances. If your man falls into this category, be a positive role model instead of a drain on his wallet. Remember, a man wants to look at his partner as someone who is going to help him grow. If he's looking to make a purchase – whether it's a car, a television, or a new suit – do some research and help him find the best deal. On occasion, fix him a lunch he can bring to work, to save him the expense of eating out. These gestures can be as small as clipping some coupons for your boyfriend so that he saves a few bucks on groceries. Even if he has plenty of money to throw around, you need to show that you're looking out for his best interests if you want him to respect you in the long term.

73. 'Don't sweat the small stuff'

This is about as close to a cliché as we're going to get on our list, but only because it's so true in relationships. 'With my previous girlfriend, *everything* was drama,' says Terry, 35. 'If I got a stain on the carpet, she'd freak out. One time I dented her car, and she was pissed off at me for a week. I wound up cheating on her with a girl who was way more mellow. When I went to her place, I could plop down on her couch with my shoes on and just relax.'

72. 'Make me laugh'

Most women consider a sense of humour to be a very important quality in a man. Yet if you ask most men who the people are that make them laugh, they rarely say their woman. You don't need to perform stand-up comedy routines, but understand that men value a sense of humour as much as you do.

71. 'Check your inhibitions'

We have a friend, Ben, who has a thing for women's feet, but his girlfriend is so insecure about hers that she won't even let him look at them. When he announced to us that he was sleeping with a girl on the side, we weren't surprised to find out that she had a habit of being barefoot whenever possible.

If your man has some weird fetish that creeps you out, you're not obligated to indulge him – but if it's harmless, loosen up and give it a try. The fact that it turns him on might turn *you* on.

70. 'Stand up for yourself'

Guys respect a woman who can handle her business – and other people when they deserve to be put in check. We want to know you won't allow yourself to be pushed around; this way, we'll view you as an equal instead of someone who needs to be constantly bailed out of situations.

'One of the things I love most about my girlfriend is that she won't take crap from anyone,' says Tommy, 33. 'She's never rude, she just refuses to be taken advantage of. If a guy tries to come on to her with some obnoxious line, she doesn't need me to do anything – she cuts him down to size. When she has problems at work, she'll go straight to her boss and hash it out. When we were having work done on our house, she kept tabs on things and made sure the job was being done correctly. She's a sweetheart, but she'll step up when she needs to . . . and I find something incredibly sexy about that.'

69. 'Don't mess with my sleep, unless the house is on fire (and you can't put it out yourself)'

Guys hate to be disturbed when they're sleeping. It's hard to rouse us from a deep sleep, even for sex. When we were kids, our mothers told us to tip-toe around the house when Dad was sleeping. As adults, we view our sleeping time as sacred and not to be disturbed unless necessary.

68. 'Play with me in a public place'

A squeeze of his butt or a naughty nibble on his ear is a hundred times hotter when we're out somewhere together. We like to think of the scene in *Flashdance* when Alex (Jennifer Beals) uses her foot to play with her man's crotch under the table.

Catch him off guard with a playful squeeze or caress. Let him know how bad you want him. His focus for the rest of the night will be locked on you.

67. 'If I'm driving and we're lost, don't insist on asking for directions'

As directionally challenged as your man may be, give him time to figure it out on his own. It's a male pride thing. Nuff said.

66. 'Obsessing about your looks isn't sexy'

When you spend too much time and energy worrying

about competing with other women – especially ones who are younger or thinner – you're drawing his attention to the fact that you're insecure about your looks. It shows a lack of confidence that is going to undermine his confidence in *you*. If you want to improve your looks and your body, we commend you for it – just do it in a healthy, reasonable fashion, not through starvation diets, working out obsessively or constantly asking him for reassurance that you look good. (God help us if we hear 'Do these jeans make me look fat?' one more time . . .)

65. 'Tune out the distractions, and tune into us'

From sundown Friday to sundown Saturday, observant Jewish families turn off the TV and computer, ignore the phone, and spend time together without any of the distractions of modern life. It's a concept that works. I'm good friends with a young Jewish couple who observe this rule. During the week, they work in the entertainment industry in Hollywood and run with a fast-paced crowd. But every Friday night, I know not to call them because they're at home, spending time together, focusing only on each other. And if there's one couple I know that is guaranteed to stay together for the long haul, it's this one.

With our big-screen TVs, hundreds of cable channels and high-speed internet connections, the simple act of sitting down with your spouse in the evening and having a meaningful conversation has been lost in a sea of distractions. Don't allow your relationship to settle into the routine of spending every evening watching television together on the couch (or even worse, him holing up in the other room to mess around on the internet for hours). If the two of you normally eat dinner in front of the TV, institute a new rule: from now on, or on a special night of the week, you're going to eat at the kitchen or dining-room table. If you have a flair for cooking, you can make this a special night where you cook a favourite meal and serve a nice bottle of wine. Anything you can do to encourage conversation and communication, or to give a familiar routine a fresh twist, is a good thing.

64. 'Be reliable'

By always being there when it counts, your man will know who he can count on in the long run – and what he would lose by cheating on you. This is especially important during the dating stage of a relationship, when a man has to consider whether you're a potential long-term partner or just another girlfriend to have fun with until someone more serious comes along.

When you're consistent and dependable – whether it's picking him up in the middle of the night when his car breaks down, or standing by him during a difficult period in his life – he'll begin to view you as essential. Put it this way: if he gets tossed in jail for any reason and is allowed only one phone call, you should be the first name in his mental Rolodex. In turn, he should demonstrate the same reliability towards you. We know plenty of men who've had their share of young, sexy girlfriends, yet they never took any of them too seriously because they clearly couldn't be depended upon to handle anything of importance. It was when a truly reliable woman entered the picture that they fell in love, and gladly surrendered their bachelor status.

63. 'When dining out, turn sharing dessert into an erotic gesture'

Remember, *any* gesture that strengthens the physical bond between you and your man, no matter how small, can be powerful. We'll let one of the 'enemy' – a 24-year-old husband hunter named Francesca – explain. 'I'm dating an older guy who's married,' she says. 'He's used to eating at home with his wife, sitting in front of the television and not saying a word to each other. With me, we go to restaurants and I focus on him, like he's the only person in the room. Our favourite part of the meal is always dessert. I order it, and we take turns; I take a bite, then I feed him a bite. I don't know why exactly, but there's something really erotic about it. He sure isn't getting anything like that at home.'

62. 'If you think I'm cheating, I probably am – but don't grill me for the confession'

Women always want the confession. Some women can have all the evidence in the world that their man has been cheating like mad, but they won't stop interrogating him until he admits it. The problem is that guys *hate* to confess. Some absolutely refuse to, no matter what. It's similar to someone being arrested: the cops can have the murder weapon with his prints on it, and a dozen eye-witnesses, but they're still going to sit the suspect in a room and grill him until he comes clean. If the signs are adding up and your female intuition delivers a guilty verdict, your best move is to cut him loose and move on. At this point, he might spill his guts out of desperation and beg for forgiveness; it's then up to you whether he deserves a second chance.

61. 'Don't suddenly impose restrictions just because we're married'

Help your man ease into the concept of married life; don't make him equate being married with suddenly losing his right to have fun. 'As soon as we got married, things changed,' says Bill, 28. 'She didn't want me going on my annual ski trip with my buddies. She didn't want me going out for drinks after work. She didn't want me to see my friend Joanne, who I'd been friends with since high school. My wife was fine with all these things right up until we got married. I felt like she had some plan in the back of her mind to completely re-order my life as soon as I was wearing the ring.'

60. 'Pressure is not the solution'

When trying to get men to do something, pressure often forces them in the opposite direction. If your man is tired and doesn't want to accompany you to a party, forcing him to go will result in a lousy evening for both of you. On the other hand, if you ask the *right* way, you can get us to do just about anything. Heed the words of Eva, 39: 'My husband, who was back then my boyfriend, used to hate spending time at my mother's house. I'd tell him, "We're going to my mum's house on Sunday", and he would gripe and complain. When we'd get there, he would sulk the whole time.

'Then a friend of mine suggested that I phrase it differently – turn it into a casual suggestion instead of an order. Instead of telling him what we were *going* to do, I'd say, "Honey, I was thinking maybe we could stop by my mum's place on Sunday, to see her for a little while." When I put it that way, he was okay with it.'

Men don't like feeling boxed in, like they're being given directions instead of options. A simple difference in phrasing can work wonders.

59. 'Tell me you're horny when we're in a public place'

This never fails to inject an element of excitement, and makes for extra-hot sex when you get home. Nothing turns on a man like knowing he turns *you* on.

58. 'Let me know that if I cheat, you'll walk'

You don't need to phrase this as some dramatic ultimatum. Just let him know that it's non-negotiable: if he were to ever cheat on you, you would not be able to take him back. Let him file that away in the back of his brain.

57. 'PMS is not an excuse for being impossible to deal with'

If your PMS is so severe that you're extremely difficult to be around, don't make him suffer through your mood swings. Spend time alone or with girlfriends, or encourage him to get out of the house and meet up with friends.

56. 'Know there are points of no return'

Understand that this relationship, no matter how much you have invested in it, and no matter how much you love him, will have to end if he ever crosses certain lines. If you know you would never be able to forgive him for cheating, then this is a line you must adhere to. For some women, a line would be any form of physical abuse. In other cases, it's a time frame: if your goal is to get married and have children, you should know how long you're willing to date a man before it's time to start seriously discussing these matters.

Every woman has boundaries and expectations for their relationship. Think about yours, and keep them firm in your mind. Trust your instincts about what you will and will not accept; otherwise, you might find yourself accepting behaviour from a man that you never thought you would. Plenty of women *say* they would never stay with a man who cheated or refused to ever marry them, yet they stick with dead-end relationships way past (what should have been) the expiration date. A woman with confidence and self-respect won't fall into this trap.

55. 'Never compare me to an ex'

Emphasis on the word 'never'. Men are fragile in this area. He realises he's not dating a virgin, but he wants to believe in his mind that he's the first guy that really counts. During an argument, invoking your ex's name to make a point (i.e. '*Mike* used to buy me nice things') is like dousing a fire with gasoline. But even more importantly . . .

54. 'Don't talk to me about your sexual history with other guys'

Men are all for honesty in relationships, but this particular topic is better left off-limits. Admitting that you've had one-night stands, had sex with two guys at once, etc. is going to gnaw at him, and chances are he'll throw it back at you during a heated argument. As Chris Rock said, 'Even if you say you had two [guys], it's two too many for him.'

'I had a girlfriend who admitted to me that she had sex once with a professional athlete,' says Ryan, 27. 'He plays for my favourite team, but I can't even watch them on TV any more . . . I see that guy's face and my blood starts boiling.'

Even if he enquires about your previous sex life, he doesn't really want to know the truth. It's a can of worms and there's no point in removing the lid. By the same token, don't press your man to tell you about how many women he's been with; as curious as you may be, it's something *you* really don't want to know. (He'll probably lie, anyway.)

53. 'Be openly appreciative'

One of the biggest things guys complain about to each other is when they do something and their partners don't show any appreciation. The 'other women' they cheat with tend to appreciate the smaller gestures. If your man takes you out for a nice meal or puts in some work around the house, acknowledge it. 'When I would take my chippie out for a $40 meal, she always thanked me,' says Roger, 34. 'My steady girlfriend, on the other hand, lived in my apartment free of charge for a year and never thanked me for it once. I wound up breaking up with her and getting serious with the other girl.'

Your man won't expect constant thank-yous, but show him you appreciate the things he does for you. When he doesn't expect it, give him a kiss and a thank you. In turn, he should acknowledge and appreciate the things you do for him. Neither person should ever feel taken for granted in any sense.

52. 'Set parameters for boys' nights out'

If he's going out for beers with the boys, it's okay to tell him, 'If I call your mobile phone, I want you to answer because it could be important', and hold him to that. If it's verbalised and agreed to, there's no room for argument. On the other hand, if you give vague parameters such as 'Don't stay out too late' or 'Don't drink too much', don't be surprised when he stumbles home at 4 am reeking of tequila. In his mind, he didn't break an agreement; in his opinion, ten drinks isn't 'too much', and as long as he gets home before sun-up, it's never 'too late'.

Guys need time to hang out with their guy friends. This is perfectly healthy and natural, and when he's out with them, you shouldn't be sitting at home worrying about him. Establish parameters beforehand if it makes you feel more comfortable, but don't sound like you're setting ground rules. Remember, the best scenario is for his buddies to consider you the 'cool' wife or girlfriend of the bunch, and for him to appreciate you enough to never consider straying. Let his friends be the ones who sit around at the bar and bitch about their nagging spouses. You don't ever want him to speak of you in these terms behind your back. And on this note . . .

51. 'If I'm out with the boys, don't call for the sake of calling'

No guy wants his buddies to think he's on a short leash and has to constantly answer to his woman. Calling him to 'check up' on him while he's out with his friends is only going to irritate him and make him want to avoid your calls. The other danger of doing this is that his friends are going to rib him about it. If he starts thinking he needs to assert his masculinity in front of his friends, he might do so with that cute blonde sitting at the end of the bar.

50. 'Know my favourites'

Do you know your man's favourite band? His favourite colour? The best book he ever read? The places he's always wanted to visit? The movie he loves to watch over and over again? The person who inspired him the most in his life? The more 'favourites' of his that you know, the more he'll feel that you relate to him and understand him. And as an added bonus, you'll always know the right 'small surprises' to spring on him.

49. 'Don't compare me to your dad, unless you're saying I do it better'

Women don't like being measured against their husband's mother, and men don't want to be compared to someone's father. 'My ex-wife would always make comments like, "My *father* would never let the lawn get like that,"' says Eddie, 31. 'She could've simply said, "Hon, the lawn would look so much nicer if you would mow it." That's all it takes. If you miss how your dad handles things, move back in with him.' And while we're on the subject . . .

48. 'Don't compare me to your best girlfriend'

'When I used to do something wrong, my girlfriend would always bring up her best friend Christina,' says William, 32. '"*Christina* is always there for me." Or, "*Christina* isn't boring, she likes to go out with me and have fun." I actually would rather have had her compare me to her ex-boyfriend. At least he was out of the picture. Christina was still in it, talking in her ear every day.'

47. 'Get to know my friends'

The types of guys he's close to will tell you a lot about him, and about interests of his that you might not have been aware of. His friends should enjoy your company and want to include you in activities, instead of urging your man to leave you at home.

46. 'If I have a buddy who's a cheater, it's bad news'

Men who cheat can be a poisonous influence on your relationship. They don't have to actively encourage him to cheat; their wild sex stories alone can be enough to get his hormones flaring and make him start checking out other options. If you're aware that one of his friends is a cheater, calmly explain to him that you're not comfortable with him hanging around that person. He should understand. Bear in mind, he wouldn't want *you* spending time with a girlfriend who takes home a new guy from the bar every night.

45. 'Be every woman'

Remember that kick-ass Chaka Khan tune 'I'm Every Woman'? Take that song to heart. One of the chief reasons why men cheat is that they desire variety. Counter this by expressing all the different facets of your personality. You can enjoy a quiet evening at home together on Friday, and take him out dancing at a nightclub on Saturday. You can cook him great dinners, and go out on dates to new restaurants you've heard about. You can be a buttoned-up corporate professional by day, and a bad girl in the bedroom by night. You can be a supportive, loving partner, but also show him you're an independent, assertive woman who has her own goals.

Show him the full range of who you are. Be passionate about your life and the way you live it. This diminishes the chance of him feeling there's a void in your personality, or in the relationship, that another woman might fill.

44. 'Forgive *and* forget'

Some women catch their man cheating but decide to continue with the relationship. The problem is that very few of these women are able to permanently bury their anger and resentment. The act of infidelity, even if it occurred years ago, remains a sore spot that they won't hesitate to hurl in his face during an argument.

Drawing out the pain

I met a guy named Frank who says his cheating is what ultimately destroyed his marriage — though it had been nine years since his wife busted him. 'I'd been seeing a girl on the side, a blonde,' he explains. 'One night I'm out at dinner with my wife, who's a brunette. We're at a restaurant I'd taken my girlfriend to a couple of times. The waiter comes over and I say to him, "Hey, I'd like you to meet my wife." And the idiot says, "That's your wife? I remember your wife having blonde hair."

'My wife turns bright red. She immediately knew I'd been bringing another girl to this place. She threw me out of the house and I lived in a hotel for a couple of weeks until eventually, I grovelled enough for her to take me back. I confessed everything. We did marriage counselling, the whole routine. But it was never the same. Every time we fought about something, she would bring up that incident. Stuff like, "I'm going to the hair salon today, I'm thinking about going blonde . . . You like blondes, don't you?"

'Look, I'm not saying my behaviour was excusable. But if you're going to find it in your heart to forgive the guy, you need to find a way to forget. It took nine years for my wife and I to finally split up for good, and I'm convinced that single incident was the reason why.'

43. 'Give a great massage'

Learning how to give a professional-quality massage is like owning Microsoft stock that you bought back in the '80s: it's going to pay huge dividends, either in your current relationship or the next time you want to give a guy an unforgettable evening. Men are suckers for a good massage; when the massage rises to the level of *great*, they think 'keeper'. It relieves stress, it's absolutely erotic, and it's a tool every woman (and guy, for that matter) should pack in their bag of tricks.

42. 'The way to a man's heart is through his stomach'

He won't expect you to be a world-class chef in the kitchen, but never underestimate the importance of being able to cook meals that he looks forward to and enjoys. Prior to meeting their special someone, most guys live on a bachelor diet that's barely fit for human consumption.

Preparing a great dinner and then sitting down to enjoy it together – even better, with a bottle of wine – is a recipe for romantic bonding on any night of the week. If you're not a skilled cook, take the time to master a few of his favourite dishes. On special occasions, he'll appreciate a home-cooked meal more than an expensive trip to a restaurant.

41. 'Be careful about fantasies'

Therapists who counsel couples sometimes encourage them to explore 'mutual fantasies'. In reality, this phrase is an oxymoron. An impossibility. As comedian Bill Maher said, 'Our fantasies disgust you, and yours bore us.' Your man's secret fantasies might be dirtier than you think – and if you indulge him, he may lose respect for you.

Colin, 40, used to fantasise about watching his wife having sex with another man – a well-hung African-American man, to be precise. One night at a party, while in an experimental mood, they took home a guy who fitted the bill and Colin's wife made his fantasy come true. 'It was a mistake; I hate to say it, but I could never look at her the same way again,' Colin says. 'The next day, the mother of my kids was a slut in my eyes. I didn't expect it to affect me that way. I felt terrible about it, because it was all my idea, and she was only doing it to please me.'

40. 'Don't obsess about catching me'

If your man finds out you've been trying to 'catch' him at it, he may never feel comfortable around you again. No guy wants to feel like he's under surveillance, and it's only going to make a cheater act more secretively. If you're sincerely worried that he's creeping around with other women, you can confront him about it, at which point he's bound to deny everything. You only have two logical options in this situation: trust him and put the issue to bed; or, if you don't believe him, cut him loose.

But never tell him about the 'evidence' that you've been gathering. Don't tell him you followed him the last time he went out, that you quizzed his best friend about what he's been up to, or that you checked his phone calls or emails. Doing so is going to wreck his sense of trust in you, whether he's actually been cheating or not.

39. 'Don't feel threatened by my friends'

For some women, preparing their boyfriend to become 'husband' material is a process that involves isolating him from his guy friends. One by one, she insists on eliminating his buddies from his life until his entire world revolves around her. (The first to go are his single friends who she considers to be 'players', and therefore bad influences.)

If you love him, respect the choices he's made as far as who his close friends are. If you feel certain friends of his might tempt him to stray, then express your feelings to him. But never *force* him to abandon his close friendships. It will only make him resent you.

38. 'Change your look'

Surprise him with new hairstyles and hot additions to your wardrobe; it keeps the relationship feeling fresh and demonstrates that you want to look good for him. But before you do anything *too* radical . . .

37. 'Know what I find sexy about you'

Have you ever asked him what it is about you, specifically, that turns him on? You might be surprised by his answers. 'I used to always wear jeans or long skirts because I have big calves,' says Lucy, 27. 'I came to find out, after being with my boyfriend for a year, that my calves are his favourite part of my body. He's got a thing for big, strong calves. Who would've thought? Now, when we go out together, I know what to wear in order to turn him on – and I feel much more comfortable and sexy.'

On the flip side, we know a guy named Mark who never bothered to tell his girlfriend that her long hair drove him wild. Her waist-length hair was his favourite aspect of her appearance. Then, one day she cut it all off, trying a new look that she thought he'd like. He broke up with her a week later.

36. 'Tell me what you find sexy about me'

Men get turned on by details. From your man's point of view, it could be your legs, your lips, or the way you laugh. Tell him about the details that *you* love. If you can make him feel sexy, he'll love being around you even more.

35. 'Never go to sleep angry'

Pretty obvious advice, but extremely true. Before you turn off the lights, do your best to resolve the argument. Kiss and make up – even if it means conceding some ground. You can resume the discussion tomorrow, with a clear head. Don't let your man lie next to you, staring at the ceiling and wishing he was in bed with someone else.

34. 'Ignore the gossip machine'

Just about every woman has one of these: the friend, roommate, co-worker, sister or mother who always has a negative thing to say about your man. Sometimes they're simply jealous of your relationship; other times, they may suspect that he's cheating on you or feel he's not treating you right. Whatever the case may be, these are things you need to address with your man, not discuss with them. Inform these gossipers that your relationship is not their business. And on this note . . .

33. 'Consider the source when getting "advice"'

A lot of people who give advice about your relationship are biased by past break-ups perhaps, or might even have ulterior motives. Kim, 29, says: 'My roommate, Dawn, used to always warn me about my boyfriend Jerry. She would tell me he wasn't right for me, that he was a "player" and was only going to break my heart. Well, she wound up being a bridesmaid at our wedding. The night before, she broke down and confessed that she only said those things because she was worried about losing me, her best friend. She actually thought Jerry was a great guy.'

32. 'Take it easy on my cell phone'

Women possess a chromosome, as yet unidentified by science, that makes them think nothing of calling their best friend ten times a day or chatting on the phone for hours on end. Guys have a much lower threshold for phone chats. Resist the urge to call him with constant updates or to ask questions that can wait until you see him. If he's out with his buddies, check in with him once and let him be. His friends will ridicule him if you're constantly calling him, and it makes him view you as needy.

31. 'Don't argue with me when one of us is drinking'

Even if the two of you are just having a couple of cocktails, alcohol loosens the tongue and causes things to be said that one of you might regret later. This isn't the right time to get on a topic that you know will instigate an argument. And when a man is drunk, just remember that his brain can only focus on three subjects (in order of importance): sex, food and sleep. It's useless trying to work out a problem with him when he's in this mindset.

One of the rules they teach in police work is that you can't reason with a crazy person, or a drunk person. This carries over into relationships.

30. 'Little white lies aren't always harmless'

Some men have the ability to lie and feel absolutely no remorse. It took Grace, 25, over a year to finally realise she'd been royally burned by her boyfriend Ian, who constantly lied to people whenever it suited his interests.

She overlooked it at first, since they generally seemed to be 'little white lies' that weren't hurting anyone. He would lie to his parents about his job, exaggerating his role at the company he worked for. He would lie to his friends about how much money he made. Every time he had to cancel plans he'd made with her, instead of offering a simple explanation he always gave some crazy, complicated story: his car broke down, his brother was in the hospital, etc.

Grace eventually discovered proof that he'd been lying to her all along, but these lies weren't little white ones. She found out that Ian was dating another girl, who was pregnant with his child. **Lying is an integrity issue.** If he has a habit of spouting little white lies every time he runs into difficulties, we'll lay odds that he's saving the biggest lies for you. Accept nothing but complete honesty.

29. 'Know each other's views on infidelity'

We've explained how important it is to define the parameters of fidelity in your relationship, and to let him know what you consider to be cheating. If you're uncomfortable with the fact that he hangs out socially with a former girlfriend, you need to express this to him. If his job requires him to have business lunches or dinners with women on occasion and it bothers you, don't allow yourself to grow suspicious and jealous – but do talk to him about your feelings and set parameters. Maybe you'd feel more comfortable if he's always home before a certain time or calls you to check in.

The problems arise when the two of you aren't on the same page about what's acceptable to you and what isn't. Of course *he* doesn't think it's a big deal if he's staying in touch with his ex-girlfriend or going out for drinks with his pretty young co-workers; he'll always claim it's completely innocent. But if it bothers you, you simply need to express how you feel and set parameters. Say it nicely, and he should respect it. *He* sure isn't going to appreciate you having lunch with your ex or hanging out at bars with single guys from your work.

The best way to have this discussion with your man is to use the Entrance Exam found at the beginning of this book. We designed it for this exact purpose. Use it!

Christopher Curtis says . . .

Here's an actual interrogation technique that police officers use to extract confessions from suspects, that you can use during the 'infidelity' discussion with your man. If a guy is suspected of killing his girlfriend, the cops usually won't get anywhere by yelling at him and accusing him of the crime. Instead, they'll pretend to take his side: 'I understand how women can drive a guy crazy. Sometimes you have to put them in their place. It's not like you meant to hurt her ...' By phrasing it like it's not a big deal, the cops prompt him to admit how he really feels, or to confess what he did.

I taught this technique to my friend Emma. She laid out a 'cheating scenario' to her new boyfriend, Joe, but phrased it like she didn't think anything of it.

'I used to have a guy friend who was married,' she said with a smile. 'Sometimes when we all went out to clubs without his wife, he'd wind up dancing and kissing other girls. But he was just having fun, it wasn't like he was sleeping with them or anything.'

Emma shrugged and looked at Joe, prompting him to offer his opinion. 'Yeah, it's not like he was cheating by kissing some chick at a club,' he agreed.

Joe had busted himself. By using smart phrasing, Emma got him to state one of his beliefs about cheating that he wouldn't normally admit. She then told him, in no uncertain terms, that in her mind kissing any other girl absolutely constituted cheating. From that point forward, there would be no grey area in Joe's mind about this.

28. 'Don't view it as your money/my money'

Don't expect him to whip out his wallet every time you want something when you're together. If he usually picks up the take-away and pays for it, you should reciprocate on occasion. 'With my girlfriend, I got tired of always picking up the tab for everything,' says Tyler, 29. 'After a while, she didn't even thank me any more – it was expected that I'd pay for every meal and every round of drinks. I didn't want to say anything because

I didn't want to sound cheap. I think the guy *should* pick up the cheque in most instances, but when you've been dating for over a year I think the woman should at least offer sometimes. Especially when they've known you long enough to know your financial situation, and you're obviously not made of money.'

27. 'Don't grow new inhibitions'

Don't stop doing certain things in bed just because you're married, or because you've been together a long time. The sex life you share is a big reason why he's with you. Developing sudden inhibitions is a sure-fire way to send him on the hunt for a chippie. Remember that nine times out of ten, a man is going to cheat with a woman who represents what his spouse *used* to be. This usually means a woman who enjoys sex and makes him feel like a man in the bedroom.

26. 'Save the dirty talk for the bedroom'

Here's another song lyric to bear in mind, this one courtesy of rapper Ludacris: 'I want a lady in the street but a freak in the bed.' Make it a habit to stop using profanity in your day-to-day language. That way, when you talk dirty in the bedroom it's going to hit him with twice the impact – and drive him wild.

25. 'Sexy text messages can go a long way'

Trent, 42, is a bartender at a beach resort who's been with more than his share of beautiful women – most of them quick flings that he quickly forgot about. But he met his match with a girl named Natalia, whom he met while she was on vacation at the resort where he worked. Once she returned home to Europe, she'd occasionally send him a dirty text message out of the blue, saying the things she wished she could do to him right now. Now Trent says, 'I can't get her out of my head.' Use this bit of modern cell-phone technology to spark his imagination, and guarantee a hot time the next time you see him.

24. 'Know the enemy'

Many women wrongly assume that if their man is going to have an affair, he'll cheat with some hot young bimbo. But the idea of a married man hooking up with his hot young secretary is more suited to the movies than to real life. In reality, men usually have affairs with women who are more goal-oriented than their current spouse. Keep this in mind.

23. 'Don't pump my friends for info'

Don't try to get his best friend to divulge info about where they went last night, or who your man has been hanging out with. He's going to report this back to your man, and it's going to irritate him. It also puts his friends in an uncomfortable position. They're not going to want to be around you if they know you're going to put them on the spot. And what's the point, anyway? You can't expect his friends *not* to cover for him.

22. 'Show interest in my job'

Even if he doesn't like his job, you should express interest in it and be aware of what's going on in his workplace. It brings the two of you closer when you're able to talk to him about the project he's working on, a problem he's having with his boss or a promotion he's hoping to get.

21. 'Let's take our relationship in stages'

Don't let your age, your biological clock or the opinions of your friends and family make you rush him into uncomfortable territory. Take the relationship in steps. This means don't expect him to spend all his free time with you when you've just begun dating. Don't move in together too quickly. And definitely don't have a child or get married before you're absolutely committed to each other. One guy we know was faithful to his girlfriend for three years. It wasn't until she started pressuring him into marriage that he started cheating. Subconsciously, he wanted to get busted so he'd have a way out of the relationship. He got his wish.

20. 'Remember the importance of polarity'

Sexual attraction between two people can only remain strong over time if one person projects masculine energy and the other projects feminine energy. This way, you complete each other. If you're the feminine partner and he's the masculine partner, encourage him to continue playing his role. Don't belittle him, order him around or do things that threaten his masculinity. If he's secure in himself as a man, he's going to make you feel secure and loved as a woman.

19. 'Understand my long-term goals before committing to the relationship'

This means being aware of his career goals, his views on having children, etc. Felecia, 28, married a struggling musician named Steve with the expectation that he would eventually abandon his music and get a 'real' job. But Steve had no intention of doing so, and this led to their break-up. In other cases, we've seen women marry men that already had children from an earlier relationship and didn't want any more kids. The woman believes he'll 'come around' and eventually want a baby with her; when they finally realise it's never going to happen, they're devastated.

18. 'Don't marry a guy who you consider a work in progress'

If he can't hold a job, has a history of cheating or has some other serious character flaw, don't assume that marriage is going to correct or tame him. You know the saying about old dogs and new tricks.

17. 'Don't start fights for the sake of fighting'

We all know high-drama couples: the ones who are constantly arguing, having huge 'break-ups' and then reconciling two days later. These are desperately insecure people who need constant validation from their partner that they're still loved. If you need to pick a fight or threaten to leave him, just to get him to show he cares, you're with the wrong person . . . and you really should work on your self-esteem before you commit to another relationship.

16. 'Find a romantic getaway and make it our special place'

This can be as simple as a picnic spot, or as exotic as a city in Europe. When he associates a special place with a romantic time you've shared, you can always take him back there to rekindle the sparks.

15. 'Don't be a "Bridezilla"'

If your heart is set on a huge fairy-tale wedding, knock yourself out. He wants you to have the wedding of your dreams. It only gets problematic when women get so obsessed with making wedding plans that they forget the reason behind the event. If money is an issue, men would rather spend big on an unforgettable honeymoon than a blow-out wedding that's going to cause stress and drain the finances.

14. 'Don't insert yourself into my problems with my family members'

Understand the dynamics of his family and respect those dynamics. He's known them a lot longer than you have, and his issues with them probably run deeper than you're aware of.

13. 'An "unexpected" pregnancy is never going to cement our relationship'

Intentionally getting pregnant, when he's not looking to be a father, will only lead to disaster. Best case scenario: he marries you out of a sense of obligation, resents you for it, and your child is raised by two parents that can't stand to be around each other. Worst case scenario (and the usual outcome): he breaks up with you, moves on with his life, and you join the ranks of bitter single mothers.

12. 'Make me shine at work-related events'

Whether you're his date at the Academy Awards or accompanying him to a company Christmas party, look your best and go out of your way to make a great impression on his co-workers. Few things make a man prouder than introducing his charming, beautiful wife or girlfriend to his professional colleagues.

11. 'Be less like work, and more like a vacation'

Spending time together shouldn't feel like work. Making plans shouldn't involve bickering or drawn-out debates about where to go, what to do, etc. If he associates his job with stress, he should associate you with fun, spontaneity and romance.

10. 'Excel at an equal pace'

If you're ambitious about your career, it's important that you find a man who is similarly motivated. Your partner should inspire you to greater heights, not serve as a distraction or resent your success. If he's less successful than you are, do your best to encourage and inspire him; if he refuses to get his act together, save yourself the frustration and move on.

'I never would have imagined my boyfriend Darren would cheat on me,' says Annie, 31. 'I was out there working 60 hours a week to pay the bills, while he sat at home and played video games. He didn't even have a car, but that didn't stop him from sleeping with a bunch of different women. Maybe it was because he had too much time on his hands and got bored. But more likely, he resented my success, and cheating was his way of getting back at me.'

9. 'Protect my feelings and my best interests'

'I'm only five foot five, so my buddies rib me sometimes about my height,' says Richie, 25. 'One time they cracked a joke in front of my girlfriend, and she shot right back at them: "Trust me, he more than makes up for it where it counts." I didn't need her to defend me, but she did anyway. It's cool to know she has my back.'

8. 'There's no such thing as a good kisser'
Two people 'kiss good' together. Keep this saying in mind, because it translates into all areas of a relationship – especially in the bedroom. No guy can be 'great in bed' without an enthusiastic sex partner.

7. 'Set aside time each day to be alone'
This is especially important if you have children. You need time to think and reflect, whether it's an hour at the gym, a yoga class, taking up a creative hobby or just reading a book. By using this time to decompress, you'll be better equipped to take problems in your stride and not start arguments over trivial matters.

6. 'Pace yourself'
Spread out projects over time. When you attempt to juggle the demands of a career, raising kids, taking classes, home-improvement projects, etc., tension is going to build until there's an explosion on the home front. If you need a helping hand, let your man know before your stress level gets out of control.

5. 'Remind yourself that you're not the general manager of the universe'
It's great if you're a source of support and comfort for your friends, but don't get so wrapped up in their problems that you neglect your man. He really doesn't care about the latest break-up your drama-queen friend is going through. Be there for your

friends when they need you, but make him feel that your relationship is always the number one priority.

4. 'Remind me why you love me'

Never forget the reasons why you fell in love with him in the first place – and don't let him forget. Maybe it's his sense of humour, the way he's always been able to make you laugh; maybe it's because he always stood by you through difficult periods. Remind him of the little things he does that make you smile or turn you on, and of the experiences the two of you have shared as a couple. Show him that you appreciate him in ways that no other woman could.

3. 'Understand the male biological clock'

There are two major misconceptions related to the concept of the 'biological clock', the impulse to start a family before it's too late. Firstly, a woman's biological clock isn't some genetic mechanism that kicks in around age 30; its timing is set according to the status of the women close to her. If your close friends are settling down and having children, you're going to feel it's time to do the same. For some women, this means their mid-twenties; for others, it's their late thirties.

The other falsehood is that only women have internal clocks. Men have them as well. But theirs run by a different standard: the age of the women they're still able to attract and sleep with. Max, 38, is an example. 'This girl I was dating told me, "You're pushing 40 and you're still partying in nightclubs all the time. When are you going to grow up?" Well, the truth was, I was in those nightclubs picking up 22-year-old women. I figure as long as I can still score younger chicks, what's the sense in settling down with a woman my age? When they start dissing me, that's when it's time to start thinking about starting a family with the right woman.'

Be aware of this mentality. If your man has a history of sleeping with much younger women, his 'clock' is probably telling him to keep it up while he can still pull it off.

2. 'Know when to walk away'
If he's cheating and the relationship is damaged beyond repair, cut your losses. The best way to prevent cheating in your next relationship is to enter into it with your self-respect intact.

1. 'Love yourself'
Women tell us that the sexiest quality a man can possess is confidence. This goes both ways. Nothing turns on a man like a woman who is comfortable with herself and her sexuality and knows what she wants. The more you love yourself and your life, the easier it will be to find a man who'll love you for it.

Chapter 22
In Conclusion . . .

After seven years of marriage, I am sure of two things. First, never wallpaper together and second, you'll need two bathrooms . . . both for her. The rest is a mystery, but a mystery I love to be involved in.

Dennis Miller

As two single guys, we wrestled with our own feelings on infidelity throughout the year we spent researching and writing this book. In some ways, working on *The Cheat Sheet* changed us – for the better, we'd like to believe.

As you know, we've got a lot of buddies who confide in us every juicy detail of their affairs. We admit, we've covered for them on occasion – usually because they come to us in a fit of last-minute desperation, needing an alibi for their whereabouts last Saturday night or an excuse for why their wife found a condom in their pants pocket. ('I was holding on to it for Rob!' one friend told his furious wife. 'His pockets were full.')

We used to find their escapades somewhat amusing. Constantly scrambling to cover their tracks, they acted like naughty kids trying to avoid a scolding from Mum. Sometimes, we'd just assume that their wives or girl-friends weren't giving them what they needed, so they were only doing what they felt was necessary to find satisfaction. But now, after all we've seen and heard about infidelity, we take a different view. We find this type of behaviour pretty pathetic. In some cases we can only pity these guys, since we know what kind of disaster looms on their horizon.

We know the consequences far outweigh whatever fun they think they're having, sneaking away from their wives or girlfriends to have flings with other women. The fact that they're getting away with it doesn't make them slick or clever. It just means they've become good liars. And when a guy makes lying a part of his daily routine – to the women he supposedly loves, no less – what does that say about his character?

It reminds us of a story we once heard about a Mafia boss, which we related in *M.A.C.K. Tactics*. In Mafia culture, it used to be normal for the guys to spend certain nights of the week with their wives and kids, and other nights with their mistresses. They all had at least one. But this particular boss had a different attitude towards cheaters. He didn't trust them. His attitude was, how could he expect loyalty from a guy who couldn't even be loyal to his wife, the one person in the world he'd sworn to be faithful to?

Sure, we still see our cheating buddies when we're all hanging out at the bar, and we still hear their scan-dalous sex stories. But now they just seem confused, desperate and trapped in a no-win situation. And we can tell you this after writing *The Cheat Sheet*: if we stay single much longer, it's only because we want to make sure we marry the right woman for the right reasons. After all the train-wreck relationships we've seen and included in this book, we have no intention of joining their ranks.

In writing this book, we also saw the depressing aftermath of infidelity. For most of the cheaters we got to know, there were only three outcomes. One, they wind up getting caught and suffer through a horrible divorce, which crushes them financially and estranges them from their kids. Two, they abandon their marriage to run off with another woman who doesn't offer one-third of what their wife does, and eventually they wind up alone and regretting their stupidity. Or three, they stay married, continue to cheat and get away with it, and have to live with constant guilt and anxiety.

It's been our message throughout this book, and we'll state it once more for the record: **catching your man cheating should never be the priority.** Your efforts should be focused on making your relationship as strong, honest and mutually fulfilling as possible. When the heat in the bedroom begins to cool off, there are methods for taking your sex life to a new level. When he starts taking you for granted, there are ways to remind him of what a precious, unique, desirable individual you are. When he's not willing to put in the work, it's up to *you* to step up and make the effort, and this book has shown you how to do that.

As long as you're willing to roll up your sleeves and put the necessary work into your relationship, a good man is going to respect and appreciate you for it, and step up his game in return. If he doesn't, then you need to respect yourself enough to move on and find happiness with someone else. Refuse to be the victim, and refuse to be taken for granted.

Good luck. Take it from two guys who've seen it all, it's a jungle out there. Every relationship is a long and winding road that contains twists, turns and challenges. May *The Cheat Sheet* be your compass, and may you find the happiness – with or without him – that you deserve.

Sources and Further Reading

About.com, www.marriage.about.com

AP Global News Network, www.associatedpress.com

Ashley Madison Agency, www.ashleymadison.com

AskMen, www.askmen.com

Rabbi Shmuley Boteach, *Kosher Adultery: Seduce and Sin with Your Spouse*, Adams Media Corporation, Cincinnati, OH, 2002

Cheaters, www.cheaters.com

China Window, www.chinadaily.com

Court TV, www.courttv.com

Daily News (New York), www.nydailynews.com

Divorce magazine, www.divorcemag.com

Divorce Statistics, www.divorcestatistics.net

Bonnie Eaker Weil, *Adultery, The Forgivable Sin*, Hastings House, Winter Park, FL, 1994

Fact Monster, www.factmonster.com

Fox News, www.foxnews.com

Hidden Spy Cameras, www.4spycameras.com

Hideaway Couples, www.hideawaycouples.com

J.L. King, *On the Down Low: A Journey into the Lives of 'Straight' Black Men Who Sleep With Men*, Broadway Books, New York, 2004

Los Angeles Times, www.latimes.com

Manhaters, www.manhaters.com

Modem Spy, www.modemspy.com

MSNBC, www.msnbc.com

New York Post, www.nypost.com

Passion Parties, www.passionparties.com

Anthony Robbins, www.tonyrobbins.com

Telegraph (Calcutta), www.telegraphindia.com

USA Today, www.usatoday.com

Peggy Vaughan, *The Monogamy Myth: A Personal Handbook for Dealing with Affairs* (3rd edn), Newmarket Press, New York, 2003

Rob Wiser & Christopher Curtis, *M.A.C.K. Tactics: The Science of Seduction Meets the Art of Hostage Negotiation*, Penguin, New York, 2005

Acknowledgments

Rob Wiser says . . .

The Cheat Sheet would not have reached this point without the tireless efforts of my manager, Peter Miller, the encouragement and enthusiasm of Jeanne Ryckmans at Random House Australia, and the editing prowess of Jon Gibbs. After hearing a thousand stories of infidelity and break-ups in the course of researching this book, I'd like to give a special thanks to my uncle, Jimmy Reardon, and his wife Siobhan, whose marriage gives me hope that it *can* be done correctly. (May we celebrate your fiftieth anniversary at Hudson Yards some day.) I dedicate this book to Sheila Reardon, the greatest mother, mentor and friend I could have ever wished for.

Christopher Curtis wishes to thank . . .

God for always being there for me; Peter 'The Lion' Miller; everyone at Random House Australia; and Moms, Pops, Shawn and Curt Wills for supporting all of my endeavours.

I also want to thank my ace, Rob 'Bass' Wiser, and everyone else who has encouraged and inspired me – you know who you are.